To the student

How do you learn a language? There is no easy answer to this question. People learn languages in many different ways. The **Innovations** series starts from the basis of natural conversations people have every day, then teaches you the language you need to have similar conversations in English.

To make this process as interesting, motivating, and productive as possible, the **Innovations** series:

- contains numerous examples of the way grammar and vocabulary are naturally used. You can learn a lot of useful vocabulary from good grammar exercises, and good vocabulary activities will give you practice with the grammar of English.
- introduces you to many new features of spoken grammar and useful idiomatic language, followed by opportunities to practise them in meaningful contexts.
- includes reading texts that are intriguing and challenging, giving you plenty to talk – and think – about.
- features 'Learner advice' pages, which will help you study better.

We hope you find **Innovations** as fun and interesting to learn from as we did to write!

Acknowledgements

The authors and publishers would like to thank Clare West and Jeremy Ottewell for their valuable input on this material at various stages during production.

Hugh Dellar has taught EFL, ESP and EAP in Indonesia and Britain, where he is now a teacher and teacher-trainer at the University of Westminster, London. He trains both native-speaker and non-native speaker teachers. He has also given papers and teacher development workshops all over the world. He would like to thank the following people: Lisa, as ever; his mum and dad; Julian Savage; Andrew Walkley, Darryl Hocking, Sally Dalzell, Andrew Fairhurst; Scott Thornbury and Ivor Timmis for their support and help over the years. He would also like to thank The Untouchable Arsenal team of 2003–04 and King Tubby's for inspiration and joy.

Andrew Walkley has taught mainly in Spain. He currently divides his time between teaching general English, writing materials and maintaining a family life. He also does teacher training and regularly gives talks and workshops to teachers. He would like to thank Macu, Rebeca and Santiago, Harry and Shirley Walkle – great parents and true internationalists – and Harry Dancey, his first friend made through teaching English.

Hugh and Andrew would both like to thank:
Jimmie Hill, Howard Middle, Chris Wenger, Stuart Tipping, Helena Taylor, Liz Driscoll, Nick Broom, Ian Martin and all at Thomson Heinle for their support and belief in us. We'd also like to thank Nick Barrett, and to send out a shout to all the good folk at The Social, all our former CELTA trainees, the people we've met on our travels around the world, McVities' Jamaica Ginger Cake and PG Tips. This book wouldn't have happened without you!

Contents

Unit 1
Where are you from? 8

Conversation
Starting a conversation 8
Making friends 8

Reading
I'm not from here originally 10

Listening
Meeting people for the first time 12

Using Grammar
Past simple: *My father got a job there. Did you go out last night?* 11
There's and **there are:** *There's a lot of crime and violence there. There are lots of parks and trees.* 12

Using Vocabulary
Geography quiz: *I've no idea where it is. I think it's somewhere in West Africa.* 10
Key words: miss and lose: *I missed my bus. I got lost on the way here.* 13

Pronunciation
Getting the stress right 9
Weak forms 13

Unit 2
Likes and dislikes 14

Conversation
Talking about music you like 14
Answering questions 15

Reading
Family or friends 17

Listening
Talking about going out 18

Using Grammar
Too: *I'm too tired to think. You drive too fast!* 19

Using Vocabulary
What kind: *What kind of things do you write? Mainly just a diary.* 15
Key word: go: *How's it going? The meeting went on for hours.* 18

Pronunciation
Stress in expressions 18

Unit 3
Have you got ... ? 20

Conversation
Explaining where things are 20

Reading
I haven't got one! 22

Listening
Seven short conversations 24

Using Grammar
Questions with have you got: *Have you got a cloth? Have you got a stapler?* 21
I'm thinking of + -ing form: *I'm thinking of getting a new mobile.* 23
Using one and ones: *I prefer the ones we saw earlier. Have you got a larger one?* 24

Using Vocabulary
People's houses: *What's her place like? It's a bit cramped.* 21

Unit 4
Times and dates 26

Conversation
Telling the time 26
Making plans 26

Reading
Special days 28

Listening
Six short conversations 30

Using Grammar
Present continuous for arrangements: *We're going to Spain for the weekend.* 27
Present simple with hope: *I hope it goes well. I hope it doesn't rain.* 29
Time expressions: *It's just gone half past six. It's almost three o'clock.* 30
Talking about the future: *I've got an exam next week.* 31

Using Vocabulary
Birthdays, holidays, anniversaries: *It's a public holiday. It's my birthday.* 28

Pronunciation
Linking words 30

Review: Units 1-4 32

Unit 5
Buying things 36

Conversation
Talking about things you've bought 36

Reading
Good mothers – real men 38

Listening
Conversations in shops 40

Using Grammar
That and those, it and them: *I love that shirt. Where did you get it? I really like those shoes. Where did you get them?* 37
Prepositional expressions: *It's three doors down from the bookshop.* 37
Not enough with nouns and adjectives: *I'm not old enough to vote. I don't have enough qualifications.* 40
Negative questions: *Don't you think it's a bit too bright? No, it really suits you.* 41

Using Vocabulary
Clothes and accessories: *Who's that guy with the red trainers?* 36
Verbs around the house: *Can you lay the table, please? I hate doing the washing-up.* 39
Problems with clothes: *It's too old-fashioned. They're too trendy!* 40

c o u
Inr   ns

a c   sh

THOMSON
™

United Kingdom • United States • Australia • Canada • Mexico • Singapore • Spain

THOMSON

Innovations Pre-intermediate Coursebook
Dellar/Walkley

Publisher: *Christopher Wenger*
Series Editor: *Jimmie Hill*
Director of Development: *Anita Raducanu*
Director of Marketing: *Amy Mabley*
Editorial Manager: *Howard Middle/HM ELT Services*
International Marketing Manager: *Eric Bredenberg*
Editor: *Liz Driscoll*
Production Development: *Oxford Designers & Illustrators*

Sr. Print Buyer: *Mary Beth Hennebury*
Associate Marketing Manager: *Laura Needham*
Illustrator: *David Mostyn*
Photo Researcher: *Suzanne Williams*
Cover/Text Designer: *Studio Image & Photographic Art*
(www.studio-image.com)

Printer: *Seng Lee Press*

Cover Images: Kandinsky: © *2003 Artists Rights Society (ARS), New York/ADAGP, Paris;* Da Vinci: © *Bettmann/CORBIS;*
Guggenheim Museum: *Tim Hursley/SuperStock*

For more information, contact Thomson Learning, High Holborn House, 50/51 Bedford Row, London WC1R 4LR United Kingdom or Thomson Heinle, 25 Thomson Place, Boston, Massachusetts 02210 USA. You can visit our Web site at http://www.heinle.com

ISBN: 0-7593-9620-5
(Coursebook)

Illustrations

David Mostyn pp 40, 12, 36, 37, 40, 42, 52, 53, 66, 120, 132;

Photo credits

The publishers would like to thank the following sources for permission to reproduce their copyright protected photographs:

Alamy pp 10br (Apply Pictures), 12 (Janine Wiedel Photolibrary), 13 (Leslie Garland Picture Library), 13 (Alan Copson City Pictures), 20br (Andy Ridder/fl online), 41/D (Patti McConville), 54 (Banana Stock), 56bl (StockShot/J Stock), 56tl (Steve Hamblin), 59 (Patrick Ray Dunn), 68b (Inmagine), 68t (Robert Lawson), 74l (Dennis Hallinan), 74r (Comstock Images), 76/B (S Sarkis/Sarkis Images), 76/D (GP Bowater), 78 (Robert Harding World Imagery), 79b (Paul Ridsdale), 079tl (Andy Myatt), 079tr (Christine Osborne), 080c (Paul Baldesare), 082r (Eye Candy Images), 099 (Alex Segre), 102/2 (Foodcollection), 102/4 (Robert Kalb), 102/6 (Liam Bailey), 102/7 (Jacky Chapman), 102/8 (Elizabeth Whiting & Associates), 114 (Shout), 120/A (© Image Source), 120/B (Medical-on-Line), 120/D (Brand X Pictures/C Anderson), 120/E (Comstock Images), 120/F (Bart's Medical Library/Phototake Inc.), 122cr (Brand X Pictures /P Coblentz), 122tl (RubberBall Productions), 122tr (Janine Wiedel), 126 (David Bishop), 130/A (Judith Collins), 130/B (bobo), 130/D (ImageState), 135l (A Parada), 135r (Tim Graham), 136/1 (Janine Wiedel), 136/2 (Robert Llewellyn), 136/3 (PCL), 138 (Richard Greenhill); **Corbis** pp 8 (Wolfgang Kaehler), 9 (Jeremy Horner), 14/A (Bettmann),14/B (Derick A. Thomas; Dat's Jazz), 14/E (Rainier Jensen/dpa/Landov), 17br (Tom and Dee Ann McCarthy), 18b, 22ct (Norbert Schaefer), 22t (Rob & Sas), 25b (Obremski), 25cbc (David Raymer), 25ctc, 31b, 38 (William Gottlieb), 43r (George Shelley), 47bc (David Turnley), 47br (Michael S. Yamashita), 47t (Robert Estall), 48 (Patrick Ward), 49b (Jennie Woodcock; Reflections Photolibrary), 49cl (Jennie Woodcock; Reflections Photolibrary), 49cr (Jack Hollingsworth) 50 (Bryn Colton), 56tr (David Raymer), 65/F (Miki Duisterhof), 71t (Gary Houlder), 72t (Karin Kohlberg), 73b (Roman Soumar), 75 (Kaveh Kazemi), 76/E (Gideon Mendel), 80/B, 82 (Robbie Jack), 84/A & 84/B (Matt Brown), 84/C (Joe Skipper/Reuters), 85/D & 85/E (Reuters), 85/F (Ray Stubblebine), 86l (Dan Lamont), 86r (Tom & Dee Ann McCarthy), 94l (Bob Krist), 94r (Darren Maybury), 95c (Jon Hocks), 95l (Judy Griesedieck), 95r (Dex Images), 96b (Revillon Patrick), 96c (Norbert Schaeffer),

98l (Jim Sugar), 98r, 102/3 (Jonathan Torgovnik), 102/5 (Carmen Redondo), 107t (Susan Mullane), 108b (Jeff Mitchell/ Reuters), 108tl (Alex Segre/Alamy), 110 (LWA-Stephen Welstead), 115 (Reuters), 122cl (Ludovic Maisant), 124, 128 (Peter Turnley), 130/C, 130/E (Michael Porsche), 130/F (Herrmann/Starke), 134 (Pawel Libera), 136/4 (James Leynse), 14/G (Lyn Goldsmith); **Getty Images** pp 92l (Frank Herholdt), 112, 140bl (Hulton Archive/Evening Standard), 140br (Gabrielle Revere), 140t, 142 (Mel Yates), 143 (Mel Yates), 76/A (Justin Kase); **Ronald Grant Collection** pp 102/1 (© 20th Century Fox); **Robert Harding World Imagery** p 10; **Hemera Photo Objects** pp 20tr, 20bl, 20cb, 20ct, 25tl, 25tr, 130/G, 130/H; **Index Stock Imagery** pp 10bc (Heinle), 14/C (Steve Dunwell), 17bl (Benelux Press), 17tc (Benelux Press), 17tl (Heinle), 18t (Barry Winiker), 19tl (Ed Lallo), 19tr (BSIP Agency), 22b (Heinle), 22cb (AbleStock), 25cbl (Dan Gair Photographic), 25cbr (Walter Geiersperger), 25ctl (Wendell Metzen), 25ctr (Michael Howell), 30b (Omni Photo Communications Inc.), 31t (Zefe Visual Media – Germany), 43l (AbleStock) 44 (Heinle), (46bl IT Stock Int'l), 49c (Heinle), 56bl (Barry Winiker), 64 (Dave Bartruff), 65/A (Peter Johansky), 65/B (Dave Bartruff), 65/C (Peter Ardito), 65/D (IPS), 65/E (FotoKia), 68c (Dave Bartruff), 70 (ThinkStock LLC), 71b (Jim Corwin), 76/C (Mark Gibson), 96t (Mitch Diamond), 122cr (Tina Buckman), 17tl (Steve Dunwell), 41/A (ThinkStock LLC), 41/B (Mark Segal), 41/C (Image Source Limited); **The Kobal Collection** pp 104/A (Paramount), 104/B (Paramount/Miramax /Coote, Clive), 104/C (Universal /MC Broom, Bruce), 104/D (Concord/Warner Bros), 104/E (Warner Bros), 107/b (Dreamworks/Kraychyk, George); **Landov** pp 14/D (David Mercado/Reuters), 14/F (Adrees Latif/Reuters); **ODI** p 20tl (George Palmer); **Photofusion** pp 80/A (Paula Solloway), 81/D (Paul Doyle), 100b (Brian Mitchell), 100t (Crispin Hughes), 108tr (Sally Lancaster), 122cl (Christa Stadtler); **Science Photo Library** p 120/C (Dr P. Marazzi)

Unit 6 How are you? 42	*Conversation* Talking about being ill 42 *Reading* The sleeper 44 *Listening* Greeting people 46	**Using Grammar** **Infinitives of purpose:** *I'm just phoning to see how you are.* 43 **Can't and couldn't:** *I can't eat peanuts. They make me ill.* 45 **Using Vocabulary** **Not feeling well:** *I've got an upset stomach. I've got a bit of a cold.* 42 **Feeling tired:** *I couldn't get to sleep last night. I was up till four reading.* 44 **Good news:** *Hey, guess what? We're getting married! Congratulations!* 47 *Pronunciation* Sounding pleased and surprised 47
Unit 7 School and studying 48	*Conversation* Talking about university 48 *Reading* Students these days! 51 *Listening* Talking about class rules 52 Asking for permission 52	**Using Grammar** **Going to + verb:** *What're you going to study? I'm going to take a year off.* 49 **Asking for permission:** *Is it OK if I close the window? Yes, of course. Go ahead.* 52 **Could you for requests:** *Could you turn it down a bit, please? Yes, of course. Sorry.* 53 **Using Vocabulary** **Your academic career:** *I'm going to do a Master's.* 48 **Studying at university:** *I fell asleep in her last lecture. He dropped out.* 50 **Different subjects:** *You can earn more money if you do business management.* 51 *Pronunciation* Linking words 52
Unit 8 Work and jobs 54	*Conversation* Talking about your job 54 *Reading* Work or life 56 *Listening* Looking for a job 58 Applying for jobs 58	**Using Grammar** **Have to and don't have to:** *I have to start work at six in the morning.* 55 **Present perfect simple:** *Have you done this kind of work before? No, never.* 57 **Want + me + to:** *My parents want me to study economics, but I want to do history.* 59 **Using Vocabulary** **Expressions with get:** *He got sacked. I get six weeks' holiday a year.* 55 **Jobs:** *I'm a bus driver. I'm an estate agent.* 56 **Good at / with:** *I'm terrible at maths. I'm quite good with young children.* 59 **Career or job:** *I'd like to work in the media. I'd like to be an accountant* 59 *Pronunciation* Compound nouns 56

Review: Units 5–8   60

Unit 9 Eating out 64	*Conversation* Deciding where to eat 64 Recommending a restaurant 64 *Reading* I wouldn't recommend it! 66 *Listening* Ordering in a restaurant 68	**Using Grammar** **Some and any:** *Do you want to get something to eat? Have you anywhere in mind?* 65 **Irregular past simple verbs:** *I fell over and hurt myself.* 67 **Using Vocabulary** **Describing food:** *I don't really like anything spicy. It's delicious!* 64 **Restaurant vocabulary:** *Can I book a table for two for tonight, please?* 68 *Pronunciation* Using stress to correct a mistake 69
Unit 10 Family 70	*Conversation* Questions about families 70 Talking about your family 70 *Reading* Eighth time lucky! 72 *Listening* Talking about how you know friends 74	**Using Grammar** **Comparatives:** *She's easier to talk to than my dad. He's a lot older than I am.* 71 **Better / worse:** *My English is better than it was six months ago.* 71 **Using Vocabulary** **A lot in common:** *We've got a lot in common. We both like cats.* 72 **Collocations:** *I live on my own. She got pregnant. I grew up by the sea.* 73 **Key word: die:** *She died in a car crash. He died of cancer. I'm sorry to hear that.* 75 **The internet:** *They met in an internet chat room. I booked the tickets on-line.* 75

5

Unit 11 Getting around 76	*Conversation* Asking for directions 76 *Reading* It drives me mad! 78 *Listening* Four conversations about journeys 81	*Using Grammar* **Indirect questions:** *Do you know how old he is? Do you know if she's married?* 77 **Comparatives:** *Let's get a taxi. It'll be quicker.* 79 *Using Vocabulary* **Around town:** *It's near the crossroads. There's a mosque just past the bridge.* 76 **Talking about time:** *How long does it take you to get to work? About 20 minutes – on a good day.* 78 **Key words: right and wrong:** *Is this the right platform for Leeds? I got on the wrong bus..* 81 *Pronunciation* Sentence stress 76
Unit 12 Free time 82	*Conversation* Talking about your free time 82 *Reading* The other team in Manchester 84 *Listening* Talking about a course 86 Making enquiries about a course 87	*Using Grammar* **Expressions of frequency:** *Not that much. Maybe once or twice a year.* 83 **Superlatives:** *He's one of the nicest people I've ever met.* 85 **Present simple for the future:** *What time do you arrive in Vienna?* 87 *Using Vocabulary* **Team sports:** *I really like watching football. It's really exciting!* 84 **Different kinds of course:** *I'm thinking of doing a German course.* 86 *Pronunciation* Pausing when adding information 83
Review: Units 9–12 88		
Unit 13 Places to stay 92	*Conversation* Booking a hotel room 92 *Reading* The best place I've ever stayed 94 *Listening* Staying with a friend 96	*Using Grammar* **First conditionals:** *I'll do it later if I don't forget. If you wait there, I'll go and see.* 93 **Asking for permission:** *Is it OK if I turn the TV over? Yes, of course.* 97 *Using Vocabulary* **Places to stay on holiday:** *We stayed in a little campsite by a lake. We stayed in a five-star hotel.* 92 **Hotels:** *It had a swimming pool. Has it got somewhere you can leave the children?* 94 **Hardly:** *There were hardly any people there. It cost us hardly anything.* 95 **Describing places:** *It's lovely. It looks out over the mountains.* 95 *Pronunciation* As long as 97
Unit 14 What was it like? 98	*Conversation* Talking about holidays 98 *Reading* What's your life like? 100 *Listening* Eight people answer questions 102	*Using Grammar* **Present perfect questions:** *Have you ever been there? No, but I've never really wanted to. Yes, I went there last year on holiday.* 99 **Asking longer questions:** *What was that film you saw the other day like?* 103 *Using Vocabulary* **Key word: have:** *I had a really nice time. I had the day off.* 101 *Pronunciation* It was great. The food, the wine, everything! 103
Unit 15 What's on? 104	*Conversation* Arranging to go to the cinema 104 *Reading* Saturday night TV 107 *Listening* Booking tickets 108	*Using Grammar* **Passives:** *The show's been cancelled. I'm being picked up from the airport.* 109 *Using Vocabulary* **Different kinds of film:** *horror films, action movies, a drama* 104 **Fixed questions:** *When's it on? What's it about?* 105 **Describing who famous people are:** *Who's Curtis Mayfield? He's a famous old American singer.* 105 **Kinds of TV programme:** *There's a quiz show on later I'd like to see.* 106

Unit 16 **Telephoning** 110	*Conversation* Answering and talking on the phone 110 *Reading* Telephone stories 112 *Listening* Four conversations 115	*Using Grammar* **Reporting what people say:** *Alan told me to ask you if you could call him.* 114 *Using Vocabulary* **Key word: phone:** *Why don't you phone in sick?* *She put the phone down on me.* 110 **Adjectives ending with -ed / -ing: tired / tiring:** *I've had a really tiring day.* *I was so annoyed I wanted to hit him!* 113

Review: Units 13–16   116

Unit 17 **Accidents** 120	*Conversation* Hurting yourself 120 *Reading* It really hurt! 122 *Listening* Two unfortunate situations 124	*Using Grammar* **Have + something done: have it looked at:** *You should have it checked out.* *Maybe you should have it X-rayed.* 120 **Past simple and past continuous:** *I was chopping vegetables, and the knife slipped and cut my finger.* 123 **Will:** *I'll call you a taxi if you like.* 125 **Let me:** *Let me take your coat. Let me help you.* 125 *Using Vocabulary* **Health problems:** *I woke up with horrible toothache.* 121 **Describing accidents:** *It was icy and I slipped. I cut myself shaving.* 121 *Pronunciation* *I'll* 125

Unit 18 **Problems** 126	*Conversation* Things you can't live without 126 *Reading* The queue 128 *Listening* Problems with machines 131	*Using Grammar* **Present perfect questions:** *Have you phoned the bank and cancelled your cards? No, not yet, but I'm going to.* 127 **Must:** *I must go or I'll be late. Listen, I must go. I'm meeting a friend of mine at six.* 129 *Using Vocabulary* **Key word: sort out:** *Did you sort out the problems with your passport?* 127 **Machines and technology:** *Can you bring your camcorder and film it?* 130 *Pronunciation* *must* 129

Unit 19 **Money** 132	*Conversation* Borrowing money 132 *Reading* Eight things I hate about banks 134 *Listening* Money problems 136	*Using Grammar* **Making offers:** *Do you want me to turn the heating on? Would you mind?* *No, of course not.* 133 **Comparing prices:** *Food is much cheaper here than it is in my country.* 136 *Using Vocabulary* **Time and money:** *It's a waste of time. I spend a lot of money on clothes.* 133 **Key word: pay:** *Can I pay in euros? How are you paying?* 137 *Pronunciation* Sentence stress 133

Unit 20 **Society** 138	*Conversation* Talking about life in your country 138 *Reading* The changing faces of Britain 140 *Listening* Comparing young people today with those in the past 142	*Using Grammar* **Questions with how long:** *How long've you been here?* 138 **Describing changes:** *Unemployment is falling at the moment.* *He's changed a lot over the last few months.* 139 **Used to:** *I used to, but I don't anymore. I never used to, but I started last year.* 143 *Using Vocabulary* **The economy:** *Inflation is very low. The economy is in a mess.* 139 *Pronunciation* *of* 139

Review: Units 17–20   144

Tapescript 148	**Grammar commentary** 165	**Student A/B/C material** 176
Grammar introduction 164	**Expression organiser** 171	

Where are you from? • Oh really? Whereabouts in China? • Oh, I've been there. • I've never heard of it. • Sorry. Have you got a light? • Where are you from again? • It's in the south-west. • It's by the sea. • It's up in the mountains. • It's right up in the north. • Do you come from Berlin originally? • I really miss the food. • I really miss my friends and family. • There's a lot of unemployment there. • There are lots of parks and trees there. • Their kids are growing up bilingual.

1 Where are you from?

Conversation

1 | Starting a conversation

Discuss these questions.

1. Are you a quiet person or do you like talking a lot?
2. Do you like talking to people you don't know?

Match the conversation starters with the replies. The first one has been done for you.

1. Is anyone sitting here?   d
2. It's hot, isn't it?
3. Have you been waiting for a long time?
4. Do you know anyone here?

a. Yes, I know. I'll open a window.
b. Ten minutes. The bus should be here soon.
c. No. This is my first class here.
d. No. Go ahead. Take a seat.

Now match these conversation starters with the replies.

5. What a horrible day!
6. What's your name?
7. Where are you from?
8. Is this the bus stop for the centre of town?

e. Yes, it is. You need to get a number 63.
f. Italy. What about you?
g. I know, it's terrible. It's so wet and cold.
h. Andrew. And yours?

Which of the conversation starters above do you use in your language? When?

2 | Making friends

🎧 **Listen to this conversation between two people, Caroline and Danko. They don't know each other very well. The first time you listen, note anything you hear about Danko. Don't look at the conversation while you listen.**

Compare what you heard with a partner.

Listen again and complete the conversation.

C: Do you smoke?

D: No, thanks. I'm trying to stop.

C: Yes, I should too. (1) ...., what's your name again?

D: Danko. And yours?

C: Caroline. Hi, so where are you from, Danko?

D: Croatia.

C: Oh yes? (2) ....? Zagreb?

D: No, Split. It's on the coast. Do you know it?

C: I've heard of it, but I've never been there. There was a tennis player from there, wasn't there? What's his name?

D: Goran Ivanisevic.

C: Yes, that's the one. He was lovely.

D: Yes, well, you should come to Split. There are lots of lovely people there. It's a beautiful city.

C: I'd love to go one day. So how long (3) .... ?

D: Almost six months now. I came here in September.

C: Right. When are you (4) .... to Croatia?

D: In May. I've got to go back then.

C: Why? What do you do back home?

D: Oh, I'm a student. I'm at university. I have to (5) .... June.

C: Oh right. What are you studying?

D: English language and culture. That's (6) .... I'm here.

C: Right, right. Well, you speak English very well.

D: Thanks. I hope so.

C: No, really.

With a partner, practise reading the conversation.

Goran Ivanisevic is one of the most famous people from Croatia. Who is the most famous person from your country?

3 | Where are you from? Whereabouts?

Put the sentences in order and make conversations. The first in each has been done for you.

Conversation 1

a. It's OK. It's quite a big city, but it's a nice place to live.

b. France.

c. Grenoble. It's in the south-east. Do you know it?

d. Oh right. Whereabouts exactly?

e. No. What's it like?

f. So where are you from?

1. [f]   2. [ ]   3. [ ]   4. [ ]   5. [ ]   6. [ ]

Conversation 2

a. Yes, I do, actually. My grandparents lived there!

b. So where are you from originally?

c. Oh, yes. Whereabouts exactly?

d. Oh, a place just near Blackpool.

e. St Anne's. Do you know it?

1. [b]   2. [ ]   3. [ ]   4. [ ]   5. [ ]

Conversation 3

a. Not that far. Haringey.

b. Haringey? Whereabouts exactly?

c. Yes, yes. I used to live in Hewitt Road!

d. So do you live near here?

e. Allison Road. It's just past the shops where the church is. Do you know it?

1. [d]   2. [ ]   3. [ ]   4. [ ]   5. [ ]

In which conversation do you think the people live:

a. in the same country?

b. in the same city?

c. in different countries?

Find out whereabouts exactly in your town or city the other people in your class live. Who lives nearest to you?

4 | Pronunciation: getting the stress right

🎧 **When we speak English, we say words in groups. In each group, we stress one or two important sounds – we say them more loudly than others. Listen and practise these sentences. The stressed parts are in CAPITAL letters. The groups of words are separated by spaces.**

1. It's quite a BIG TOWN   on the SOUTH COAST, about SIXty MILES from LONdon.

2. It's a BIG CIty   RIGHT in the CENtre of ENgland.

3. It's a NICE little SEAside TOWN   on the NORTH-EAST COAST.

4. It's a SMALL TOWN   JUST outside LONdon.

5. It's a FAmous OLD CIty   in the SOUTH-WEST of ENgland.

6. It's a SMALL TOWN   RIGHT up in the NORTH of SCOTland.

7. It's an ARea   in the NORTH-WEST of ENgland.

Now look at the map of Britain and decide which places are being described in the sentences above.

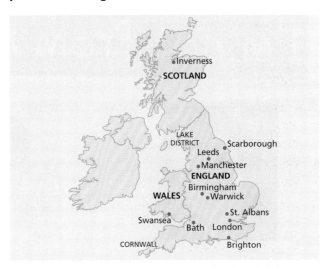

Describe where these places are on the map.

| Cornwall | Leeds | Manchester | Swansea | Warwick |

5 | Practice

Work in pairs.

Student A: You are from England.

Student B: You are from your own country and you meet Student A while you are on holiday.

Have a short conversation like Conversation 1 in Activity 3. Use the information on the map to help you. Then change partners and have a similar conversation.

Reading

1 | Geography quiz

How good is your geography? Do you know where these countries are?

Albania	Ecuador	Oman
Bangladesh	Japan	Somalia
Cuba	Luxembourg	Tunisia
Denmark	Nicaragua	Wales

Tell a partner what you think. Use these expressions.

*   I've no idea where ... is.
*   I think ... is somewhere in South-east Asia but I don't know where exactly.
*   ... is in Eastern Europe. It's next to Poland.
*   I've actually been to ... ! I went there a few years ago on holiday.

2 | Before you read

You are going to read about three people and the reasons why they moved to London. Before you read, think of three reasons why people move to a capital city like London.

3 | While you read

🎧 **Read the article and find out if any of these people had the same reasons you thought of.**

I'm not from here originally

Faten

I'm from Tunisia. I came to London when I got married to Faisal. I met him in Tunisia. He was born in London, but his family used to go to Tunisia every year on holiday to stay with his uncle, who lived in Tunis. My father knew his uncle, so that's how we got to know each other. We went out together every summer when he was there. I really like it here most of the time, but I miss the food in my country and the people. Back home in Tunisia, we visit each other's houses more than people do here in the UK. We cook for each other and share things more. I think we're more friendly and generous. Anyway, two of my sisters also now live here in London, and my children go to school here and they have lots of British friends. It's good and of course they grow up knowing another language.

Hung

I'm from Vietnam originally. I came over here about 25 years ago to escape the problems in my country. Back home in Vietnam, I was a doctor. But when I wanted to work here, they told me I had to get a British degree. The problem was, I lost everything when I came here. I didn't have enough money to study and I needed to support my wife and children. To begin with, I worked in two different places – I did cleaning jobs during the day and at night I worked in a pizza take-away. I hated it, but after a few years, I saved up enough money to do a nursing course and now I work in a big local hospital.

Ian

I was born in the north of England and grew up there. The factory I was working in closed down and so I lost my job. I couldn't find another job – there was a lot of unemployment in my town at the time. So I decided to come here to look for work. I moved down to London around ten years ago. I got a job painting people's houses and I've been doing that since then. Five years ago, I started doing a part-time degree. I work during the day and go to classes in the evenings. I'm going to finish in June this year. I hope I can get a better job after I graduate.

4 | Comprehension

Answer these questions about the three people.

1. Who is originally British?
2. Which of them are immigrants?
3. Who was a refugee?
4. Who had a better job before they lived in London?
5. Whose husband is from London?
6. Which of them are growing up bilingual?

> **Real English: refugee**
>
> A refugee is someone who had to leave their home country – perhaps for political reasons.
>
> An immigrant is someone who decided to move from their own country to live in a new country.

5 | Word check

Complete the sentences with words from the text. Try not to look back at the text.

1. I .... married to Faisal.
2. His family .... to go to Tunisia every year.
3. I .... the food in my country.
4. I came over here about 25 years ....
5. I needed to .... my wife and children.
6. I .... up enough money to do a nursing course.
7. The factory I was working in .... down.
8. I .... my job.
9. There was a lot of .... in my town.
10. I work .... the day and go to classes in the evenings.

6 | Speaking

Discuss these questions with a partner.

1. Do you know anyone who is bilingual? What languages do they speak?
2. Do you know anyone who is married to someone from a different country?
3. Would you like to live in a different country?

7 | Using grammar: past simple

We form the past simple of regular verbs by adding -ed or -d to the verb:

* My grandfather worked in a bank.
* We lived in France for two years.

We make negatives by using didn't before the verb:

* We didn't have any money, so I had to get a job.
* I didn't see you yesterday. Were you ill?

We make questions by using did you / did she / did they before the verb:

* Did you go out last night?
* Where did he work before here?

Some common verbs have irregular past simple forms. Which verbs have these past simple forms?

bought	found	had	lost	told
brought	got	knew	made	took
came	grew up	left	said	went

Complete the sentences with the past simple form of the verbs.

1. We .... to Tokyo because my father .... a job there. (move, get)
2. I .... Bolton when I .... my job. It was easier to find a job here. (leave, lose)
3. I .... here when my husband's father .... He .... to live nearer his mum so we could look after her. (move, die, want)
4. We .... to move because we .... the area. There was a lot of crime. (decide, not like)
5. We had to leave because of the war. We .... safe living there. (not feel)
6. We moved to the country because we .... living in a big city. It was too crowded and the children .... anywhere to play. (hate, not have)
7. When .... you .... here? (move)
8. Why .... they .... Cuba? (leave)

> ▶ For more information on using the past simple, see G1.

8 | Speaking

Discuss these questions with a partner.

1. How many times have you and your parents moved? Why?
2. Do you know anyone who is not originally from the place they live now? Why did they move?
3. Are there any reasons in sentences 1–6 in Activity 7 that you think are bad reasons to move?

Listening

1 | Meeting people

When you meet someone for the first time, which of these things are you happy to do?

a. give them your address

b. give them your e-mail address

c. give them your home telephone number

d. invite them back to your house or flat

e. go back to their house

f. accept a lift in their car

Tell a partner about your choices. Try to explain them.

2 | Before you listen

Discuss these questions.

1. Who do you think the two people in this picture are?

2. What do you think they are talking about?

3. What do you think happens next?

3 | While you listen

🎧 **Listen to the conversation between the two people in the picture and see if you were right. Tell a partner:**

1. who the two people are.

2. where they are from.

3. what these places are like.

4. what you think is going to happen.

Listen again if you need to.

4 | Using grammar: *there's / there are*

In the conversation, you heard that:

*   there are a lot of tourists in Burlington.

*   there's so much to see and do in London.

*   there's so much crime and violence in Washington DC.

We use there are with plural nouns.

We use there's with singular nouns or uncountable nouns.

Look at these examples.

*   There are lots of hotels near the station.

*   There are lots of nice beaches on the south coast.

*   There's only one cinema in the whole city.

*   There's quite a lot of unemployment in my country. It's about ten per cent.

Complete the answers to the question 'What's it like there?' with there's or there are.

1. It's great. .... a really good transport system, so it's very easy to travel round.

2. It's nice. .... lots of big shops and malls, so it's good for shopping.

3. It's not that nice. .... lots of factories, so it's quite an ugly place.

4. It's OK, but .... too many people. It's really crowded.

5. It's nice. .... lots of parks and trees. It's beautiful.

6. It's not very nice. .... quite a lot of crime, so it's not safe at night.

7. It's great. .... lots of really nice old buildings. It's beautiful.

8. It's OK, but .... not much to do. .... a cinema and .... a few bars, but that's about it.

> ▶ For more information on using *there's* and *there are*, see G2.

Real English: There's a lot of ...

Some people use There's with plural nouns, especially when they use a lot of before the noun. Look at these examples:

There's a lot of cars on the road this morning.

There's a lot of policemen outside. What's happening?

It's easier and quicker to say There's a lot of than There are a lot of!

5 | Pronunciation: weak forms

When we say there's and there are, we usually use their weak forms: /ðez/ and /ðerə/.

⌒ **Listen to the sentences in Activity 4 and check your answers.**

Now practise the sentences in Activity 4. Try to use the weak forms.

6 | Practice

Tell a partner the names of three places you know well. Your partner will ask you What's it like there? Try to answer as in Activity 4. Use there's and there are.

What's the best / worst place in your country to live? Why?

7 | Key words: *miss* and *lose*

In this unit, Ian lost his job and a tourist called George missed the last bus. Complete the sentences with the words in the box.

my address book	the beach	2–1
my train	the class	weight
on the way	the end	

1. Can you give me your phone number again? I've lost ....
2. Sorry, I'm late. I got lost .... here. I've been walking around for hours.
3. Did you see the game on Saturday? Chelsea lost .... to Liverpool.
4. I really miss going to .... now we live in London. I lived by the sea when I was younger.
5. Have you seen Andrew? He's so thin. He's lost a lot of .... He used to be really fat.
6. Sorry, I missed .... yesterday. I had to go to an important meeting.
7. Did you see that film last night? I missed .... because I had to go out.
8. Sorry I'm late. I overslept and I missed ....

Now cover the sentences. How many of the expressions with miss and lose can you remember?

Complete these sentences with the correct form of miss or lose.

1. I don't believe it! I've .... my keys!
2. My boyfriend has been in Australia for three months studying English. I really .... him.
3. Hurry up. I don't want to .... the beginning of the match.
4. It was terrible. I got .... on the way to the airport and I .... my flight.

8 | Speaking

Discuss these questions with a partner.

A: What's the worst thing you've ever lost?

B: I once lost …

A: Have you missed a class or a meeting recently?

B: I missed a … recently because I …

A: Have you ever missed a flight or a train?

B: I once missed a … to …

A: What would you miss if you lived in a different country?

B: The thing I'd miss most is …

2 Likes and dislikes

What kind of music do you like? • I can't stand traditional folk music. • I'm thinking of going to the Travis concert and I'm trying to find someone to go with. • All their songs sound the same. • I've never heard of him. • She's OK, I suppose. • I love anything by Mark Smith. • I like anything with Jackie Chan in. • I like lots of different things, but mainly I read crime fiction. • I ring my mum every weekend. • He sounds really nice. • How long have you known each other? • It went really well. • The meeting went on for hours.

Conversation

1 | Speaking

What kind of music is being played in each photo?

classical	folk	jazz	soul
country	heavy metal	punk	

Do you know any famous people who play these kinds of music?

2 | Likes and dislikes

🎧 **Listen to this conversation between two people – Ken and Joyce. The first time you listen, note the kinds of music they like. Don't look at the conversation while you listen.**

Listen again and complete the conversation.

K: Do you like opera?

J: No, I (1) .... I find it really boring. Why do you ask?

K: Oh, I'm (2) .... going to see something at The Opera House and I'm trying to find someone to go with.

J: No, sorry. I always think operas go on too long. I can't sit still for four hours.

K: Never mind. I'll try someone else.

J: Have you asked Miriam? I think she likes that kind of music.

K: Oh, right. OK. Maybe I'll ask her. So (3) .... music do you like?

J: Lots of things, really. Jazz, pop, Latin music. I love Tito Lopez.

K: Really? I hate him. All his songs sound the same. I like jazz, though. Do you like Louis Armstrong?

J: Yes, he's OK. I quite like some of his tunes, but (4) .... Gato Barbieri.

K: Oh, right. I've never (5) .... Who is she?

J: He's a man. He's an Argentinian musician. He's really good. I'll lend you a CD if you like.

K: Yes, OK. Thanks.

Now look at the tapescript and practise reading it with a partner. Remember to stress the sounds in CAPITAL LETTERS and try to say each group of words together.

14

3 | Answering questions

Complete the conversations with the expressions in the box.

It's OK, I suppose.	No, not really.
I've never heard of it.	Yes, I love it.
No, I can't stand him.	Yes, they're OK.

1. A: Do you like football?
    B: .... I play every week.
    Why do you ask?

2. A: Do you like Coldplay?
    B: .... I quite liked their first
    album. Why do you ask?

3. A: Do you like modern art?
    .... I find it a bit boring
    sometimes. Why do you ask?

4. A: Do you like reading?
    B: .... I find most books
    really boring. I prefer watching TV. Why do you ask?

5. A: Do you like Tom Cruise?
    B: .... I think he's awful.
    He can't act. Why do you ask?

6. A: Do you like the song *Can you get to that?*
    B: .... How does it go?

Now add these replies to the conversations.

1. ☐   2. ☐   3. ☐   4. ☐   5. ☐   6. ☐

a. I'm thinking of going to see them in concert and I'm
    trying to find someone to go with.

b. I'm thinking of going to an exhibition this afternoon
    and I'm trying to find someone to go with.

c. I'm thinking of going to see the Inter Milan game on
    Sunday and I'm trying to find someone to go with.

d. I'm thinking of going to his new film tonight and I'm
    trying to find someone to go with.

e. I think it goes *Can you get to that? I want to know if you
    can get to that. Da di da.*

f. No reason. I just wondered.

Practise the conversations with a partner.

🎧 **Listen and practise the sentences. Notice the
difference between the way we say OK and OK,
I suppose.**

4 | Practice

**Think about your answers to these questions. Try
to answer as in the conversations in Activity 3.
Then ask some other students the same questions.**

1. Do you like horror films?
2. Do you like going shopping?
3. Do you like swimming?
4. Do you like cooking?
5. Do you like clubbing?

5 | Vocabulary: *What kind?*

Complete the lists with the expressions in the box.

anything by Steven Spielberg	nature programmes
e-mails to friends	old coins
fashion magazines	traditional folk music

1. jazz / classical / rock / techno / ....
2. anything on history / anything on politics /
    biographies / novels / ....
3. foreign stamps / modern paintings / anything to do
    with Star Wars / ....
4. documentaries / sitcoms / news programmes /
    game shows / ....
5. a diary / poems / short stories / ....
6. anything with Chow Yun Fat in / action movies /
    comedies / ....

**Compare your answers with a partner. Then add one
more thing to each list. Find out if your partner likes
any of the things.**

6 | Practice

Complete the questions with the verbs in the box.

collect	listen to	write
go and see	read	watch

1. A: What kind of things do you .... ?
    B: Lots of things really, but mainly Brazilian and Cuban
    music. I love anything you can dance to.

2. A: What kind of things do you .... on TV?
    B: Anything really, but mainly nature programmes.
    I love anything about animals.

3. A: What kind of things do you usually ....
    at the cinema?
    B: Mainly action movies. I love anything with Arnold
    Schwarzenegger in.

4. A: What kind of things do you .... ?
    B: Mainly old Spanish coins, but I also have some
    Roman ones. I also collect stamps.

5. A: What kind of things do you .... ?
    B: I mainly just keep a diary, but I've also tried writing
    some short stories.

6. A: What kind of things do you .... ?
    B: I don't really like novels. I prefer non-fiction, like
    biographies. I love anything on politics or history.

**With a partner, have conversations which are true
for you. For example:**

A: What do you do in your free time?

B: I like listening to music.

A: Oh really. What kind of things do you listen to?

B: Lots of things really, but mainly blues and soul.

Reading

1 | Introduction

🎧 **Read the beginning of this article about best friends. Do you agree with Professor Morris? Why / why not?**

Professor Morris, from the University of Thameside, has just written a book about friends and relations. In it, he says that people in Britain today believe that their friends are more important than their families. He says, 'These days, many people in Britain move away from their family and home to look for work or to study. If children and parents live in different cities, families cannot help each other in the way they did in the past. Grandparents can't babysit their grandchildren and children can't look after their parents when they get old. Brothers and sisters can't go out together or see each other much. Personally, I don't think this is a bad thing. We choose our friends in a way we can't choose our families. With friends, we have a lot of things in common, which we often don't have with our families.' Not everyone agrees with Professor Morris, so we decided to ask a few people in the street who their best friends are and why.

2 | Vocabulary

Match the sentence beginnings with the endings to make sentences about family relationships.

1. I chat
2. I often cook
3. I sometimes go
4. My brother and I both support
5. My parents sometimes babysit
6. I usually ring
7. I often take
8. I usually get on

a. shopping with my mother.
b. really well with my younger sister.
c. on the phone a lot with my brother.
d. my sister when I have a problem.
e. my brother out for dinner.
f. Hull City football club.
g. for us.
h. dinner for my parents.

Are any of the sentences above true for you and your family? What other things do you do together with your parents / brothers / sisters?

Real English: my brother and I

Using I like this is always correct in both spoken and written English. However, you will hear young people say:
Me and my brother or Me and some friends or Me and Jane.
We don't usually start with me like this when we write. Some older people even think it is wrong. Are there things like this in your language?

3 | While you read

🎧 **Now read the rest of the article about best friends on the opposite page. Who agrees with Professor Morris and who doesn't?**

4 | Comprehension

In pairs, tell your partner if you think you could or couldn't be friends with each of the people in the article. Say why. Use these expressions.

I don't think I could be friends with ...
- I don't really like walking.
- I hate animals.
- He sounds really boring.
- I could never be friends with someone who was older than me.

I think I would get on with ...
- I love the same things as him.
- He sounds really nice.
- I usually get on with people who talk a lot.

5 | Speaking

Put the words in order and make questions.
1. does / she / do / What
   ....?
2. How / each / you / know / do / other
   ....?
3. known / How / have / you / each / long / other
   ....?
4. Do / together / go / out / you / much
   ....?

Tell some other students about your best friend. Ask each other the questions.

Family or friends

◇ Katy (27)

My mum is a nice woman, but we're very different. If I have a problem or if I really want to talk to someone, I ring my friend Marian. I've known her since I was at school. We often go shopping together. We spend the whole day going to different shops, trying things on. We stop for coffee and lunch, and chat to each other about everything. We get on really well.

◇ Charlotte (34)

I'm a twin and I think my sister and I will always be best friends. I see her a lot. We both love cooking – really hot, spicy food like Indian curries and things like that – so we often invite each other round for dinner.

◇ Graham (48)

I don't believe what this guy Morris is saying! I live with my mother and she is still the most important person for me. We do lots of things together. We both like the theatre, so we go a lot. We like similar kinds of music. We're both big fans of Andrew Lloyd Webber. I can talk to her about anything.

◇ Damien (22)

My best friend is James. We both really love Star Wars. We actually met at a Star Wars club and we get on really well. We watch the films together once or twice a month and go to conventions with other Star Wars fans. We went to America together on holiday last year. If I had a problem, I might talk to him. It's never really happened.

◇ Ron (37)

My best friend's my dog. Dogs don't lie; they don't criticise you and they like going for a walk. What more do you want from a friend?

◇ Edna (67)

I'm not sure I would call my children my best friends. Professor Morris is probably right. My best friend is my husband. We've been married for over 30 years, so I suppose we must get on quite well! We met in Nigeria, where we were both teaching. Apart from both being teachers, we are both Christians and that's a very important thing we share. Having said that, our best friends aren't religious at all. Joyce and Zola used to be our neighbours. That's how we became friends. We just found we had a lot of other things in common. They'd also lived in Africa, for example. We all love walking and I suppose we are all active in politics.

◇ John (26)

I actually don't have very much in common with my best friend, Colin. I've known him since I was six or seven. When we left university, he joined the army and I became an art teacher. He plays a lot of sport like football, and he hates going to art galleries and places like that. We're still friends because he's really funny, and maybe just because we've known each other so long. Also, I think we actually both love arguing about films and things in the news.

Listening

1 | Key word: *go*

Find twenty-one expressions with the word **go**. Mark the end of each expression using /. The first one has been marked for you.

```
Itwentreallywell/itwentbadlyI
wentonmyownIwentwithafriend
I'mgoingswimminglaterareyou
goingonholidayinthesummerdo
youwanttogoforawalkI'mgoing
backhomeonTuesdayI'mgoingout
laterhow'sitgoingpriceshavegone
upalotrecentlyhowdiditgothe
meetingwentonforhoursIwent
roundtoafriend'shousegoonthere
yougoI'mjustgoingtothetoilet
sure,goaheadIwentshoppinghe's
justgonetogetanewspapergotobed
early
```

When you translate the above expressions into your language, how many of the translations use the word **go**? Which expressions use a different verb in your language?

2 | Pronunciation: stress

Very common verbs like **go**, **have**, **take** and **get** are used in lots of different expressions. We do not usually stress these verbs. We usually stress the word which carries the main meaning of the expression.

🎧 Listen and practise the expressions.

3 | Listening

🎧 Listen to this conversation between three people – Mario, Tina and Hugh. Tick the expressions you hear from Activity 1. Then compare your answers with a partner.

Now listen again and try to answer these questions.

1. What's the relationship between the three people?
2. What problems does Mario have?
3. What's Hugh's problem?

4 | Speaking

Discuss these questions with a partner.

1. What was the last exam or test you did? How did it go?
2. Have you ever been travelling on your own? When? Where to?
3. When did you last go round to a friend's house? What for?
4. What's the longest meeting you've been to? What's the longest film you've seen? How long did it go on for?

> **Real English: How did it go?**
>
> If a friend has just done something difficult (sat an exam, had an interview, had a meeting, etc.), you can ask How did it go? or How was it?

5 | Using grammar: *too*

Mario didn't do well in his speaking test because he was **too tired to think.** When was the last time you felt like that?

Match the statements with the follow-up comments.

1. It's too hot here. ☐
2. It's really hot here. ☐

a. I love this kind of weather.
b. I hate this kind of weather.

We often use too + adjective to explain why we don't like something or cannot do it.

Complete the sentences with the adjectives in the box.

busy   hot   late   old   tired   young

1. I don't want you to go to that party. You're only 15. You're too .... to stay out all night.
2. Be careful with the coffee. It's too .... to drink at the moment.
3. I've had a really long day. I'm too .... to cook tonight. Let's just get a pizza.
4. Listen, I'm too .... to do it now, but I'll try to do it sometime this afternoon, OK?
5. I'm 45. I can't go to a disco! I'm too .... to go clubbing.
6. It's nearly midnight. It's too .... to call her now. Phone her tomorrow.

Did you notice what comes after too + adjective in the sentences above?

Now complete these sentences using your own ideas.

a. I'm too old to ....
b. I'm too young to ....
c. It's too cold to ....
d. It's too hot to ....

Compare your ideas with a partner.

We can also use too with other words. Look at these examples.

A: He drives too fast.
B: I know. He's going to have an accident one day.

A: He drives too fast.
B: I know. I get scared when I'm in the car with him.

Match the problems with the bad results.

1. She talks too quickly. ☐
2. He eats too much. ☐
3. She does things too quickly. ☐
4. They play their music too loud. ☐
5. I ate my dinner too quickly. ☐
6. He talks too much. ☐

a. I feel sick.
b. He's always saying the wrong thing.
c. He's going to get really fat.
d. It's hard to understand her.
e. I can't get to sleep at night.
f. She's always making mistakes.

With a partner, think of another bad result for each problem above.

> For more information on using *too*, see G3.

19

Have you got any plasters? • I think there are some in my bag somewhere. • Have you got any brothers or sisters? • I'm an only child. • Have you got time for a coffee? • Have you got the time on you? • Have you got a light? • Yes. There you go. • There's one in the bathroom. • It's on the shelf. • Have you got a torch? • I'm thinking of getting a laptop. • This one is much nicer than the blue one. • That one was a bit complicated to use. • Have you got anything a bit cheaper? • They've got a tiny flat.

3 Have you got ... ?

Conversation

1 | Explaining where things are

Why would you ask for the things in the pictures?

🎧 **Listen to this conversation between Paul and Steven, and find out what Steven asks for and why. Don't look at the conversation while you listen.**

Listen again and complete the conversation.

P: Ouch!

S: What's up?

P: I've just (1) .... on this nail.

S: Let's have a look. Oh, yes. That's quite nasty.

P: I'd better run it under the tap.

S: Have you got (2) .... ? I'll go and get you one.

P: Yes, I think there are some on the shelf (3) ....
....

S: I can't see any. Are you sure they're here?

P: Do you see the cupboard (4) .... ?
Have a look in there. I think there are some in the top drawer.

S: I've found them.

P: Thanks.

S: I also found these.

P: Oh, er ... right ... er ... Where did you find those?

S: They were (5) ....

P: Whose are they?

S: Well, (6) .... !

What do you think Steven found in the bathroom? Begin your answer Maybe he found some ... .

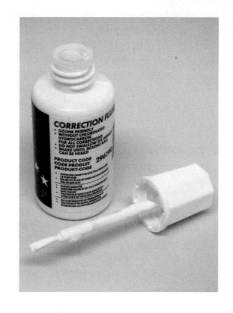

2 | Using grammar: questions with *have you got … ?*

With a singular noun, we use **Have you got a … ?**

With a plural or uncountable noun, we use **Have you got any … ?**

Complete each conversation with one of the questions above and an appropriate noun.

1. A: Oh no! .... ?
   I've just spilt wine all over your carpet.
   B: Yes, there's one in the kitchen by the sink.

2. A: Ouch! .... ? I've just
   cut myself.
   B: Yes, there are some in the drawer in the kitchen.

3. A: .... ? I've just met an
   old friend and want to make a note of his phone
   number.
   B: Yes, just a minute. There's one in my bag
   somewhere.

4. A: .... ? I just need to
   cut this bit of string.
   B: Yes, there's a pair on the table in the front room.

5. A: .... ? I just need to
   open this plug up to see if the fuse is OK.
   B: Yes, there's one in a box in the garage, I think.

6. A: .... ? I just need to
   change this word here.
   B: Yes, one minute. There's some on my desk.

🎧 **Now listen to the conversations and check your answers.**

Look at the tapescript and practise reading it with a partner.

Remember to stress the sounds in CAPITAL LETTERS and try to say each group of words together.

▶ For more information on using questions with *have you got*, see G4.

3 | Practice

With a partner, have conversations like those in Activity 2 about these things.

a corkscrew	a knife	a stapler
a dustpan and brush	a needle	a torch
an envelope	a rubber	

4 | Speaking

Tell a partner what YOU keep in these places.

1. in the drawers in the kitchen
2. in the cabinet in the bathroom
3. under the sink in the kitchen
4. on the floor in your bedroom
5. in your wallet or purse

5 | Talking about people's houses

Complete the conversations with the words in the boxes.

Conversation 1

bedrooms	garden	the country

A: What's their place like?
B: It's really nice. They've got a really big house in
.... I think it's got six ....
or something like that. It's huge. And then they've got a
huge .... with a swimming pool.

Conversation 2

bathroom	cramped	lounge	modern

A: What's their place like?
B: It's OK. It's a small flat in a .... building.
It's only got one bedroom. Then there's a small
.... where they eat as well. Then they've
got a tiny kitchen and a tiny .... , which
has room for a shower and a toilet, and that's about it.
It's a bit .... now they've got a baby, so
they're thinking of moving.

Conversation 3

balcony	building	floor	lift

A: What's his place like?
B: It's really nice. He's got this huge flat on the top
.... of an old .... in the
centre of town. It's got a lovely big ....
It looks out over the park. The flat is very light
inside, but the building hasn't got a .... ,
so they have to walk up the stairs every day.

Real English: a three-bedroom house

In Britain, people generally talk about the size of a
house by saying how many bedrooms it's got rather
than how many square metres (m^2) it is. Look at
these examples:

He's got a huge mansion. It's got 25 bedrooms!
They've got a tiny one-bedroom flat.

What's the best / worst flat you know? What's it like?

Reading

1 | Before you read

Look at the people in the photos and read about the things they **HAVEN'T GOT**. What reasons do you think they will give for not having the things?

**Amparo is a doctor.
She hasn't got a mobile phone.**

**Muriel is a manager.
She hasn't got any children.**

2 | Jigsaw reading

Work in two groups.
Group A: read about Amparo and Muriel.
Group B: read about Andrew and Boris.
Find out what reasons each person gives for not having certain things.

Group A

**Andrew is a teacher.
He hasn't got a watch.**

**Boris is a student.
He hasn't got a TV.**

I haven't got one!

Amparo

I haven't got a mobile phone and I don't want one. I don't really know why – I just hate them. If you've got a mobile phone, it means people can contact you at any time. Personally, I sometimes want to get away from the hospital, my kids and my mother, and be on my own. I don't want people ringing me all the time. The other thing is, I hate the way some people behave when they have mobile phones. Sometimes when I talk to patients and their relatives, their phone rings and they answer it. I'm trying to tell them they've got some terrible disease and they've only got a few months to live, and they're talking to some friend about going shopping or where they get their hair cut! I just think it's so rude!

Muriel

We haven't got any children. My husband Liam and I can't have any. We thought about getting medical treatment, but it was very expensive. Now I'm happy we didn't have any. I look at my friends and I feel sorry for them. They don't get enough sleep because the baby wakes them up in the middle of the night. They can't go out because they haven't got anyone to babysit. They haven't got any money because they spend it all on nappies, clothes, food and child care. And it never stops because when your kids get older, you'll have to pay their school fees and university fees. Someone told me it costs £10,000 a year to have a child! It's cheaper to go on holiday to the Caribbean every year. I know what I'd prefer! Sometimes Liam gets upset when people ask 'Have you got any kids?', but I don't. I just say 'No, thank goodness!'

Group B

I haven't got one!

Andrew

I haven't got a watch. I don't like wearing them. They feel uncomfortable, so when I do wear one, I always end up taking it off. The problem is, I usually forget to put it back on and then I leave it somewhere. I've probably lost four or five watches like that. I don't want to waste my money buying another one. It's not a big problem. There's always a clock nearby and if there isn't, you can always ask someone the time. It's actually a good way of starting conversations with people. In fact, that's how I first met my wife! She was in the university coffee bar and the first time I spoke to her was to ask the time. We got married last year. I don't wear my wedding ring because it feels uncomfortable and I don't want to lose it like I lost all those watches.

Boris

I haven't got a TV. I used to have one, but one day my three-year-old nephew poured water down the back of it and the TV exploded. I didn't have enough money to buy a new one immediately. I tried to save some money, but I found it really difficult because I went out more. I went to the cinema and to concerts, and I went out with my friends more. When I was at home, I read or listened to music and studied more. I even started learning to play the guitar and teaching myself English. I suddenly realised how much time I wasted watching TV. I didn't miss it at all. So when my sister offered to buy me a new TV and DVD for my birthday, I said I didn't want one. She bought me a lovely old guitar instead.

3 | Information exchange

Check with somebody else from your group to make sure you found the same reasons.

Now tell somebody from the other group about what you have read.

4 | Language work

Work with a partner from the other group. Can you remember who talked about these things? What exactly did they say about each one?

conversations	offered	sleep	water
get away from	rings	upset	wedding ring

Now read the text again. Underline exactly what the people said about the things. Did your partner forget to tell you anything? What?

Which of the four people do you agree with? Why / why not?

5 | Speaking

Tell a partner about:

1. something you can't live without.
2. something you used to have, but that you haven't got any more.
3. something you've got now, but want to get rid of.
4. something you haven't got at the moment, but would like to have.

6 | Using grammar: *I'm thinking of …*

Match the sentence beginnings with the endings to make sentences about what people haven't got.

1. I'm thinking of getting a bicycle because
2. I'm thinking of getting a new car because
3. I'm thinking of getting a laptop because
4. I'm thinking of getting a new laptop because
5. I'm thinking of trying to find a new job because
6. I'm thinking of buying a flat because
7. I'm thinking of getting a mobile phone because
8. I'm thinking of getting a new mobile phone because

a. the one I've got now is really slow and doesn't have enough memory.
b. the one I've got keeps breaking down all the time!
c. I really hate wasting all my money on rent.
d. you can't send pictures with the one I've got now.
e. I really hate the one I've got now. My boss is really horrible!
f. I'm out of the office a lot and I need to be able to contact people.
g. then I could do some work on the train.
h. I really hate taking the bus to work every day.

Spend two minutes trying to memorise as many of the sentence endings as you can.

Now close your book. Your partner will read out the sentence beginnings. How many endings can you remember?

What are YOU thinking of getting / buying / trying / doing? Why?

> For more information on using *I'm thinking of*, see G5.

23

Listening

1 | Speaking

Ask some other students these questions.

a. Have you got a car?

b. Have you got any children?

c. Have you got a computer at home?

d. Have you got a mobile phone?

e. Have you got any brothers or sisters?

f. Have you got any pets?

g. Have you got a degree?

2 | While you listen

🎧 **Listen to seven short conversations and decide which of the questions from Activity 1 each person is answering.**

1. ☐   2. ☐   3. ☐   4. ☐

5. ☐   6. ☐   7. ☐

Discuss with a partner what you can remember about each person's answer. Did any of the speakers have any similar answers to you?

3 | Word check

Can you remember the missing words from these extracts?

1. a. I sometimes got a bit ………………………… because I didn't have anyone to play with.
    b. I often used to go ………………………… to friends' houses.

2. a. Do you want to …………………………… it?
    b. You have to ………………………… that green button there.

3. a. I haven't even got a driving ……………………………… !
    b. Public ………………………… is usually fine for me.

4. a. I graduated ……………………………… mechanical engineering in 1995.
    b. decide to offer you the …………………………

5. a. It's very slow and it ……………………………… all the time.
    b. Why don't you get …………………………… of it and get a new one?

6. a. He's very ………………………… on it.
    b. He's forgotten to ……………………………… it.

7. a. quite hard …………………………
    b. I can …………………………… .

Listen to the conversations again and check your answers – or read the tapescript.

Discuss these questions.

1. When was the last time you got upset? Why?

2. How often do you use public transport?

3. What kind of things are you very keen on?

4 | Using grammar: reference words

Look at this extract from Conversation 5. Can you remember what the two people are talking about?

A: It's a really old one.

B: Yes? Why don't you get rid of it and get a new one?

A: I don't know. I don't really need a new one. The old one does everything I need it to.

We use one or ones to talk about something that has already been talked about.

When we are comparing things, we can avoid repeating the noun:

*   I like this sofa. It's much nicer than that blue one you had.

*   It was a good film, but his last one was better.

*   I'll have to wear these shoes until my other ones have been repaired.

*   I don't like those jeans. The other ones were nicer.

Complete the conversations with one or ones.

1. A: I've just bought Jean a really nice present for her birthday.
    B: Oh, that reminds me. I must get her ………………………… too. What did you get her?

2. A: Which curtains do you prefer? These ………………………… or those red ………………………… we looked at earlier?
    B: The red ………………………… , I think.

3. A: Have you heard The Warlocks' latest CD?
    B: Yes. It's great. It's much better than their last ………………………… .

4. A: Which plates do you want me to use? These ………………………… ?
    B: No, not those ………………………… . I don't think they're big enough. Try the other ………………………… over there, by the sink.

> ### Real English: I can imagine
>
> When someone tells you how they feel and you want to tell them you understand, you can say I can imagine. Here are some examples:
>
> A: *I've worked late every day this week. I'm really tired.*
> B: *I can imagine.*
> A: *I was really pleased when I heard the news.*
> B: *I can imagine.*
> A: *I felt terrible when he told me the news.*
> B: *Yes, I can imagine.*

5 | Practice

Look at the pairs of photos. With a partner, discuss which of the two choices you prefer and why. Use these questions.

*   Which one **do you prefer?** This one **or that one?**
*   Which ones **do you prefer?** These ones **or those ones?**

6 | Further practice

Eight people are talking in shops. Match their problems with the questions they then ask.

1. This one's a bit small.
2. These ones are a bit big on me.
3. This one's a bit complicated to use.
4. This one's a bit bright on me.
5. This one's a bit expensive for me.
6. I don't really like the colour of this one.
7. I don't really like the length of this one.
8. I don't really like the style of this one.

a. Have you got something a bit more modern?
b. Have you got something a bit longer?
c. Have you got any smaller ones?
d. Have you got anything a bit easier to understand?
e. Have you got anything a bit darker?
f. Have you got anything a bit cheaper?
g. Have you got a larger one?
h. Have you got a pink one?

We don't stress one in what the people say above. We stress the word which goes before it.

⌒ **Listen to what the people say and mark the words before one which are stressed.**

▶ For more information on using *one* and *ones*, see G6.

7 | Speaking

Discuss these questions with a partner.

1. This unit has been about things. Do you have enough things or too many things?
2. How often do you throw things out? Do you have any things at the moment you really should throw out?
3. What do you do with things you don't need any more?
4. Are there any things you really need to get?
5. Could you live in a room like this one?

It's just gone ten to seven. • What time does the film start? • I'm going out for dinner later. Do you want to come with me? • Shall we say half past nine? • I'm having my hair cut tomorrow. • It's our anniversary. • I hope you get better soon. • I'll never forget it. • When was the last time you went to the doctor's? • The other day. • In a few days' time. • I'm really looking forward to it. • I need to make an appointment. • I've got an exam next Thursday. • A friend's coming over to watch a video. • I hope you pass.

4 Times and dates

Conversation

1 Do you know what the time is?

Match the times with the clocks.

1. It's just gone three.
2. It's five o'clock exactly.
3. It's half past two.
4. It's almost three o'clock.
5. It's one thirty.
6. I don't know exactly, but it must be around four.
7. It's a quarter to six.
8. It's just gone a quarter past six.

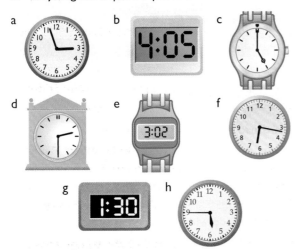

Now ask a partner the time in the clocks below.

Real English: half past nine

This is the normal way to say the time. In informal spoken English you will also hear half nine, half one, etc. You will also hear It's half past if it is clear to everyone that the hour is nine. In the same way, you can say It's ten to, It's a quarter past, It's twenty-five to.

---

2 Making plans

You are going to listen to a conversation between two friends – Syd and Emily. Some of the words they use are below. Look quickly at the words. Try to guess what Syd and Emily are talking about. Discuss your ideas with a partner for three minutes.

S: party – tonight?
E: think so – you?
S: nice – meet – new people
E: free!
S: never say no
E: time – start?
S: seven – later – don't want – first one
E: neither
S: meet – before – go together?
E: where?
S: café? – drink first
E: time?
S: quarter past seven? – miss – food and drink
E: fine
S: doing now? – coffee?
E: time?
S: half past nine
E: go – late
S: see – café – seven
E: bye

🎧 **Now listen to the conversation and see if you were right.**

Look at the tapescript and listen again. Was there anything you missed?

Practise reading the tapescript with a partner. Remember to stress the sounds in CAPITAL LETTERS and try to say each group of words together.

Spend five minutes trying to memorise the conversation. Then have the same conversation again. This time, just use the notes above to help you remember.

Have you been to any places for free? Where? Were they good? For example:

* My boss took us all out for dinner once to this really nice restaurant.
* I went to a reception for business people at the American Embassy once.
* I won a free trip to Disneyland once.

3 | Making arrangements

Complete the conversations with the questions in the box.

> how about around seven at Tom's Diner?
>
> how about 11 a.m. at my house?
>
> how about half past nine at my house?
>
> how about nine in front of Victoria Coach Station?
>
> how about outside here at a quarter past twelve?

1. A: I'm going shopping later. Do you want to come with me?
    B: Yes, OK. What time?
    A: My class finishes at twelve, so ....
    ....

2. A: We're going on a trip to Oxford on Sunday. Do you want to come?
    B: Yes, OK. What time?
    A: Well, the coach leaves at twenty-five past nine, so
    ....

3. A: I'm going to a party later. Do you want to come?
    B: Yes, OK. What time?
    A: It starts at about nine, so ....
    ....
    We could walk to the party from there. It's not far.

4. A: We're going for a picnic on Saturday. Do you want to come?
    B: Yes, OK. What time?
    A: We're going in the car so ....
    ....
    You've got my address, haven't you?

5. A: I'm going to the cinema tonight to see *The Beast*. Do you want to come?
    B: Yes, OK. What time?
    A: Well, it starts at eight, so ....
    ....
    We could go and have a coffee first.

Now practise the conversations. In each case B should end the conversation by saying OK. That sounds fine.

Real English: Shall we say … ?

In everyday spoken English, another common way of saying How about … ? is Shall we say … ? Look at these examples:

A: *So where do you want to meet?*
B: *Shall we say outside the cinema at eight?*

With a partner, practise the conversations above again. Try to use Shall we say … ? instead of How about … ?

4 | Using grammar: present continuous for arrangements

We often use be + -ing to talk about things we have arranged to do in the future.

*   We're catching the 7.45 train tomorrow morning.
*   I'm not working this Friday. I'm taking a day off.

Read the conversations in Activity 3 again. Underline examples of the present continuous for arrangements. Notice the time expressions.

Complete the sentences with the present continuous form of the verbs in the box.

> come   go   have   meet

1. I .... a friend of mine for a coffee in ten minutes.
2. I .... for a picnic with my family at the weekend.
3. Some friends .... over to my house for dinner tonight.
4. I .... to the cinema with a friend on Thursday.
5. I .... to the Africa Funk concert in two weeks.
6. I .... my hair cut this afternoon.
7. We .... a party a week on Friday.
8. I .... my brother later.
9. I .... out in an hour.
10. I .... on holiday in two weeks.
11. I .... on a trip to Paris with some friends.
12. We .... a barbecue on Sunday afternoon.

Have you arranged to do any of the things above? When? Tell a partner.

> ▶ For more information on using the present continuous for arrangements, see G7.

5 | Practice

Practise making arrangements with a partner. Have conversations like this:

A: What are you doing later / tonight / tomorrow / at the weekend?
B: I'm meeting a friend for something to eat. Do you want to come?
A: Yes, OK. What time?
B: I'm meeting her at 6.30, so shall we say here at six o'clock?

Reading

1 | Special days

When are these special days?

> your mum and dad's wedding
>   anniversary
> your wedding anniversary
> your mum's birthday
> your grandfather's birthday
> the next public holiday
> your birthday
> Christmas Day
> Valentine's Day

Tell a partner about the special days. Use expressions like these:

* I'm not sure when it is.
* It's in two weeks' time.
* It's in a few months' time.
* It was the other day, actually.
* It was the other week, actually.

Do you usually celebrate any of these days? How?

Real English:
December 25th

We write December 25th or 25th December. We say December the twenty-fifth or the twenty-fifth of December. In Britain, December 25th is called Christmas Day. December 26th is called Boxing Day. January 1st is New Year's Day. Most British people usually celebrate on the night before – New Year's Eve.

Do you have any days with special names? Do you celebrate them?

2 | While you read

⌒ **Read the article. Six people are talking about special days in their lives. Which day do you think is the most special? Why?**

Special days

Ian
June 14th is a big day for me because it's the anniversary of the day I finally stopped smoking! When people ask when I gave up, I always say 'June 14th 2001' – not just '2001' or 'a few years ago', but the exact date. It took me so many years to finally stop that I'll never forget that day.

Murdo
June 21st is a big day for me because it's the longest day of the year. Where I live, in the north of Scotland, the light changes a lot during the year. The winters are very dark, and summer days go on for ever. In summer, the sun sets at about half past ten at night, but it never really gets dark before the sun rises again at four. It feels really special, watching the sun come up on the longest day, but it's also a bit depressing. Even though you know that July and August will be warmer, you also know the days will be getting shorter, and you've started the long journey back to winter and the endless cold dark days.

Alison
December 8th is important to me because it's the anniversary of the day John Lennon was shot in New York. I grew up listening to The Beatles and my dad loved them too. I can still remember coming home from school that day and finding my dad sitting in the kitchen, crying like a baby. I started crying too, and every year on December 8th I always listen to lots of Beatles songs and John Lennon songs.

Shinji
March 14th is quite a big day in Japan. We call it White Day. It's exactly a month after Valentine's Day and in Japan, on Valentine's Day, women give men chocolates. On White Day, men return the favour. Women have become very clever about this, and often buy tiny little chocolates and give a few out to lots of people. We call this 'duty chocolate'. They then hope they get bigger, better presents back on White Day!

Maria
An important date in Italy is 25th April. We call it Liberation Day and every year on this day we celebrate the end of the Second World War in Italy.

Nick
There are two dates that are more important for me than any others. October 5th is the birthday of my son, Lewis, and on that day in the year 2000 I became a father for the first time. Also, December 10th – it's my daughter Sam's birthday. She was born in 2002. I'll never forget those dates for as long as I live.

3 | After you read

Cover the text. Compare with a partner what you can remember about these dates. Who can remember the most?

14th June	21st June	8th December
14th March	25th April	5th October

<u>Underline</u> any new expressions in the text which you could use or would like to remember. Compare your expressions with a partner.

On your own, write down a date which is:

1. personally important for you.
2. nationally important in your country.
3. internationally important.

Compare your dates with a partner. Explain why the dates are important. Begin like this:

- I'll never forget ...
- I can still remember ...

4 | Using grammar: present simple with *hope*

We often use hope to talk about things we want to happen in the future. Notice that the verb after hope is in the present simple tense:

- I hope I get lots of chocolate on White Day.
- A: It's my birthday on Tuesday.
  B: Oh really? I hope you have a good time.

Complete the conversations with the words in the box.

it doesn't cost too much	you get better soon
it isn't that bad	you get the job
the weather is OK	you like it
we meet again sometime	you pass

1. A: I've got my second interview tomorrow.
   B: Oh really? Good luck. I hope ....

2. A: I've got my German exam next Friday.
   B: Oh really? Good luck. I hope ....

3. A: We're having a barbecue on Sunday.
   B: Oh really? I hope ....
   They said it might rain.

4. A: Thanks for the present.
   B: That's OK. I hope ....

5. A: It was lovely to meet you.
   B: You too. I hope ....

6. A: Sorry I can't come. I've got a horrible cold.
   B: Oh no! I hope ....

7. A: I've got to get my car fixed next week. I'm worried it's going to be really expensive.
   B: Oh really? Good luck. I hope ....

8. A: I'm going on holiday tomorrow, but it's a public holiday so the traffic will be awful.
   B: Oh no! Good luck. I hope ....
   .... and it doesn't take you too long.

Spend two minutes trying to memorise B's replies. Then close your book. Your partner will read out A's comments. How many replies can you remember?

Complete these sentences using your own ideas.

a. I hope .... tomorrow.
b. I hope .... some time soon.
c. I hope ....

Compare your ideas with a partner.

> For more information on using the present simple with *hope*, see G8.

Listening

1 | Using grammar: time expressions

Match the sentence beginnings with the time expressions. Then compare your answers with a partner. Do you both agree?

1. I went there ... .   ☐ ☐ ☐ ☐ ☐ ☐ ☐ ☐
2. I'm going there ... .   ☐ ☐ ☐ ☐ ☐ ☐

a. last week
b. a few weeks ago
c. in a couple of months
d. in a few weeks' time
e. ages ago
f. when I was a kid
g. a week today
h. the day after tomorrow
i. in a minute or two
j. sometime next year
k. the other week
l. the day before yesterday
m. in 1999
n. the other day

Now put the time expressions for talking about the future in order: 1 = the time expression nearest to now, 6 = the time expression furthest in the future.

1. in a minute or two
2. ....
3. ....
4. ....
5. ....
6. some time next year

▶ For more information on using time expressions, see G9.

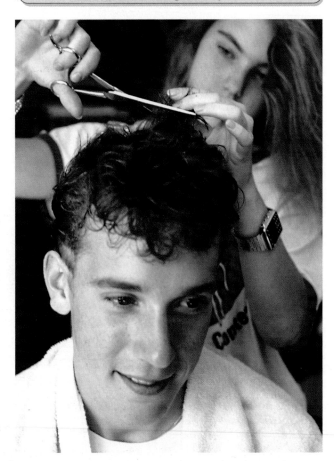

2 | Pronunciation: linking

In spoken English, we link words together if one ends with a consonant – *b, c, k, m*, etc. – and the next starts with a vowel sound – *a, e, i*, etc. For example:

ages ‿ ago

Which time expressions in Activity 1 include links like that above? Mark the links. Then compare your ideas with a partner.

🎧 Listen and practise the time expressions.

Use four of the time expressions to tell a partner something interesting about yourself.

> ### Real English: in a few weeks' time
>
> In spoken English, in a few weeks' time and in a few weeks are common ways of talking about things which are going to happen in the future. They mean exactly the same thing. Notice the apostrophe (') after weeks when you add the word time to the expression. Here are some more examples:
>
> *in a couple of hours' time*
> *in a few days' time*
> *in a few years' time*

3 | Before you listen

Think about your answers to these questions.

a. When was the last time you saw your parents?
b. When was the last time you went on holiday?
c. When was the last time you had an exam?
d. When was the last time you went to the dentist's?
e. When was the last time you went shopping for clothes?
f. When was the last time you had your hair cut?
g. When was the last time you had a day off school?
h. When was the last time you went out for dinner?

Now ask a partner the same questions. When you answer, try to use some of the time expressions from Activity 1 or answer like this:

*   I think it was about (five) or (six) days / weeks / months ago.

4 | Listening

🎧 Listen to six short conversations and decide which of the questions from Activity 3 each person is answering.

1. ☐   2. ☐   3. ☐   4. ☐   5. ☐   6. ☐

5 | Comprehension check

These sentences are all a little bit different from what you actually heard in the six conversations. Work with a partner. How many sentences can you correct?

Conversation 1: I'd like it cut really short, please.

Conversation 2: There's a sale on at the shoe shop in the High Street.

Conversation 3: He's going to tell me I need to have a filling.

Conversation 4: I'm not really looking forward to going away.

Conversation 5: I'm really excited about their visit.

Conversation 6: It was nearly twenty years ago, just before I graduated from university.

Listen again and see if your corrections were right.

6 | Speaking

Discuss these questions with a partner.

1. When you go to the hairdresser's, what do you usually say when they ask 'How do you want it?'

2. Do you like shopping for clothes?

3. Do you get nervous before exams? Before flying? Before going to the dentist's?

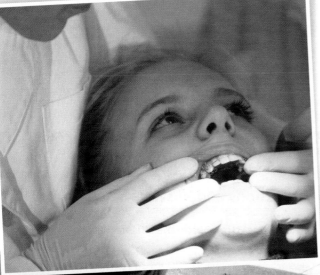

7 | Feelings about the future

Match the sentence beginnings with the endings to make four sentences about the future.

1. I've got a job ☐
2. I've got a dentist's ☐
3. I'm meeting my boyfriend's ☐
4. One of my cousins is coming ☐

a. appointment this afternoon.

b. to stay with me for a couple of weeks.

c. parents for the first time this weekend.

d. interview next Monday.

Now match these sentence beginnings with the endings.

5. I've got an English ☐
6. I'm going out for dinner ☐
7. I'm going ☐
8. I've got to give ☐

e. with my grandparents on Friday.

f. a presentation at work next week.

g. exam next week.

h. to Stockholm for the weekend.

8 | Free practice

With a partner, decide which of the sentences in Activity 7 you would follow with I'm really looking forward to it and which you would follow with I'm not really looking forward to it.

What are you looking forward to at the moment? Is there anything you're really dreading – something you're not looking forward to all? Share your ideas with some other students. For example:

A: I'm going on holiday next month. I'm really looking forward to it.

B: That's nice. I hope you have a good time.

A: I'm going to the doctor's next week. I'm really dreading it.

B: Don't worry. I'm sure it'll be OK.

Review: Units 1-4

1 | Act or draw

Work in pairs. Take turns to choose five of the words or expressions in the box. Don't tell your partner which ones you have chosen! Without speaking, draw or act out the words for your partner to guess. Your partner has one minute to guess the words you have chosen.

a diary	classical music	heavy metal
a laptop	change the batteries	mop and bucket
a plaster	crowded	murder
a shopping mall	dustpan and brush	pour
a stapler	have a barbecue	ring someone
baby-sit	have a filling	some wine
celebrate	have a haircut	spill something

Were there any words you didn't know?

2 | Tenses

Choose the correct alternative.

1. We don't / didn't have enough space in our flat, so we decided to move.

2. We all speak English at home. The children speak Spanish at school, so they are growing up / grew up bilingual.

3. A: I like that picture. Where did you get it?
   B: I bought it / brought it in a market in New York. It's really nice, isn't it?

4. A: Do you like / Are you liking Alicia Keys?
   B: I don't hear / I've never heard of her.

5. I didn't know you two are friends. How did / do you know each other?

6. I'm thinking / think of getting rid of my TV. I waste too much time watching it.

7. A: What will you do / are you doing tonight? Do you want to go out somewhere?
   B: Sorry, I'm meeting / meet a friend later.

8. I took my driving test the other day / a week today.

9. I went / 'm going on holiday in a few days' time.

10. I've got a present for you. I hope you'll like it / you like it.

3 | Grammar

Complete the sentences. Write ONE word in each space.

1. A: Whereabouts .... Scotland do you live?
   B: Fort William. It's a small town .... the west coast.

2. A: Where's the Isle of Wight? I've never heard of ....
   B: It's a small island just .... the south coast of England.

3. A: Have you got .... dictionary? I want to check a word.
   B: Sorry, I haven't. Ask Hans. I think he's got ....

4. A: Have you got .... correction fluid? I've made a mistake.
   B: Yes. There's .... in my bag somewhere.

5. A: Have you seen my keys?
   B: Yes. They're .... the table .... the living room. Why don't you keep them with the other keys?

6. A: .... you like horror films?
   B: Yes, I .... actually.

7. Let the coffee cool down a bit. It's .... hot to drink now.

8. I don't like the new Brainstorm CD, but I like some of their old ....

Compare your answers with a partner and explain your choices.

4 | Questions and answers

Match the questions with the answers.

1. Where are you from? ☐
2. Whereabouts exactly? ☐
3. Are you from there originally? ☐
4. What's it like? ☐
5. Have you got a pen I could borrow? ☐

a. No. I'm actually from a small town on the coast. I moved to Lima to study at the university.

b. It's great, but it's a bit dangerous. There's quite a lot of street crime.

c. Peru.

d. Sure. Wait a second. There's one in my bag somewhere.

e. The capital, Lima.

Now match these questions with the answers.

6. Do you like Larry and The Blue Notes?
7. What kind of things do you listen to?
8. How long have you known each other?
9. How did your exam go?
10. When was the last time you had a haircut?

f. They're OK, I suppose, but I'm not that keen on them.

g. It must be about ten years now. We used to be at school together.

h. Really well. I'm sure I've passed.

i. About a month ago. It's not that long, is it?

j. Lots of things really, but mainly pop music. I love anything by Celine Dion or Kenny G.

In pairs, ask each other the questions above. This time give different answers.

5 | What can you remember?

With a partner, write down as much as you can remember about the people you read about in the texts in Unit 1 and Unit 3.

Unit 1: I'm not from here originally

a. Faten from Tunisia

b. Hung from Vietnam

c. Ian from the North of England

Unit 3: I haven't got one!

a. Amparo, the doctor, and the mobile phone

b. Muriel, the manager, and children

c. Andrew, the teacher, and a watch

Now work with another pair of students and compare what you can remember. Who remembered more?

Which person do you think you would like the most / least? Why?

6 | Verb collocations

Complete the collocations with the verbs in the box.

cut   join   save   share   stop

1. .... the army / you
2. .... my finger / a piece of string
3. .... some money to buy a TV / a seat for a friend
4. .... a flat with someone / a pizza
5. .... smoking / talking

Now complete these collocations with the verbs in the box.

collect   do   make   support   waste

6. .... a degree / me a favour
7. .... a lot of time / a lot of money
8. .... a mistake / a mess
9. .... stamps / old coins
10. .... my city's football team / my family

Work in pairs. Take turns to memorise the words above that collocate with the verbs. Then close your book. Your partner will read out the verbs. Can you remember both collocations?

With your partner, try to think of one more collocation for each verb.

7 | Look back and check

Work in pairs. Choose one of these activities.

a. **In Unit 2, we looked at twenty-one expressions with go. How many of the expressions can you remember in two minutes? Then look back to page 18 and see if you forgot any of the expressions.**

b. **Look back at the conversation in Unit 4 on page 26. How much of the conversation can you remember? Have the conversation together.**

8 | Expressions

Complete the expressions with the words in the box.

idea love rather round stand

1. I'd .... to go there one day.
2. I've no ....
3. It's just .... the corner.
4. I'd .... you didn't.
5. I can't .... it.

Now complete these expressions with the words in the box.

believe great keen live say

6. Shall we .... seven?
7. I'm not very .... on it.
8. That sounds ....
9. I don't .... you!
10. I'll remember it for as long as I ....

Discuss these questions with a partner.

1. Is there anywhere you'd love to go to one day?
2. Is there anything you can't stand?
3. Is there anything you'll remember for as long as you live?

9 | Vocabulary quiz

Discuss these questions in groups of three.

1. If you have a cigarette, do you ask Have you got fire? or Have you got a light?
2. What's the opposite of pass an exam?
3. If there's a lot of unemployment, what is it difficult to find?
4. Do you miss or lose a class?
5. If you get on with someone, do you argue a lot?
6. What can happen if you drive too fast?
7. If you take your parents out for dinner, who pays?
8. What do you use to cut string or paper?
9. What can you press?
10. If your house is cramped, what's the problem?
11. Do you feel sad or happy if you're upset?
12. Can you think of two things which can break down?
13. If it's just gone nine, is it 8.57 or 9.03?
14. Name three things you could celebrate.
15. What date is New Year's Eve?
16. Can you think of two situations when you might say I'm not really looking forward to it?

Pronunciation

Pronunciation is important. You need to spend time practising it if you want to improve. In this book, there are lots of activities where you listen to and copy English speakers. There is a lot of work on stressing the right sounds in a sentence. At the end of each Review section, we will look at how you can record pronunciation features in your notebook and practise pronunciation at home. We will look at how we make and stress sounds in individual words. You will learn phonetic symbols. This will help you to use your dictionary and to understand how words are pronounced.

1 | Recording word stress

It is important to remember the main stress of a word. Look at these three different ways of marking the main stress.

I'talian   I<u>ta</u>lian   Italian

Mark the stress on these adjectives.

Asian	British
European	Spanish
American	Mexican
Chinese	Japanese
Brazilian	Peruvian

⌂ **Listen and check your answers in the tapescript.**

Work with a partner. Use the adjectives above and these expressions to talk about your life and what you like.

- I really like ... food.
- I don't really like ... food.
- ... are the best in the world.
- I've never met a ... person!

2 | Consonant sounds

🎧 There are some special phonetic symbols for consonant sounds. Do you know these sounds? Tell a partner how you think each sound is pronounced. Then match the sounds with the words.

1. /ʃ/ ▢   a. th<u>i</u>nk
2. /j/ ▢   b. <u>ch</u>urch
3. /dʒ/ ▢   c. plea<u>s</u>ure
4. /tʃ/ ▢   d. <u>sh</u>eep
5. /ʒ/ ▢   e. si<u>ng</u>
6. /θ/ ▢   f. <u>th</u>ese
7. /ð/ ▢   g. <u>y</u>ellow
8. /ŋ/ ▢   h. <u>j</u>am

🎧 Listen and practise the sounds.

🎧 Now listen to the sounds again. This time they are in a different order. Write down the phonetic symbols.

1. ....
2. ....
3. ....
4. ....
5. ....
6. ....
7. ....
8. ....

Look at these words. They are written in phonetic script. Try and say the words, and then write them down.

1. /θɪŋk/ ....
2. /ʃɒt/ ....
3. /kræʃ/ ....
4. /tʃeɪndʒ/ ....
5. /eɪʒə/ ....
6. /refjʊˈdʒiː/ ....

Now try and say these expressions, and then write them down.

7. /rɪŋ miː ˈleɪtə/ ....
8. /aɪ kən ɪˈmædʒɪn/ ....
9. /ˈdʌspæn ən brʌʃ/ ....
10. /ðiː ˈʌðə deɪ/ ....

🎧 Listen and check. How many words and expressions did you get right?

3 | Difficult sounds: /s/ and /ʃ/

🎧 Look at the pictures. They show how we make these sounds. Listen and practise the sounds.

/s/   /ʃ/

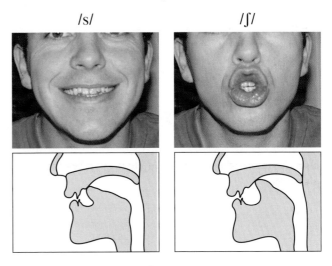

Now say these expressions.

1. Can you save me a seat?
2. I stopped smoking last year.
3. Do want to share a sandwich?
4. Shall we say six in the shopping mall?
5. He can't sit still.
6. It all sounds the same to me.
7. When does your class finish?
8. He was shot outside his house.

Try to write your own sentences using the sounds above. Read your sentences out to the class.

Who had the most sounds? Which was the funniest sentence?

Who's the guy with the baseball cap? • I really like that top. Where did you get it? • It was £20 – reduced from 50. • It's directly opposite the bank. • Oh no! I forgot to buy some toilet paper! • Could you help me tidy up this mess? • Could you lay the table? • I hate doing the hoovering. • It's too tight. • I don't have enough experience. • Don't you think it's a bit too bright? • It really suits you. • That looks ridiculous! • He always looks very scruffy. • You look very smart. • I love the design. • It was on special offer.

5 Buying things

Conversation

1 | Using vocabulary: clothes and accessories

Use these words to label the clothes in the pictures.

baseball cap	jacket	skirt	trainers
boots	jeans	sunglasses	T-shirt
bracelet	necklace	top	watch

2 | Practice

Work with a partner. Check you remember the names of all the people in your class by asking each other questions like these:

- Who's the girl / woman with the brown top?
- Who's the boy / guy with the red and white trainers?

Real English: guy / woman

In spoken English, we call men guys, we call young men boys or lads, we often call young women girls even if they are in their twenties. Some women don't like being called girls. Some do!

3 | Talking about things you've bought

Listen to this conversation between two friends – Charlotte and Lisa. The first time you listen, find out what Lisa bought and what's good about it. Don't look at the conversation while you listen.

Listen again and complete the conversation.

C: Oh, I like those shoes. (1) ....
.... ?

L: Yes, I only bought them a few days ago.

C: They're really nice. They really (2) ....
....

L: Thanks. I wasn't sure about them to begin with, but I really like them now.

C: Yes, I love the design. Where did you (3) ....
.... ?

L: From this great shop in Hockley. They've got a sale on at the moment, and I just couldn't resist them.

C: I can imagine. How much were they?

L: They were 29.99, (4) .... 65.

C: Wow! That's brilliant! Whereabouts exactly is this shop? I might try to go there later.

L: Well, (5) .... where Castle Street is?

C: Yes, I think so.

L: Well, as you're going down the hill, it's about halfway down, (6) .... I think it's called Barrett's.

C: Oh right. Well, thanks for telling me.

L: That's OK. Let me know if you buy anything!

Now look at the tapescript and practise reading it with a partner.

4 | Using grammar: reference words

Some things are always plural. For example: jeans, shorts, glasses. Cross out the words that are wrong in these sentences. The first one has been done for you.

1. I really like ~~that~~ / those sunglasses. Where did you get it / them?
2. I really like that / those shirt. Where did you get it / them?
3. I really like that / those skirt. Where did you get it / them?
4. I really like that / those boots. Where did you get it / them?
5. I really like that / those jeans. Where did you get it / them?
6. I really like that / those jumper. Where did you get it / them?
7. I really like that / those jacket. Where did you get it / them?
8. I really like that / those earrings. Where did you get it / them?

5 | Using grammar: prepositional expressions

Match the shops in the sentences with places A–F on the map.

1. There's a great shoe shop next to the cinema.
2. There's a great clothes shop on the corner of Jones Street and Wimpole Street.
3. There's a great sports shop just round the corner from the church.
4. There's a great bookshop directly opposite the cinema.
5. Do you know where the bookshop is? Well, there's a great camping shop right next door to it.
6. Do you know where the bookshop is? Well, there's a great CD and record shop about four doors down from it.

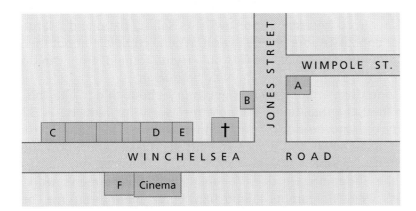

➤ For more information on using prepositional expressions, see G10.

6 | Practice

Walk round the class and compliment some other students on their clothes and accessories. Have conversations like this:

A: I really like that / those ... . Where did you get it / them?

B: From this shop in Leith / on the High Street.

A: Oh right. Whereabouts exactly is it?

Use as much of the language from Activities 4 and 5 as you can.

Reading

1 | Speaking

Discuss these questions with a partner. Decide who likes shopping more.

1. Do you like going shopping?
2. Do you prefer to go on your own or with someone else? Why?
3. What kind of shops do you like most?
4. If you're shopping for clothes, do you decide quickly what you want or do you like to shop around?
5. Who shops for the food in your house? How often do they go? How long does it take?
6. Do you like to keep an eye open for any special offers in the shops?

2 | While you read

⋒ **Read the article about shopping and housework. Do the husband and wife remind you of people you know? In what way?**

3 | Comprehension

Cover the text. With a partner, use the words in the box and try to remember what the writer said.

a real man	sell-by date
business	special offer
hospital	thirty-two
make fun	two hours
rice	washing machine

Look at the text again and check your ideas if you need to.

Good mothers – real men

My husband has just come home from the supermarket. He doesn't usually do the shopping. In fact, he doesn't usually do any housework, but today I'm very busy. I had an appointment at the hospital, so he said he'd give me a hand and buy some food for dinner and some things for the house. It has taken him two hours more than it normally takes me!

As we unpack the bags, he suddenly says, 'Oh no! I forgot to buy the oil!' Then, a moment later, 'Oh no! You wanted me to get some sugar as well, didn't you? Sorry, I forgot.'

Then I ask, 'Did you get any rice?'

'You wanted rice?' he replies.

'Of course I wanted rice. What do we normally eat every day? It was on the shopping list I gave you.'

'Sorry. I left it in the car.'

I then notice what he HAS bought. He's got six tins of pineapple – they were on special offer; two kilos of cheese – it was reduced because tomorrow is its sell-by date; and a large jar of chocolate spread – he likes it. When I complain about this, he gets upset and says he was only trying to help, and I can do it next time if I don't like the way he does it.

I don't know. Sometimes I get angry about things like this, but then at other times I almost feel sorry for him. He is 32 years old and he doesn't know how to look after himself. He can't cook, he can't iron his own shirt, he doesn't know how the washing machine works and obviously he doesn't know how to do the shopping. He doesn't really think this is men's work. That's what his parents taught him. Before he married me, he lived at home. His mother and sisters did everything for him. Now, I sometimes have to go away on business – I'm a marketing manager for a multinational company – and when I do, he gets his mother to come and stay with him and the children.

I think my husband is too old to change now, but I'm bringing up my son and daughter in a different way. I want my son to know how to cook and sew and keep the house clean, just like my daughter can. My son's friends made fun of him one day when they found out he was making cakes. They said he was a girl and he would never be a real man. But I tell him, if you don't learn, you will always be a child. A real man can look after himself and support his wife by sharing the housework. When he is older, he will thank me – and so will his wife!

4 | Word check

Complete the sentences with words from the text. Try not to look back at the text.

1. I .... most of the housework.
2. I've got an .... at the hospital tomorrow.
3. I'll .... you a hand.
4. It usually .... me an hour.
5. I'll write a .... list before we go out.
6. We need six .... of peaches.
7. I .... sorry for him!
8. I work for a multinational ....
9. I like to .... the house clean.
10. I can look .... myself.

5 | Speaking

Discuss these questions with a partner.

1. What do you think of the writer? Do you think you would get on with her? Why / why not?
2. Do you agree with her comments about 'real men'? What else do you think 'real men' should be able to do?
3. What about 'real women'?
4. Do you think her husband is really 'too old to change?'

Real English: do the shopping

We often use *do the ...* when we talk in general about jobs in and around the house.
My wife hardly ever does the cooking. I do it almost every night.
My husband sometimes does the ironing, but I do it most of the time.
I hate doing the washing up, so I usually get my children to do it.
I hate doing the cleaning, so I pay someone else to do it.

Here are some other jobs:
do the hoovering	*do the ironing*
do the tidying	*do the housework*
do the repairs	*do the paperwork*

Who does these jobs in your house? Make similar sentences to the examples above and tell your partner.

---

6 | Using vocabulary: verbs around the house

Put the activities in the order in which you would do them.

1. put the things away / do the shopping / unpack the bags / go to the shops
2. clear the table / wash up / lay the table / have dinner
3. invite some friends round / tidy up / make a mess / have a party
4. peel the vegetables / clean up the kitchen / do the shopping / cut them up / cook dinner
5. iron them / put them in the washing machine / sort out the dirty clothes / hang them up / put them away
6. make some tea / drop the cup on the floor / sweep up the bits / mop the floor / put some water on to boil

Close your book. Your partner will act out the activities for you. How many can you remember?

7 | Practice

Complete the conversations with ONE word in each space. Can you do this without looking at Activity 6?

1. A: Can I do anything to help?
   B: Yes, could you .... the table? The knives and forks are in that drawer over there.

2. A: Can I do anything to help?
   B: Yes, there's a bag of potatoes over there. Could you .... them and then put them in a saucepan? You don't need to cut them up.

3. A: Can I do anything to help?
   B: Yes, could you just help me .... these bags and put everything away?

4. A: Can I do anything to help?
   B: Yes, there are some clothes in the washing machine. Could you just .... them outside for me, please?

5. A: Can I do anything to help?
   B: Yes, I'd love a cup of tea. Could you put some water on to .... ?

6. A: Can I do anything to help?
   B: Yes, you could help me .... this mess if you want! Do you want to do the living room and I'll do the kitchen?

7. A: Can I do anything to help?
   B: Yes, you could help me .... these things .... if you want. Everything in that bag needs to go in the fridge.

8. A: Can I do anything to help?
   B: Yes, you could .... that dirty washing over there and .... it in the machine. It's been lying there for weeks!

Now have similar conversations with some other students in the class. Begin by asking Can I do anything to help?

Listening

1 | Using vocabulary: problems with clothes

Match the problems with the pictures.

1. I can't wear this. It's too big. ☐
2. I can't wear this. It's too tight. ☐
3. I can't wear this. It's too small. ☐
4. I can't wear this. It's too bright. ☐
5. I can't wear this. It's too old-fashioned. ☐
6. I can't wear these. They're too trendy! ☐

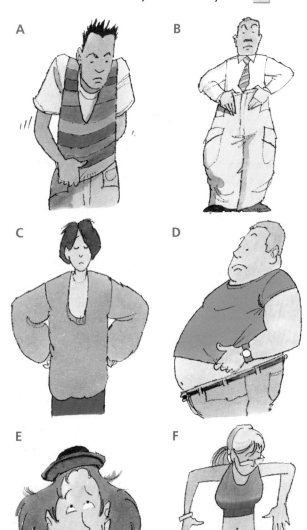

A B

C D

E F

In which picture(s) would the speaker add It doesn't fit me and in which would they add It doesn't suit me?

Do you have any clothes that you don't wear any more? Why?

What kind of clothes suit you? What colours suit you?

2 | Using grammar: *not enough*

We often use not + enough to talk about problems:

- I don't have enough money on me. I might come back and get it later.
- It's not big enough for me. Have you got a larger size?

Did you notice that enough comes before a noun, but after an adjective?

Add enough to these sentences.

1. I'd like to vote in the next election, but I'm not old.
2. This doesn't taste right. It's not sweet.
3. This computer is terrible. It doesn't really have memory for me.
4. I didn't have time to finish all the questions in the exam.
5. I didn't get the job. They said I didn't have experience.
6. I didn't get the job. They said I wasn't qualified.

> For more information on using *not enough*, see G11.

3 | Practice

Complete the sentences so that they are true for you.

1. I'm not rich enough to ....
2. I'm not tall enough to ....
3. I'm not clever enough to ....
4. I'm not fit enough to ....
5. I don't have enough time to ....
6. I don't have enough qualifications to ....

Tell a partner what you have written and why.

4 | While you listen

🎧 **Listen to three conversations in three different shops. What kind of shop does each conversation take place in?**

Now try to complete these summaries of the conversations.

Conversation 1

They didn't have his size, so he had to ....
....

Conversation 2

They only had litre bottles of shampoo, so he decided to
....

Conversation 3

He bought the wrong batteries, so he had to ....
....

They didn't have any £5 notes, so they had to ....
....

Compare your ideas with a partner. Listen to the conversations again if you need to.

5 | Speaking

Discuss these questions with a partner.

1. Have you ever been camping? Where did you go? Did you enjoy it? What did you buy before you went?

2. What kind of shampoo do you use? Why?

3. What do you think about Frank's decision not to wash his hair for a few days?

4. Have you ever taken anything back to a shop? Why? Did they let you change it? Did you need the receipt?

6 | Using grammar: negative questions

Look at this extract from Conversation 1.

A: What do you think of this?

B: It's really nice. It really suits you.

A: Don't you think it's a bit too big?

B: Yes, maybe a bit. Have they got anything smaller?

We often ask negative questions like A's when we are shopping with friends. This question means 'I think it's a bit too big. Do you agree?'

Complete the conversations with Don't you think it's and the words in the box.

a bit too big	a bit too old-fashioned
a bit too bright	a bit too trendy
a bit too expensive	

1. A: .... ?
   B: Yes, maybe a bit. Have they got anything in a darker colour?

2. A: .... ?
   B: No, I don't think so. You still see lots of people wearing things like that.

3. A: .... ?
   B: No, not really. I think it's actually quite good value for money. It's very good quality.

4. A: .... ?
   B: No, not at all. You look good in things that are a bit baggy and loose.

5. A: .... ?
   B: Yes, maybe you're right. Maybe you are a bit too old for a mini-skirt!

Practise reading out the conversations, but begin each conversation like this:

A: What do you think of this?

B: It's really nice. It really suits you.

> For more information on using negative questions, see G12.

7 | Using vocabulary: talking about clothes

Look at the expressions for talking about how people look. Translate them into your language. DON'T use a dictionary. Ask your teacher to explain any expressions you don't understand.

1. It really suits her.

2. I love the way he's dressed.

3. That shirt doesn't go with the trousers.

4. She looks very smart.

5. He looks really trendy.

6. He looks a bit too boring for me.

7. She looks a bit too scruffy.

8. That looks ridiculous!

9. That's so old-fashioned!

10. I don't really like her hair.

Compare your ideas with a partner who speaks the same language as you.

Look at the photos. Use the expressions to tell a partner what you think about the people's clothes. Would you wear any of these clothes?

A

B

C

D

I'm just phoning to ask what you're doing tonight. • I've been in bed all day. • I've got a stomach bug. • Why don't you take some herbs? • I'm phoning to apologise for what I said. • I was up till three last night studying. • I couldn't get to sleep last night. • He fell asleep in the middle of dinner! • I had a terrible nightmare last night. • I overslept this morning. • There's no cure for it. • It's a chronic illness. • I got woken up by the noise. • You're in a very good mood today. • I'm feeling a bit better. • All right. How's it going?

6 How are you?

Conversation

1 Using vocabulary: *I'm not feeling very well*

Match the sentences with the pictures.

1. I've got an upset stomach.
2. I've got a bit of a cold.
3. I've got a bit of a headache.
4. I've got a really bad cough.

When was the last time you had any of these problems?

A

B

C

D

2 Talking about being ill

🎧 **Listen to two conversations. The first is between Sarah and her friend Pete; the second is between Teresa and her friend Janet. The first time you listen, note Sarah and Teresa's problems. Don't look at the conversations while you listen.**

Listen again and complete the conversations.

Conversation 1

P: Hello. Is that Sarah?

S: Yes, hi. How are you?

P: I'm fine. (1) .... ? You weren't in class today. I'm just phoning to make sure you're OK.

S: Oh, thanks. That's really nice of you. I'm (2) .... , actually.

P: Oh no. What's the problem?

S: I've got a really bad cold. I've been in bed all day.

P: Oh no! I'm sorry. Have you been to (3) .... about it?

S: No, I'll be all right. I just need to stay in bed for a while. I already feel (4) .... than I did this morning.

Conversation 2

J: Hello.

T: Hi, Janet. It's Teresa. (5) .... ?

J: Great, thanks. How are you?

T: Not very well, actually. That's why I'm phoning. Can you tell Ralph I can't come to class tonight?

J: Yes, of course. What's the problem?

T: Oh, I've just got a really upset stomach. I've been in and out of the bathroom all day.

J: Oh no, (6) .... ! I'm sorry. Can I do anything to help?

T: That's really kind of you, but I'm all right. I'll be fine tomorrow.

J: Have you taken anything for it?

T: No, I'm just drinking lots of water and trying to (7) ....

J: Right, that sounds sensible.

T: Listen, I've (8) ....

J: Yes, of course. I'll phone you tomorrow and see how you are.

T: OK. Thanks. Bye.

Now look at the tapescript and practise reading it with a partner. Remember to stress the sounds in CAPITAL LETTERS and try to say each group of words together.

3 | Questions and answers

Match the questions with the answers.

1. What's the problem? ☐ ☐ ☐ ☐ ☐
2. Have you taken anything for it? ☐ ☐ ☐ ☐
3. Have you been to see anyone about it? ☐ ☐ ☐

a. I've got this stomach bug. I've been sick all night.

b. Yes, I took some painkillers earlier, and I'm feeling a bit better now.

c. No, I don't like taking anything.

d. I've got a really bad headache. I've had it all afternoon.

e. Yes, I went to the hospital yesterday, but they said it was fine.

f. I've got this really horrible cough. I've had it for days.

g. Yes, I went to the doctor this afternoon and he just told me to take it easy.

h. Yes, I took some herbs earlier and I'm feeling a bit better now.

i. Nothing really. I'll be fine. I just need to go to bed.

j. Yes, I took a couple of pills earlier.

k. No, it's OK. I don't need to go to the doctor. I'll be fine tomorrow.

l. I just feel really weak and tired. I've been in bed all day.

With a partner, have conversations like those in Activity 2. Use some of the answers above.

What do you normally do when you're feeling ill?

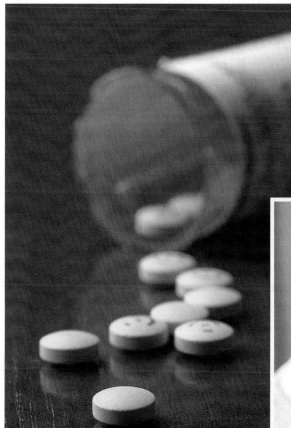

4 | Using grammar: infinitives of purpose

We often say I'm just phoning to + verb to explain why we are telephoning someone:

- Oh hello, Tom. I'm just phoning to see if you want to go out tonight.

Put the words in brackets in order and complete the explanations.

1. I'm just phoning to see ....
(are / how / you)

2. I'm just phoning to ask ....
(what / tonight / you're / doing)

3. I'm just phoning to arrange ....
(to / tomorrow / where / meet)

4. I'm just phoning to apologise ....
(birthday / for / forgetting / your)

5. I'm just phoning to enquire ....
(your / about / courses / English)

6. I'm just phoning to make ....
(sure / home / OK / you / got)

7. I'm just phoning to check you're ....
(tonight / still / coming)

8. I'm just phoning to let you know ....
(late / I'm / to / be / going)

9. I'm just phoning to find out ....
(are / how / Chile / much / your / flights / to)

With a partner, think of one more ending for each of the explanations above. For example:

- I'm just phoning to see if you're doing anything tonight.

Write a conversation using one of the explanations above. You can begin with one of these:

A: Hello.

B: Hi, is that Alan?

A: Yes, hello. How are you?

B: Fine, thanks. Listen, I'm just phoning to ...

A: Good morning. Carnaby Language School / Iberian Airways.

B: Oh hello. I wonder if you can help me. I'm just phoning to ...

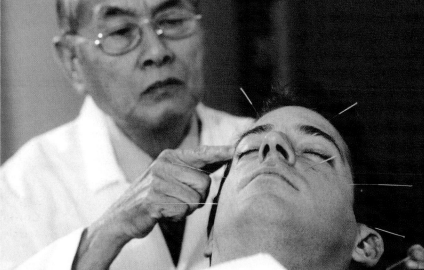

Reading

1 | Using vocabulary: feeling tired

Complete the sentences with the words in the box.

couldn't + sleep	out + home
day + lunch	up + reading
get up + catch	up + watching
gym + did	week + late

1. I've had a really busy .... I didn't even stop for ....
2. I .... get to .... for some reason last night.
3. I was .... till three last night .... TV.
4. I was .... till two last night .... a book.
5. I went .... last night and I got .... at two.
6. I went to the .... yesterday and I think I .... too much.
7. I've had a really busy .... I've worked .... every day.
8. I had to .... at five o'clock this morning to .... my flight.

Try and remember the eight reasons for feeling tired. With a partner, test each other by having conversations like these:

A: Hi B. How are you?

B: Oh, I'm really tired. I couldn't get to sleep last night.

B: Hi A. How are you?

A: Oh, I'm really tired. I was up till three watching TV last night.

How many reasons can you remember?

2 | Before you read

Discuss these questions with a partner.

1. Do you normally find it easy to get to sleep? Why can't you get to sleep sometimes?
2. When do you normally go to bed? When do you get up? How many hours a night do you sleep?
3. Have you had any late nights recently? What time were you up till? Why?

3 | Reading

🎧 **Read the introduction to this newspaper article about James Phillips. Find out why he feels tired.**

The sleeper

JAMES PHILLIPS IS SLEEPING. He fell asleep quite suddenly in the middle of our interview. Normally, I would feel angry if someone did this to me. I would think 'How rude! Am I boring you?', but with James I just feel sorry for him because James is suffering from narcolepsy. Narcolepsy is a medical condition which makes people feel tired all the time. When you suffer from it, you can't stop yourself from sleeping and when you fall asleep, it is almost impossible to wake you up. I tried to wake James up by shouting at him and ringing a loud bell, but he just continued sleeping. His wife, Michelle, told me he would probably sleep for an hour or more. Usually he sleeps between 16 and 20 hours a day. What makes it worse is the fact he often has terrible nightmares while he sleeps.

Have you heard of narcolepsy before? Think of three problems this illness could cause.

🎧 **Compare your ideas with a partner. Then read the rest of the article on the opposite page and see if you were right.**

4 | Comprehension check

Decide whether these statements about the article are true (T) or false (F). If you think they are false, can you say why?

1. James was successful at school.	T / F
2. James had a bad accident.	T / F
3. James will always have narcolepsy.	T / F
4. James has a full-time job.	T / F
5. James was late when he first went out with Michelle.	T / F
6. Michelle doesn't mind doing things by herself.	T / F
7. James didn't eat anything when they went out the other week.	T / F

Compare your ideas with a partner. Then read the article again to see if you were right.

For a long time, nobody realised James was ill. When he was younger, James often overslept in the morning and was late for school – although he didn't usually sleep at school. He often couldn't do his homework because he usually went to bed at five or six in the evening. His teachers just thought he was lazy and he often got bad grades. After leaving school, his illness got worse. He lost several jobs because he was always late or he was found asleep at his desk. Then, one day, he fell asleep while he was driving. He crashed into a wall and broke his arm. He was lucky he didn't kill himself. He finally went to the doctor to ask for help. He was told he had narcolepsy. That was ten years ago.

Unfortunately, there is no cure for the condition and doctors aren't even sure what causes it. At first, James was given some drugs which helped him to stay awake longer. As a result, he went back to school and he got very good grades. The school gave him extra time when he fell asleep during his exams so that he could finish. He can't work full-time, but he has a part-time job as a computer technician. Five years ago, he met his wife, Michelle, when they were both doing a computing course.

Michelle says, 'He's a really good-looking guy, so I was surprised he didn't already have a girlfriend. Then I found out why! He didn't actually come to the first three dates we arranged because he was sleeping. I wasn't going to give him another chance, but then he explained his problem and how the narcolepsy is worse when he is very nervous – for example, when going out with a beautiful girl for the first time! I couldn't say no after that, could I? He's intelligent, he's got a great sense of humour and he's basically a normal guy – it's just that he can't do certain things like drive or have baths or travel on his own because he can fall asleep at any moment. It's all right, though, because I'm not the kind of person who likes to go out very late, anyway. I'm a bit shy. I like to spend time on my own, so we're a good match.'

'So don't you ever get fed up with his sleeping?' I ask her.

'No, not really,' she replied, 'although the other week, we went out for dinner to celebrate our third wedding anniversary. It was a really lovely restaurant. It was really romantic. We ordered our meal and I just went to the loo for a moment. When I came back, I found him asleep with his face lying in a plate of salad. I was a bit fed up then, I must say, but then the food was fantastic and he woke up in time for the dessert, so it wasn't that bad!'

Real English: the loo

In informal spoken English, people often say loo instead of 'toilet'. For example:
I'm just going to the loo. I'll be back in a moment.
Excuse me. Where are the loos?

5 | Speaking

Discuss these questions with a partner:

1. Could you live with someone like James? Why / why not?

2. Have you ever fallen asleep in a class, a meeting, at the cinema, or on the bus?

3. Do you know anyone who has a chronic illness – one which they will have all their life?

6 | Using grammar: *can't / couldn't*

James can't work full-time because he needs to sleep. We use can't to talk about something that it's impossible for you to do:

- I can't ride a bicycle. I always fall off. (*I don't have the ability.*)

- I can't smoke in the house. My parents don't like it. (*I don't have permission.*)

- I can't eat peanuts. They make me ill. I'm allergic to them. (*Something bad will happen if I do it.*)

We use couldn't when we talk about these things in the past:

- I couldn't swim when I was younger. I only learnt when I was 22.

- Sorry I couldn't come yesterday. My boss said I had to stay and work.

Match the problems with the reasons.

1. I can't speak very loudly.
2. I can't eat things with lots of sugar.
3. I can't go up tall buildings.
4. In my country, you can't smoke in public buildings.
5. I couldn't get to sleep last night.
6. When I was at school, we couldn't talk to boys.

a. I've lost my voice.
b. I'm scared of heights.
c. It was against the rules.
d. It's against the law.
e. I was worrying about my exam.
f. I suffer from diabetes.

> For more information on using *can't* and *couldn't*, see G13.

7 | Practice

Tell a partner about some things:

1. you can't eat.
2. you can't do.
3. you couldn't do when you were younger.
4. you couldn't do in your country in the past, but you can now.
5. you couldn't do last week, although you wanted to.

Listening

1 | Greeting people

Read the beginning of five conversations. Match the conversations with the situations.

1. A: There you are!
   B: Hi. Sorry I'm late. The traffic was awful. Have you been waiting long?
   A: No, don't worry. I've only just got here myself. I thought you might've gone. So how's it going?
   B: Fine, what about you?

2. A: Hi, it's Brad, isn't it? How are you?
   B: Oh hello. Yes, not too bad, thanks. How're you?
   A: Oh, all right, I suppose. So what're you doing here? Are you doing some shopping or something?
   B: Yes, I am. What about you?

3. A: All right. How's it going?
   B: Yes, fine. Are you OK?
   A: Yes, not too bad. Did you have a nice weekend?
   B: Yes, all right. I just stayed in and took it easy. What about you?

4. A: Good morning. Do you mind if I join you?
   B: No, of course not. Have a seat.
   A: Did you sleep well?
   B: Yes, very. What about you?

5. A: Hello. Is that Barbara?
   B: Yes. Angus! How are you? It's been ages. So what've you been doing recently?
   A: Yes, I know. I'm sorry. I've just been really busy with exams and studying. What about you?

a. It's 9 a.m. on Monday morning. They work together and have just met at the photocopier.

b. They are having breakfast in a hotel.

c. They have just bumped into each other in the street. They've met once or twice before.

d. They are talking on the phone.

e. Two friends have arranged to meet outside the cinema. One has arrived late.

With a partner, practise the conversations. Try to continue each conversation for as long as you can.

> ### Real English: What about you?
>
> We often use the question *What about you?* to ask the person we're talking to the same question that they have just asked us.
>
> In each conversation above, what does the question *What about you?* mean?

2 | While you listen

🎧 **Now listen to the whole of conversations 3, 4 and 5. As you listen, decide in which conversation the speakers feel:**

a. tired and annoyed.

b. OK after feeling awful.

c. happy and excited.

With a partner, see if you can remember why the speakers feel the way they do.

3 | Word check

Complete the sentences with words from the conversations in Activity 2. There is only one word missing from each sentence. Read the tapescript if you need to – or listen to the conversations again.

1. A: How are you? Are you still feeling ill?
   B: Yes, but I'm .... a bit better today, thanks.

2. A: Morning. Did you .... well?
   B: No, I didn't, ...

3. A: I was up .... four last night writing my essay for the history class.
   B: Oh no. You .... be really tired.

4. A: Did you get .... up by that storm last night? It was really loud.
   B: No, I'm a really .... sleeper. I can sleep through anything.

5. Sorry I haven't phoned for a long time, but I've been really .... with work.

6. A: I haven't told you yet, but I'm pregnant.
   B: Really? That's brilliant. When's it .... ?

Discuss these questions with a partner.

1. Have you ever had food poisoning? What happened?

2. Are you a heavy sleeper or a light one?

3. When was the last time you got woken up? What was it that woke you up?

4. Do you know anyone who's pregnant at the moment? When's it due?

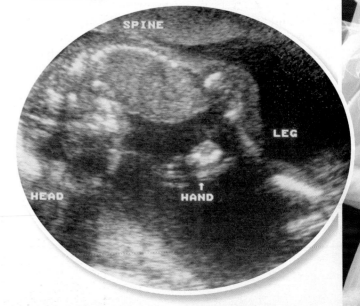

4 | Good news

Match the conversation starters with the replies.

1. Hey, guess what? We're getting married.
2. Hey, guess what? I passed all my exams.
3. Hey, guess what? I got promoted at work.
4. Hey, guess what? It's my birthday today.
5. Hey, guess what? My best friend from Greece is coming to visit.
6. Hey, guess what? I'm going on holiday this Friday.
7. Hey, guess what? I've finally found a new place to live.
8. Hey, guess what? I've finally got my visa to go to the States.

a. Oh really? Congratulations! Did you get good grades?
b. Oh really? That's great! So when're you going to move in?
c. Oh really? That's great! Are you going anywhere nice?
d. Oh really? Congratulations! Does that mean you're going to get a pay rise as well?
e. Oh really? That's great! How long is she going to stay here?
f. Oh really? Congratulations! When's the big day?
g. Oh really? That's great! So when're you going to go?
h. Oh really? Happy Birthday! How old are you?

Listen and practise the expressions in the box.

| Hey, guess what? | Oh really? |
| Congratulations! | That's great! |

Spend two minutes trying to memorise as many of the replies as you can.

Now close your book. Your partner will read out the conversation starters. How many replies can you remember?

Have you had any good news recently? Tell some other students. They should use the replies. Try to continue each conversation for as long as you can.

47

7 School and studying

Conversation

1 | Vocabulary: your academic career

Put the stages in the order in which they usually happen. The first one has been done for you.

a. go to university ☐

b. start secondary school ☐

c. do a Master's ☐

d. start primary school ☐ 1

e. do a PhD ☐

f. leave school ☐

g. graduate ☐

Which of the above have you already done? Which are you going to do in the future?

Real English: graduate

In British English, you graduate when you complete your university studies and get your degree. Notice that you graduate in (a year or a subject) from (a university):

I graduated in 1991.
I graduated in English literature.
He graduated in law from Manchester University.

Can you make some sentences about people you know as in the examples?

In American English, you graduate when you finish high school.

2 | Talking about university

🎧 **Listen to this conversation between two students – Lee and Jane. The first time you listen, note anything you hear about Jane. Don't look at the conversation while you listen.**

Compare what you heard with a partner.

Listen again and complete the conversation.

L: So what do you do, Jane? Are you working or studying or what?

J: I'm doing business management at the London Business School, actually.

L: Oh right. That sounds good. (1) .... ?

J: My third, unfortunately. I've got (2) .... in the spring. I'm really worried about them.

L: Yes, I can imagine. So what're you going to do when you graduate? Have you decided yet?

J: Yes, I'm going to (3) .... and go travelling a bit and then I'm going to try to get onto a Master's course somewhere.

L: Oh yes? (4) .... ?

J: International finance.

L: Wow. (5) .... anywhere yet?

J: Not yet, but there's a course in Leeds I'm very interested in.

L: Leeds? I've heard it's got (6) .... What do you need to do to get in?

J: Well, obviously, I need to get a good grade and then I have to (7) ....

L: Oh right. Well, good luck.

J: Thanks. I'll need it. Anyway, Lee, (8) .... ? What do you do?

How do you think the conversation will continue? Compare your ideas with a partner.

Now practise the conversation in pairs. Try to continue for as long as you can by adding how you think Lee will answer Jane's last questions.

🎧 **Listen to the rest of the conversation and see if you had any similar ideas.**

What do you learn about Lee?

3 | Using grammar: *going to*

In the conversation, Jane said: 'I'm going to take a year off and go travelling a bit and then I'm going to try to get onto a Master's course somewhere.'

We use **be going to** + verb to talk about things in the future that we have already decided to do. We often use this structure to talk about our plans for the next few weeks and months:

- I'm going to join a gym in the New Year.
- My brother is going to leave his job next month.

Put the words in brackets in order and make questions.

a. So what .... ?
   (are / study / going / you / to)

b. So how .... ?
   (you / pay / fees / going / college / are / to / your)

c. Are you .... ?
   (go / away / summer / the / going / in / to)

d. What are .... ?
   (tonight / party / wear / going / you / the / to / to)

e. So what .... ?
   (when / finish / you / are / going / you / to / do)

f. Which universities .... ?
   (apply / you / going / are / to / to)

Check your answers with a partner.

🎧 **Listen and practise the questions.**

Now match the answers with the questions.

1. I'm not sure. I might try King's College and Hull. ☐

2. We're not really sure yet. We might go to South America. I've got a friend who lives in Peru. ☐

3. My parents are going to give me some money and I'm going to get a part-time job. ☐

4. I'm going to stay on for another year and do a Master's. ☐

5. Modern languages – German and English. ☐

6. I'm going to wear a new dress and those shoes I was wearing last Saturday. ☐

Did you notice that the first two answers both use might?

We use might to talk about ideas for future plans that we are not really sure about yet:

- I might take a year off between school and university. I haven't really decided yet.
- I might call in later this evening, if I have time.

> ▶ For more information on using *going to* and *might*, see G14.

4 | Practice

Find out if anyone in your class is at university or still at school. Which of the questions in Activity 3 can you ask them? Can you ask them any of the questions below?

- Have you applied anywhere yet?
- What do you need to get in?
- What year are you in?
- When do you finish?

If no-one is at university or still at school, pretend you are one of the people in the photos. Spend three minutes thinking about how to answer some of the questions.

With a partner, have conversations using some of the questions above about what you're going to do in the future.

Reading

1 | Using vocabulary: studying at university

Translate these words into your language. Use a dictionary if you need to – or ask your teacher.

a lecture	an exam	term
an essay	course	university

Complete these lists with the words in the box.

1. have got / pass / fail / retake ....
2. a hard / do a / an English / a part-time / a full-time ....
3. the start of / the end of / a long / the summer ....
4. apply to / get into / go to / drop out of ....
5. go to / have got / fall asleep in / give ....
6. write / hand in / rewrite / the deadline for ....

Complete each of these sentences with ONE word from the lists above.

1. A: Are you going to .... to the lecture this afternoon?
   B: No. I don't like the woman who gives those lectures. She's so boring! I fell .... in the last one I went to.

2. A: What's the matter? You're looking stressed out!
   B: I've .... an exam this afternoon. I'm sure I'm going to .... I'm terrible at taking exams.

3. A: Did you go .... university?
   B: Yes, I did, but I dropped .... after the first year. I just found the course too .... and I was too lazy!

4. A: How many weeks are there until the .... of term?
   B: Six more. This term has been really .... !

5. A: When's the .... for the essay we're writing for Mr Jones?
   B: Friday, and I haven't even started it yet. He said we'd get nothing if we .... it in late.

2 | Speaking

Discuss these questions with a partner.

1. Do you get stressed out if you've got an exam? What do you do the night before an exam?
2. What's the hardest course you've done?
3. Do you know anyone who's dropped out of university / a course? Do you know why?
4. Have you got any essays or homework you have to hand in soon? When's the deadline?

3 | Before you read

Has university changed over the last twenty years in your country?

What is the difference between a grant and a loan? Use your dictionary and translate them if you want to.

4 | While you read

🎧 **Read the article on the opposite page and find out how things have changed in Britain over the last twenty years in:**

1. what students pay.
2. when students work.
3. the subjects students study.

How many changes did you notice? Compare what you found with a partner.

5 | Vocabulary focus

Can you remember what Danny and his father said using these words?

demonstrations	essays	lectures
drop out	grant	pay back

Compare what you can remember with a partner. Then read through the text again and <u>underline</u> how these words were used.

Students these days!

My son, Danny, is in his second year at university studying computing. He's not enjoying it. He tells me it's boring and too hard. He says he has to go to too many lectures, and he doesn't really have enough time to do the essays and projects he has to write. He wants to drop out and apply to do American studies at a different university, but I say he shouldn't. Last night we had a big argument about it while we were having dinner. 'You don't understand. It was different when you went to university!' he shouted and then he left the house.

Actually, I really do understand and he is right to say things were different when I went to university. Twenty-five years ago, being a student in Britain was really easy. We didn't have to pay anything to study at university. It was completely free. In fact, when I went to university the government actually GAVE me money. And I mean, gave. I got a grant of over two thousand pounds (which was a lot of money in those days) and I was free to spend it, and I never had to pay any of it back at all. Nowadays, lots of students (or their parents!) have to pay two or three thousand pounds for their course. They also have to pay for food, somewhere to live, books, bills and everything else. The government gives you a loan, which you then have to pay back after you graduate. Most people have to get a part-time job while they're studying.

I used to work in the summer holidays, but I didn't have to get a job during term-time, so I could just concentrate on studying. I say concentrate on studying, but actually a lot of the time we just sat around and chatted to each other, watched French films, read books, went on demonstrations or went to parties. I only had to go to ten hours of lectures each week, so I had lots of time to write my essays and do everything else I wanted to do. And of course, almost all students lived away from home. We had a lot of freedom – we didn't have to worry about coming home late or bringing friends home, because our parents weren't there. It was fun and easy.

I just chose the course I wanted to do, which was politics and history. I don't think you can do that now. I know Danny really wants to do American studies, and I'm sure it'd be interesting, but who would give him a job when he finishes his degree? I went travelling for six months after I graduated because it was easy to find work. I got a job in banking very quickly, but he'll have to pay back the money he's borrowed. So he needs to get a job which pays good money straight after graduating. That's why I want him to do his computing degree. It'll be better for him in the end.

6 | Speaking

Discuss these questions with a partner.

1. Are any of the things mentioned in the text the same in your country?
2. What do you think of Danny and his dad?
3. Who do you think is right in their argument?

Now work on your own for three minutes. Look at the list of choices. Decide which of the two choices is better. Why?

Is it better:

1. to do a course you enjoy OR to do a course that leads to a good job?
2. to study in your home town and live with your parents OR to go to a university in a different city?
3. to do what your parents think is best OR to do what YOU want to do?
4. for the government to give you a grant to study OR for students to get a loan to pay for university?
5. to start work straight after graduating OR to travel around the world a bit?
6. to get a job after you leave school OR to go straight to university?

Now discuss your ideas with some other students. Have conversations like this:

A: I think it's better to study a course you enjoy, because you'll do better in your exams if you're interested in the subject.

B: Maybe, but if you study a strange subject, you won't get a good job after you graduate.

OR

B: Me too. If you don't like the course, you'll probably fail.

7 | Which degree?

Which of the degree courses below would you like to do? Mark them like this:

1 = this course sounds really interesting

2 = this course sounds OK

3 = this course sounds really boring

fine art	business management
media studies	biochemistry
computing and IT	English literature
Russian and Chinese	Middle-eastern history
pure mathematics	philosophy

Compare your answers with a partner and explain your decisions. Try to use these expressions.

- You can get a good job if you do ...
- You can earn more money if you do ...
- It's more difficult to get a job if you do ...

Listening

1 | Class rules

Tell some other students how you feel about the class rules below. Use these expressions.

- I totally agree with this one.
- I'm not sure about this one. It depends.
- I totally disagree with this one.

1. If you arrive late for class, you shouldn't be allowed in.
2. You should always turn your mobile phone off in class.
3. You shouldn't eat or drink in class.
4. Only one student should speak at a time.
5. You should always do your homework.
6. You should always bring a notebook and pen to class.

Can you decide on two other rules you'd like to have in your class?

2 | While you listen

🎧 **Listen to the conversation between a teacher and her class and decide which of the rules above are broken during the lesson. Can you remember why Adam broke these rules? Listen again to check if you need to.**

3 | Speaking

Discuss these questions with a partner.

1. What do you think of Adam's teacher?
   a. She sounded really nice.
   b. She sounded horrible.
   c. She needs to be a bit stricter.

2. Do any of the problems you heard about in the conversation ever happen in your class? How do you feel about that?

3. Have any teachers ever got annoyed with you? Why? What did you do?

4 | Asking for permission

Can you remember how Adam asked for permission to answer his telephone call? Complete this question.

.... just answer this?

🎧 **Listen and check your answer.**

Match the questions with the answers.

1. Is it OK if I open the window a bit? It's boiling in here. ☐
2. Is it OK if I leave about half an hour early today? I've got a doctor's appointment at 12.15. ☐
3. Is it OK if I close the window? I'm freezing. ☐
4. Is it OK if I smoke in here? ☐
5. Is it OK if I sit here? ☐

a. Well, actually, I'd rather you didn't. I'm quite cold myself.
b. Well, actually, I'd rather you didn't. Not while I'm eating.
c. Well, actually, I'd rather you didn't. I was saving that seat for a friend.
d. Yes, of course – but don't forget to do the homework for tomorrow.
e. Yes, of course. Go ahead. I'm a bit cold myself.

🎧 **Listen and check your answers.**

5 | Pronunciation: linking

In Unit 4, we saw that we link together words when one ends in a consonant sound and the next starts with a vowel sound. Look at the way we link the sentence starter below:

Is‿it‿OK‿if‿I

Practise the conversations in Activity 4 with a partner. Make sure you link Is it OK if I ... ?

> **Real English: Do you mind if I ... ?**
>
> We also ask for permission using the sentence starter Do you mind if I ... ?
> We reply to questions like this by saying No, of course not or Well, actually, I'd rather you didn't.

Practise the conversations in Activity 4 again, but this time one of you should begin by using Do you mind if I ... ? Can your partner answer without looking at the book?

With a partner, think of two more questions to ask your teacher or another student. Use Is it OK if I ... ? or Do you mind if I ... ?

Now with a new partner, have conversations using your questions.

> For more information on asking for permission, see G15.

6 | Making requests

Match the requests with the responses.

1. Could you just open the door there for me, please? ☐

2. Could you just move up a bit so I can sit down? ☐

3. Could you just turn that tape up a bit? I can hardly hear it. ☐

4. Could you just open the window a bit? Just to let a bit of fresh air in. ☐

5. Could you lend me a pound for a coffee? I left my money upstairs. ☐

a. Yes, sure. Sorry. It is a bit quiet, isn't it?

b. Sorry, but I'm really cold. Can we keep it closed?

c. Yes, sure. There you go. Do you want me to open the next one there as well?

d. Sorry, but I've only got enough for my own tea.

e. Yes, sure. There you go. Have you got enough space?

With a partner, have short conversations like those above for the situations in the pictures. Decide if you want to do what your partner is asking you to do or not.

> For more information on making requests, see G16.

53

Work and jobs

I think I'm good with people. • She works in the media. • He got sacked! • The interview was a disaster! • Could you send me an application form? • I sent it off the other day. • Have you done this kind of work before? • I got promoted last year. • I have to work very long hours. • I don't have to work tomorrow! • She's a fitness instructor. • My dad's an estate agent. • I have to wear a suit to work. • He's very good at languages. • I get twelve euros an hour. • She's a very reliable worker. • Why don't you take a day off sick?

Conversation

1 | Questions about work and jobs

Complete the questions with the words in the box.

boss	enjoy	hours	people	travel
do	get	money	studying	weekends

1. Are you working or .... or what?
2. So what do you .... ?
3. Do you .... it?
4. Do you have to work .... ?
5. And do you .... much holiday?
6. And do you have to .... far to work?
7. What are the .... you work with like?
8. And what's the .... like? Is it OK?
9. What's your .... like?
10. And what are the .... like?

Now translate the questions into your own language. DON'T use a dictionary. Ask your teacher to explain any expressions you don't understand.

Compare your ideas with a partner who speaks the same language as you.

Are there any questions you WOULDN'T ask in your language? Why not?

2 | Talking about what you do

🎧 **Listen to this conversation between Jenny, an English woman, and Nori, a Japanese man. The first time you listen, tick the questions from Activity 1 you hear being asked. Don't look at the conversation while you listen.**

Compare what you heard with a partner. Can you remember how Nori answered these questions?

Listen again and complete the conversation.

J: So what do you do, Nori? Are you working or studying or what?

N: Well, I graduated (1) .... and now I'm working in Osaka.

J: Oh right. So what do you do?

N: I'm a (2) .... I work for the government.

J: Oh, do you? Do you enjoy it?

N: Yes, it's OK. I have to do a lot of paperwork, which is (3) .... , but it's quite well paid.

J: Oh, that sounds good.

N: Yes, it is, but sometimes I get (4) .... with it. I have to work (5) .... most days. A lot of the time, I don't really have much to do, so I just sit around and kill time.

J: Do you have to work weekends?

N: No, thank goodness! Five days a week is enough.

J: Yes, I know what you mean. Do you get much holiday?

N: It's not too bad. I get (6) .... , so that's OK.

J: And do you have to travel very far to work?

N: Yes, quite a long way. It's about an hour on the train, so I have to (7) .... commuting. Anyway, what about you, Jenny? What do you do?

How do you think the conversation will continue? Compare your ideas with a partner.

Now practise the conversation in pairs. Try to continue for as long as you can.

🎧 **Listen to the rest of the conversation. What do you learn about Jenny?**

3 | Speaking

Discuss these questions with a partner.

1. Who do you think has the better job – Nori or Jenny? Why?

2. Why do you think Nori has to stay in the office if he doesn't have much work to do?

3. Do you know anyone with a stressful job?

Now have a conversation like that in Activity 2. Use the questions from Activity 1.

4 | Using vocabulary: expressions with *get*

Lots of useful words for talking about work go with – collocate with – get. Complete the sentences with the words in the box.

a half-hour break	sacked
an interview	six weeks' holiday
a job	ten euros an hour
bored	to work

1. A: Hey, guess what? I've finally got .... !
   B: That's great! When do you start?

2. Do you remember that job in the big computer company that I applied for? Well, guess what? I've got .... for it. They want to see me tomorrow afternoon.

3. My job's OK, but I get a bit .... with it sometimes. There's not really enough work for us all to do.

4. A: How long does it take you to get .... ?
   B: About an hour usually. It depends on the traffic.

5. It's not a very well-paid job. I only get ....

6. It's great where I work because I get .... a year.

7. A: Do you want to meet for lunch sometime?
   B: I'd love to, but it's quite difficult because I only get .... at lunchtime.

8. I was late every day for two weeks and after that I got .... ! I'm looking for a new job at the moment!

In Unit 2, we saw that when we use expressions with common verbs, we don't stress the verbs – we stress the words which follow.

🎧 **Listen and practise the expressions with get, paying attention to the stress.**

5 | Speaking

Discuss these questions with a partner.

1. Do you know anyone with a really well-paid job? How much do they get a year?

2. Do you ever get bored with your job? Why?

3. Do you ever get bored with anything else? Why?

4. How do you get to work / school?

5. How long does it take you to get to work / school?

6. Do you get many breaks at school / work? How long do you get for lunch?

6 | Using grammar: *have to*

In the conversation, Nori said: 'I have to do a lot of paperwork'. We often use have to to talk about things we don't really like doing, but we have no choice about:

• I have to work late tonight. I've got something to finish before tomorrow.

We use don't have to if we have a choice:

• I usually work every weekend, so I don't have to go to work on Mondays – but I can if I want to.

Can you remember two other things Nori has to do?

Complete the sentence endings with the words in the box.

do	make	start	wear	work

It's awful where I work because:

1. I have to .... work at six in the morning.
2. I have to .... very long hours.
3. I have to .... a suit and tie to the office.
4. I have to .... a lot of travelling.
5. I have to .... the tea for everyone all the time!

Now complete these sentence endings with the words in the box.

go	start	take	wear	work

It's great where I work because:

6. I don't have to .... work until ten.
7. I don't have to .... a horrible uniform.
8. I don't have to .... to boring meetings.
9. I don't have to .... very hard.
10. I don't have to .... work home with me.

Are any of the sentences above true for you? If not, do you know anyone who they are true for?

 For more information on using *have to* and *don't have to*, see G17.

Reading

1 | So what do you do for a living?

Complete the answers to the question above with the words in the box.

agent	designer	guard
clerk	driver	instructor

1. I'm a taxi ....
2. I'm a web ....
3. I'm a security ....
4. I'm a bank ....
5. I'm an estate ....
6. I'm a fitness ....

Can you think of two other kinds of: guard, instructor, driver and designer? The pictures might help you.

2 | Pronunciation: compound nouns

A compound noun is made with two nouns. For example:

- bus stop
- database
- windsurfer

When we say compound nouns, we usually stress part of the first word. Look at these examples:

- a seCURity guard
- a TAXi driver

Practise saying the sentences in Activity 1. Then practise saying the other examples you thought of.

3 | While you read

∩ You are going to read about a man who does temping work for a living. As you read, find out:

1. what temping work is.
2. why he does temping work.

Would you like temping work? Why / why not?

Work or life?

A lot of people ask me why I do temping work rather than get a permanent job with one company. I guess it's partly because of my father. He was a computer programmer for a big multinational company. His job was very important to him. He used to work very long hours. When we were kids, he often got home after nine o'clock at night – the time that we went to bed. Sometimes I didn't see him for days and days. He did very well in his job. He got promoted. He became the manager for the whole of the country and then the whole of South-east Asia. He just worked harder and harder. I don't think he was really happy doing what he was doing, but I guess he couldn't see any other way. Then, when he retired, he didn't know what to do. He was even more unhappy. He died of a heart attack when he was 68.

I don't want to be like that. Doing temping work means I don't have to go to work every day. When I work, I don't have to do the same things or see the same people every day. That's why I like it. I've been with the same agency for about ten years now. They know I'm a good worker and I'm reliable – I've never been late for work – so I can more or less choose the jobs I want to do. Sometimes I work in the same place for a few weeks, sometimes it's for just one day. I only get paid for the days I work, so if I'm not very well and take a day off sick, or if I want a holiday, I don't get any money. I suppose that if I had a family, it would be a problem, but I don't mind. Money isn't that important to me. It's more important that I can take time off when I want to. Some of my friends only get two weeks' holiday a year. I often take five or six weeks' holiday and go travelling all over the world.

At the moment, I'm working in an office as a secretary. I've been there for about three months. It's a nice place. The people who work there are really friendly, but I'm getting a bit fed up with the work, so I think I'll probably ask to change and do something else soon. I do quite a lot of office work because I'm good at typing, but I've done lots of other jobs as well. I've been a security guard and a barman; I washed cars one summer; and I worked in a hotel in a ski resort for two winters, which was good because I went skiing a lot. Not all the jobs are good, though. The worst job I had was when I worked in an abattoir, which is a place where they kill animals. I had to cut up the meat, pack it and send it off to supermarkets. Then I had to clean the floor. It was disgusting! My best job was working in a chocolate factory for a week. I went home with lots of free chocolate bars. That was great!

4 | Word check

Complete the sentences with words from the text. Try not to look back at the text.

1. I work very long .... – I start at nine in the morning and finish at nine at night.

2. She did very well in her job. After two years, she got .... to manager.

3. He's a very .... worker. He never arrives late and he always does his work on time.

4. If you're really feeling bad, you should take a day .... sick.

5. I travel a lot with my job. I go all .... the world. It's great.

6. I work in the main university finance .... as a secretary.

7. My job is quite boring. I'm getting a bit .... up with it.

8. I have to clean all the toilets in the hotel. It's really .... !

Think of all the people you know. Who has the best / worst job?

5 | Using grammar: present perfect simple

In the text, the writer said: '**I've done** lots of other jobs as well. **I've been** a security guard and a barman'. This form is the present perfect simple. We make it by using **have** or **has** and adding the past participle. We use it to talk about experiences in the past. We don't use the present perfect with a past time expression like **last week** or **yesterday**.

Do you know the past participle of these verbs?

be	find	hear	see	try
do	go	play	travel	visit

Real English: I've been (to) and He's gone (to)

The participles been and gone are sometimes confused. Look at these examples:

A: Is Mike in?
B: No, sorry. He's gone shopping. He'll be back later. (= he's not here now)

• Sorry I'm late. I've just been shopping. I had to buy a few things for dinner. (= now I'm back)

Notice that you can't say Have you gone ... ? or I've gone because you are here!

Complete the conversations with past participles. You will need to use some twice.

1. A: Have you .... this kind of work before?
   B: Yes, I worked for a design company in Brazil for three years.

2. A: Have you .... that new film – *Shanghai Cops*?
   B: Yes, I went to see it last week. It was OK, but nothing special.

3. A: Have you .... from Jing recently?
   B: Yes, she rang me a few days ago actually, and guess what? She's .... a new job with a much bigger company. We're going out next week to celebrate.

4. A: Have you .... our country before?
   B: No, this is the first time I've ever .... here.

5. A: We're going to a Vietnamese restaurant tonight. Would you like to come with us?
   B: Yes, I'd love to. I've never .... Vietnamese food before.

6. A: Have you .... this game before? You're very good at it.
   B: No, never, but I have .... something similar.

7. A: Have you .... round Asia much?
   B: Yes, I have, actually. I've .... to Singapore, Thailand, the Philippines, Japan. Quite a few places, really.

Did you notice the answers in sentences 1–3? We often use the past simple to give details about when our past experiences happened.

With a partner, practise the conversations.

For more information on using the present perfect simple, see G18.

6 | Practice

Put the words in order and make questions.

1. much / you / have / travelled
   .... ?

2. much / food / foreign / you / tried / have
   .... ?

3. any / films / recently / you / seen / have / good
   .... ?

4. CDs / bought / any / you / good / recently / have
   .... ?

5. many / before / you / had / have / jobs
   .... ?

6. this / grammar / before / you / studied / have
   .... ?

Now ask a partner the questions. Try to answer as in the conversations in Activity 5.

Listening

1 | Looking for and getting a job

Complete the conversations with the words in the box.

advertised	fill in	good luck	looking for
applied for	go	interested in	offer

1. A: I've started .... a job.
    B: Oh really? What kind of thing?

2. A: There was a job in the paper this morning that you
        might be ....
    B: Really? What was it?

3. A: Hello, I'd like an application form for the job
        you .... in the paper this morning.
    B: Certainly. Could you give me your details?

4. A: I'm sorry, I can't come to your party tonight. I've
        got to stay in and .... the
        application form for a job.
    B: Don't worry. Getting a job is more important than
        my party. When do you have to send off the form?

5. A: I've got an interview for that job I
        .... It's next week.
    B: Really? That's brilliant. When is it exactly?

6. A: .... with the interview tomorrow.
        I hope you get it.
    B: Yes, so do I. I really need the money.

7. A: We'd like to .... you the job, if
        you're still interested.
    B: Definitely. That's great. When would you like me to
        start?

8. A: How did the interview .... ?
    B: Really well. In fact, I got the job!

With a partner, practise the conversations. Try to continue each conversation for as long as you can. For example:

A: I've started looking for a job.

B: Oh really? What kind of thing?

A: Anything really, but I'd quite like to work in a clothes shop or something like that.

B: Oh right. So have you applied for anything yet?

Can you remember which verbs complete these expressions?

a. Can you .... me your details?

b. I need to .... off my application form.

c. I've .... an interview.

d. When would you like me to .... ?

e. I .... the job.

2 | Before you listen

You are going to listen to a conversation between two friends – Vic and Sue. They are both in their final year at university and are talking about applying for jobs. Sue's had an interview for a job in an accountancy company. It was a disaster. Before you listen, think of four reasons why the interview could be a disaster.

Compare your ideas with a partner.

3 | Listening

🎧 **Listen to the conversation and find out why Sue's interview was a disaster. Were you right?**

4 | Comprehension check

Listen again and decide whether these statements are true (T) or false (F). Try to correct the sentences that are false.

1. Sue missed class yesterday because she was ill.   T / F
2. Vic hasn't applied for any jobs yet.   T / F
3. Sue is doing a degree in business management.   T / F
4. Sue was good at maths when she was at school.   T / F
5. Sue worked in her uncle's accountancy company
    in the holidays.   T / F
6. Sue did accountancy work at the company.   T / F

Listen to the conversation again and check your answers – or read the tapescript.

5 | Speaking

Discuss these questions with a partner.

1. Did you know what kind of job you wanted to do when you were 21? 16? 12?

2. What other jobs have you wanted to do? Why didn't you do them?

3. Sue lied a little bit about her previous work experience. Would you ever lie about:
    *   your work experience?
    *   your age?
    *   your qualifications?

4   Is there anything else you think it's sometimes OK to lie about?

6 | Using vocabulary: *good at ... / good with ...*

Complete the sentences with the words in the box.

computers	English	languages	maths	people
cooking	fixing	listening	my hands	sports

1. I'm terrible at .... I can't even add up!

2. I'm really good at .... I speak French, Russian, German and Swedish.

3. I'm quite good at .... I lived in Australia for six months, so I learnt it there.

4. I'm terrible at .... I can't even boil an egg!

5. I'm good at .... I used to play in the school football team and I play a lot of tennis.

6. I'm good at .... things. I enjoy repairing things around the house.

7. I'm not very good at .... to people's problems. I think they should sort things out themselves!

8. I'm not very good with .... I can use Word, but I don't know how to use any other software. I don't know what to do when they crash.

9. I'm good with .... I make friends quite easily and I don't usually have arguments.

10. I'm good with .... I'm good at painting and making things, and doing practical things like that.

Tell a partner whether the sentences are true for you or not. Explain why. For example:

• Number 1 isn't true for me. I'm quite good at maths. I got a good grade when I took my maths exam at school.

7 | Career or job?

You have a career when you change jobs several times within the same area. If your career is going well each new job is better than the last one.

Put these words into two groups – careers and jobs.

accountant	fitness instructor	the media
business	IT	teacher
civil servant	lawyer	tourism
doctor	marketing	vet

Which of these careers and jobs would you be good at? Which could you never do? Why?

Tell a partner what you think. For example:

A: I'd quite like to work in education, because I'm good with children and I'm good at listening to people.

B: Oh really? I couldn't do a job like that. I'm not very good at explaining things. I'd quite like to be an accountant because I'm good at maths.

8 | Using grammar: *they want me to*

In the conversation, Vic said: 'companies usually want people to have some experience of working in business'. We often use this structure when reporting what people have said to us.

Report what people have said with the correct form of want and the words in the box.

me / finish	my dad / retire
me / get a job	people / spend
me / have a party	us / get married
my boyfriend / take me out	

1. My girlfriend .... , but I've told her I'm not ready yet.

2. My parents .... when I leave school, but I've told them I want to go to university.

3. My boss .... this work by Tuesday, but I've told him I can't do it by then.

4. My mum .... , but he's told her he's not ready yet.

5. My friends .... for my birthday, but I've told them my parents won't let me!

6. I .... on Friday, but he's told me he can't afford it.

7. The government .... more money, but I don't think many people can afford it.

Tell a partner about what different people want you to do. How do you feel about each one?

Review: Units 5-8

1 | Act or draw

Work in pairs. Take turns to choose five of the words or expressions in the box. Don't tell your partner which ones you have chosen! Without speaking, draw or act out the words for your partner to guess. Your partner has one minute to guess the words you have chosen.

a demonstration	hang up clothes
a necklace	herbs
a special offer	I couldn't get to sleep
a top	iron a shirt
a uniform	pills
be sick	sort out the dirty clothes
bright	sweep up
do paperwork	tight clothes
fall asleep	trainers
fill in a form	work late
get paid	

Were there any words you didn't know?

2 | Tenses

Choose the correct alternative.

1. I've got a horrible cough. I have it / I've had it for days.

2. Sorry I can't / I couldn't come tomorrow. I forgot I'd arranged to go out with my friend, Lars.

3. I can't / I couldn't swim till I was 18. I was scared of water when I was young.

4. A: What are you going to do after you graduate?
   B: I don't really know. I'm not sure, but I might do / I'm going to do a Masters, if I get good grades.

5. A: Are you going round to Ben's house tonight?
   B: No, I might / I'm going to see Infected in concert. I got the tickets ages ago.

6. A: Have you been / gone to Mexico before?
   B: No, this is my first time here.

7. A: Have you tried snake before? It's lovely.
   B: Yes, I had / I've had some in China last year, but I didn't really like it / I haven't really liked it.

8. A: What do you think of our country?
   B: It's great. I never came here before / I've never been here before, but I'm really enjoying it. Actually, we've only arrived here / we only arrived here a few hours ago!

3 | Grammar

Complete the sentences with the words in the box.

Could you	Do you want	I don't have to	Is it OK
Do you mind	enough	I have to	too

1. A: .... open the door for me, please?
   B: Yes, of course. There you go.

2. A: .... if I turn on the TV?
   B: Yes, of course. Go ahead.

3. A: .... if I smoke?
   B: No, of course not. Go ahead.

4. A: .... me to help you?
   B: No, it's OK. I can do it, thanks.

5. My parents want me to get married, but I'm not old .... to settle down.

6. A: Do you like your job?
   B: No, I hate it. The only good thing about it is that .... get up too early. Apart from that it's awful – the money, the people, everything.

7. A: Do you want to sit outside?
   B: No way! It's much .... cold to eat outside.

8. A: Do want to go for a drink?
   B: No, I'm going to go home to bed. .... get up really early tomorrow to catch my train.

Compare your answers with a partner and explain your choices.

4 | Questions and answers

Match the questions with the answers.

1. Nice shoes! Where did you get them? ☐
2. Were they very expensive? ☐
3. Don't you think the jacket's a bit big? ☐
4. Have you got this in the next size down? ☐
5. Hey, guess what? I'm pregnant! ☐

a. That's fantastic! When's it due?

b. Yes, I think there's a small one in the store room.

c. Yeah, maybe it is a little bit, but I think a size 10 will be too small.

d. Not at all. I got them in a sale. They were half price.

e. Yeah, they're good, aren't they? I got them in Barcelona while I was on holiday.

Now match these questions with the answers.

6. What do you do? Are you working or studying or what? □

7. What are the hours like? □

8. What are the people you work with like? □

9. What's the money like? □

10. What did you do your degree in? □

f. Great, but I'm not going to tell you how much!

g. Medicine.

h. I just started work a few weeks ago, actually. I work for a drug company.

i. They're really nice. We get on really well.

j. They're normal. Nine to five, although I sometimes have to work weekends too.

In pairs, ask each other the questions above. This time give different answers.

5 | What can you remember?

With a partner, write down as much as you can remember about the texts you read about in the texts in Unit 5 and Unit 8

Unit 5: Good mothers – real men

a. The husband and shopping

b. The wife and her job

c. The son

Unit 8: Work or life?

a. His father, the computer programmer

b. Why he does temping work

c. His best and worst jobs

Now work with another pair of students and compare what you can remember. Who remembered more?

Which text did you enjoy more? Why?

6 | Verb collocations

Complete the collocations with the verbs in the box.

| arrange   enquire   keep   look after   suffer from |

1. .... a meeting / to go out

2. .... about courses / about accommodation

3. .... himself / my cat while I'm away

4. .... the house clean / in touch by e-mail

5. .... a chronic illness / asthma

Now complete these collocations with the verbs in the box.

| apply   do   drop out of   find out   go on |

6. .... university / a course

7. .... holiday / a demonstration

8. .... to go to university / for a job

9. .... a degree / a PhD

10. .... how much it costs / what's happening

Work in pairs. Spend one minute memorising the words above that collocate with the verbs. Then take turns to close your book. Your partner will read out the verbs. Can you remember both collocations?

With your partner, try to think of one more collocation for each verb.

7 | Look back and check

Work in pairs. Choose one of these activities.

a. **Look back at the questions and answers in Unit 6, Activity 3 on page 43. Check with a partner anything you've forgotten. Test each other. Student A asks a question and B gives a reply.**

   Then use the phrases to have longer conversations. Start like this:

   A: Hi is that A?

   B: Yes, hello B. How's it going?

   A: Fine. How are you?

   B: I'm not very well, actually ...

b. **Look back at the conversation in Unit 7 on page 48. Can you remember how it continues? Check in the tapescript and <u>underline</u> all the questions. Try to remember them. Then have a similar conversation with a partner.**

8 | Expressions

Complete the expressions with the words in the box.

imagine   kind   resist   sorry   telling

1. That's really .... of you.
2. Thanks for .... me.
3. I couldn't .... them.
4. I feel .... for him.
5. I can ....

Now complete these expressions with the words in the box.

better   help   interesting   see   suits

6. I'm just phoning to .... how you are.
7. It really .... you.
8. I'm feeling a bit ....
9. I wonder if you could .... me.
10. It sounds really ....

Discuss these questions with a partner.

1. Has there been anything you couldn't resist buying recently?
2. What kind of styles and colours suit you?
3. Is there anyone you feel sorry for? Why?

9 | Vocabulary quiz

Discuss these questions in groups of three.

1. Can you think of two people you could have an appointment with?
2. On what part of the body do you wear a bracelet?
3. What should you do if food is past its sell-by date?
4. What do you wear on your feet to go running?
5. Do you lay the table before or after dinner?
6. If a top doesn't go with a jacket, is the top too small or the wrong colour?
7. What happens if you have an upset stomach?
8. If you have a headache, is it a good idea to take painkillers?
9. Can you think of two things you could apologise for?
10. When might you lose your voice?
11. Do you graduate from school or university?
12. What happens if you miss the deadline for handing in an essay?
13. Why would you have to retake an exam?
14. Can you think of two reasons why someone could get sacked?
15. Do you have a career at university or after university? What in?
16. If you're good with your hands, what are you good at?

Pronunciation

1 | Word stress

Put these words into groups according to their stress pattern. If you're not sure of the stress pattern of a word, use your dictionary. Dictionaries usually mark stress with a little apostrophe before the stressed part of the word, like this: re'view.

bracelet	upset	enquire
imagine	career	necklace
library	directly	appointment
opposite	lecture	arrange
sensible	details	restaurant
revision		

Pattern 1: • •
upset
....

Pattern 2: • •
bracelet
....

Pattern 3: • • •
library
....

Pattern 4: • • •
directly
....

Unstressed sounds are usually reduced to /ə/ or /ɪ/. For example, the second 'e' in bracelet is pronounced with /ɪ/ – /breɪslɪt/.

Which of the unstressed sounds above use /ə/ or /ɪ/?

🎧 **Listen and check your answers in the tapescript.**

2 | Words with two stresses

In some words there are two stressed sounds. For example, the verb graduate has the main stress on the first syllable – gra – and secondary stress on the last syllable – ate.

Look at this list of words with two stresses. Say each word. Then mark the main stress with the number 1 and the secondary stress with the number 2. The first one has been done for you.

1 2	
graduate	lifeguard
reputation	demonstration
apologize	uniform
deadline	bus stop
drop out	sort out
go away	

3 | Consonant sounds: /b/, /d/, /dʒ/ and /g/

🎧 **Look at the pictures. They show how we make these sounds. Listen and practise the sounds.**

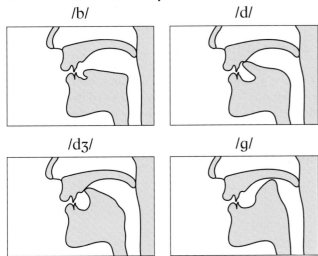

/b/   /d/

/dʒ/   /g/

Now say these English names. Notice that they begin with the sounds above.

> Bob   David   Joe   Greg

Do you know any other names which start with these sounds?

🎧 **Listen to the sounds /b/ and /p/. Can you hear the difference?**

The sounds /b/ and /p/ are formed in the same way, but we use our voice when we say /b/. Put your fingers on your throat as you say /b/. You should be able to feel your voice. Now say /p/. You can't feel anything.

🎧 **Listen and repeat these pairs of sounds. Put your fingers on your throat as you say each sound.**

1. /p/   /b/
2. /t/   /d/
3. /ch/   /dʒ/
4. /k/   /g/

🎧 **Now listen and practise these words and expressions.**

/p/ /b/	/pay/	/back/	I'll pay you back tomorrow.
/t/ /d/	/turn/	/down/	Can you turn the TV down?
/ch/ /dʒ/	/change/	/jacket/	I just need to change my jacket.
/g/ /k/	/get/	/break/	I get an hour break for lunch.

4 | Difficult sounds: consonant clusters

Do you find it difficult to say words starting with these sounds?

/pr/	/br/
/tr/	/dr/
/kr/	/gr/
/str/	/skr/

🎧 **Listen and try to say the sounds. Each pair starts with a similar position of the lips.**

Now say these expressions.

- I hate the present perfect!
- Brian Brown drives a bright green car!
- Go straight down this street.
- I get stressed out in traffic jams.
- I got a grant because of my great grades.
- I scratched my bracelet when I dropped it.

Try to write your own sentences using the sounds above. Read your sentences out to the class.

Who had the most clusters? Which was the funniest sentence?

He's mixed up our order. • Sorry, but I ordered baked potatoes, not fried. • I'm afraid we don't have any left. • Well, in that case, I'll have the lamb, please. • A table for three, please. • Should we leave a tip? • I spilled wine all over her dress! • He eats like a pig. It's disgusting! • They tried to overcharge us. • Have you got anywhere in mind? • We could try that new French place. • The portions are huge. • No, thanks. I'm driving. • No, thanks. I'm on a diet. • The service was very slow. • There was a really long queue. • I feel dizzy.

9 Eating out

Conversation

1 Using vocabulary: eating out

Match the statements about eating out with the sentences which have the opposite meaning.

1. The food was too spicy.
2. The food was really nice.
3. I was really full when we finished.
4. The waiters were great.
5. There were lots of dishes to choose from.
6. It was really crowded.
7. The food was horrible.
8. The portions were really big.

a. I was still hungry.
b. There wasn't much choice.
c. It wasn't spicy enough.
d. It was almost empty.
e. It tasted awful.
f. It was delicious.
g. They were really small.
h. The service was really slow.

2 Practice

Have you eaten in the following kinds of restaurant? What were they like? Tell a partner, using some of the expressions from Activity 1.

a fast food restaurant	a tapas bar
a French restaurant	a Thai restaurant
a Greek restaurant	a vegetarian restaurant
a Japanese restaurant	an Indian restaurant

3 Restaurants

You are going to listen to a conversation between two friends – Mel and Kenny. Some of the words they use are below. Look quickly at the words. Try to guess what Mel and Kenny are talking about. Discuss your ideas with a partner for three minutes.

M: hungry?
K: bit
M: get something?
K: OK – you – anywhere?
M: pizza place – corner
K: I – pizza last night – don't – another – anywhere else?
M: Thai place – Soho
K: spicy? – don't – like – food
M: not – bad – dishes to choose – nice food – like
K: OK – try – once
M: walk or – bus?
K: you

🎧 **Now listen to the conversation and see if you were right.**

Look at the tapescript and listen again. Was there anything you missed?

Practise reading the tapescript with a partner. Remember to stress the sounds in CAPITAL LETTERS and try to say each group of words together.

Spend five minutes trying to memorise the conversation. Then have the same conversation again. This time, just use the notes above to help you remember.

4 Speaking

Can you recommend:

1. a really top-class restaurant in your town or city?
2. somewhere good, but cheap?
3. somewhere really different?

Tell a partner your recommendations. For example:

- There's a place in … . They do really good seafood / pizzas / Indian food.

5 | Saying no to food and drink

Complete the conversations with the expressions in the box.

I couldn't eat	I don't really like anything spicy
I don't drink	I don't really like anything sweet
I'm driving	I've actually just had one
I'm full	I won't be able to sleep
I'm on a diet	

1. A: Would you like some more wine?
   B: No thanks. I mustn't have any more.
   .... One glass is enough.

2. A: Would you like some wine?
   B: No thanks. Actually, ...
   Have you got any fruit juice or something non-alcoholic?

3. A: Would you like a piece of cake?
   B: No thanks. I mustn't ....
   I'm trying to lose weight.

4. A: Would you like some more coffee?
   B: No thanks. .... if I have any more.

5. A: Would you like some chilli sauce?
   B: No thanks. .... , actually.

6. A: Would you like some more of anything?
   B: No thanks, I've had enough. ....
   A: Are you sure you don't want to finish the lamb?
   B: No, honestly. It was lovely, but ....
   anything else. Thanks.

7. A: Would you like anything for dessert?
   B: Not for me thanks. .... ,
   actually.

8. A: Would you like a cup of tea?
   B: .... , so I'm OK for the
   moment, thanks.

6 | Practice

Look at the photos. Ask a partner if they would like any of the things to eat or drink. Your partner should reply by saying No thanks. and then giving a reason, as in the conversations in Activity 5.

7 | Using grammar: *some / any*

Complete the conversations with the expressions in the box.

any more	have some more
anything in mind	not any more
any time after five	something to eat
anyone want	sometime next week
anywhere in mind	someone has taken
do something	

1. A: Do you want to go and get .... ?
   B: Yes, great. Have you got .... ?

2. A: Do you want to .... tonight?
   B: Yes, maybe. Have you got .... ?

3. A: Do you want to meet up for lunch .... ?
   B: Yes, great. How about Wednesday?

4. A: When shall I come round tomorrow?
   B: Oh, ... is fine.

5. A: Does .... to go for a
   coffee after class?
   B: Yes, I wouldn't mind.

6. A: Oh no! .... my bag!
   B: Are you sure? When did you last see it?

7. A: Would you like .... biscuits?
   B: No, thanks, but could I .... tea?

8. A: Are you still going to the English classes at
   Oxbridge House?
   B: No, ... I got fed up with
   them and stopped.

With a partner, practise the conversations. Try to continue each conversation for as long as you can.

> For more information on using *some* and *any*, see G19.

Reading

1 | Deciding where to eat

What is the most important thing for you when you have a meal in a restaurant? Mark the things in the box from 1 (= most important) to 5 (= the least important).

> the amount of food you get
>
> the cost
>
> the kind of food they serve
>
> the quality of the food
>
> the service

Compare your choices with a partner. Then work together and make a list of all the problems you could have when you go to a restaurant. Look at the picture for some ideas. See which pair in the class can think of the most problems.

2 | While you read

🎧 **You are going to read an e-mail from Enrico, an Italian student, to a friend of his in Germany. Enrico is writing about a meal he had recently in a restaurant in Britain. As you read, find out if he had any of the problems you thought of.**

3 | Comprehension check

Decide whether these statements about the e-mail are true (T) or false (F). If you think they are false, can you say why?

1. The restaurant was busy.   T / F
2. The service was slow.   T / F
3. They had a good waiter.   T / F
4. The food was really nice.   T / F
5. The bill was wrong.   T / F
6. It was rather expensive.   T / F

Compare your ideas with a partner. Then read the e-mail again to see if you were right.

I wouldn't recommend it!

From:	Enrico e.boceceli122@shotmail.com
To:	Bauer.hans@netmail.co.de
Date:	Fri, Sep1, 16:37
Subject:	Re: Disaster!
Attachments:	none

Hi Hans,

I just thought I'd send you a quick e-mail to let you know how I'm getting on. I'm studying at the school you told me about – the Oxbridge Centre. It's really nice and the teachers are very friendly. Most of the students are much younger than me, so we don't have much to talk about. Luckily though, there's a very nice Russian student in my class called Martina, who's about my age.

A few days ago we went to Michelangelo's – that Italian place you told me about. Unfortunately, it was a disaster from start to finish. When we got there, there was a huge queue. We had to wait half an hour for a table. Then we had to wait for ages for our food, and when it finally came, the waiter had mixed up our order! He brought me fish instead of chicken! Martina had ordered pasta, but she got a pizza! Unbelievable! By that time though, we were both so hungry that we decided not to complain! Unfortunately, my fish was cold and Martina's pizza just didn't really taste of anything. It was horrible!

When they brought us the bill, they'd charged us for a bottle of wine we hadn't even ordered! When we complained about it, the manager didn't even apologise! He just said it was Saturday night and they were very busy. It wasn't very cheap either. It cost us about £25 each and that was without the service charge. When I got up to leave, I spilt some coke all over Martina's dress. She wasn't very impressed, I can tell you! I rang her yesterday to see if she wanted to go out with me again, but she wasn't interested.

What do you think I should do?

Anyway, I hope you're well. See you soon.
All the best
Enrico

Real English: spilt or spilled

The e-mail said: 'I spilt some coke'. The past tense of spill is spilt or spilled. Both are correct. We often say we spill things all over something. Here are some examples:

I'm so clumsy! I've just spilt some water all over myself!

It was awful! He spilled red wine all over our new carpet.

When was the last time you spilled something?

4 | Speaking

When Enrico told his friends about the meal the following day, this is what they said:

a. 'If something like that happened to me, I would complain about the food being wrong and I'd send it back immediately.'

b. 'If my fish arrived cold, I would just walk out without paying.'

c. 'I hate situations like this. I would just eat my meal, pay the bill, and then leave without complaining – but I'd never go back!'

Which person do you agree with most? Why? What is your worst restaurant experience?

5 | Word check

Complete the sentences with words from the e-mail. Try not to look back at the e-mail.

1. I went out for a meal last night. It was a .... from start to finish!

2. The .... was so long that we decided to find another place to eat.

3. The waiter was terrible. He .... up our order and then made a mistake with the bill.

4. When they brought the bill, they tried to .... us £5 for mineral water!

5. We didn't .... any wine.

6. When I complained, at least the manager came and .... and gave us the coffee on the house.

7. It was so expensive. It .... us £30 and that was without the wine.

8. The waiter was terrible. He knocked over my glass and .... wine all over my trousers.

6 | Using grammar: irregular past simple verbs

Do you know the past simple forms of these verbs?

break	eat	feel	spill
drink	fall	send	tear

Complete the collocations with the past simple forms of the verbs above. Add one verb to each group.

1. ....
   I ... too much. / I only ... water. / They ... two litres of coke.

2. ....
   I ... wine all over the table. / I ... coffee down my shirt. / I ... some water on the floor.

3. ....
   I ... really stupid. / I ... like going home. / I ... quite ill. / I ... really dizzy.

4. ....
   I ... it into little pieces. / I ... it up and threw it in the bin. / I ... my jeans when I fell over.

5. ....
   The wine was so disgusting I ... it back. / I ... him a card. / He ... you his love.

6. ....
   I ... something that was off. / He ... like a pig! It was disgusting! / We ... a whole lamb between four of us.

7. ....
   I ... over and hurt myself. / I ... down the stairs. / I nearly ... off my chair laughing.

8. ....
   I ... a plate. / I ... my glasses. / I ... up with her last week.

7 | Practice

Choose one of these situations and spend five minutes planning how to tell a partner about it.

1. a time you ate too much
2. a time you felt really stupid
3. a time you tore your clothes
4. a time you broke something
5. a time you fell over and hurt yourself

Tell your partner about the situation you chose.

Listening

1 Restaurant vocabulary

How much restaurant vocabulary do you know already? What can you see in the photos?

Compare the words you know with a partner.

Complete the conversations with the words in the box.

bill	menu	service	waiter
book	order	tip	wine list

1. A: Hi, can I .... a table for four for eight o'clock tonight, please?
    B: Certainly, sir. What name is it?

2. A: What do you feel like drinking?
    B: I'm not sure. Let me have a look at the .... and see what they've got.

3. A: Excuse me, could we see the .... , please?
    B: Certainly, sir.

4. A: Are you ready to .... yet?
    B: Not yet. We still haven't decided.

5. A: Shall we get the .... now? I'm ready to go.
    B: OK, let me try to catch the ....'s eye.

6. A: Let's leave them a big ....
    B: Yes. OK. The .... was great, wasn't it?

2 Speaking

Discuss these questions with a partner.

1. Have you ever worked in a restaurant? Doing what?
2. Do you usually leave tips in restaurants? How much?
3. Do you ever leave tips in any other situation?
4. When was the last time you booked a table?

3 Before you listen

Look at the questions you might hear in a restaurant. Who do you think says each question and to whom? Is it waiter to customer, customer to waiter, or customer to customer?

a. Do you know what lychees are?
b. Are you ready to order?
c. Are you happy having wine?
d. Have you booked?
e. Could we have some water as well, please?
f. What a choice! Can you recommend anything?

With a partner, decide the order in which you would hear the six sentences.

1. ▢   2. ▢   3. ▢   4. ▢   5. ▢   6. ▢

4 While you listen

🎧 Listen to the conversation between two friends – Kenny and Mel – and a waiter in a restaurant and see if you were right. Who says each question and to whom? In which order did you hear the questions?

Can you remember the answers to the questions? Compare what you remember with a partner.

Listen again and check your answers – or read the tapescript.

5 Speaking

Discuss these questions with a partner.

1. Kenny and Mel ordered one of the set menus. Do you ever order set menus when you go out for dinner? Why / why not?
2. What do you usually drink when you eat out?
3. Do you like trying new kinds of food?
4. Is there any kind of food you really can't eat? Why not?

6 | I'm afraid that's off

Put the sentences in order and make conversations between a customer and a waiter.

Conversation 1

a. Oh, right. Well, in that case, I'll have the soup.

b. Could I have the prawns, please?

c. What would you like as a starter?

d. I'm afraid we don't have any prawns left.

1. ☐   2. ☐   3. ☐   4. ☐

Conversation 2

a. Could I have the paella?

b. And for your main course?

c. Oh, right. Well, in that case, I'll have the cod.

d. I'm afraid you need a minimum of two people to order that.

1 ☐   2. ☐   3. ☐   4. ☐

Conversation 3

a. Would you like anything for dessert?

b. Oh, right. Well, in that case, you have the strawberries and I'll have the lemon tart.

c. I'm afraid we've only got one portion left.

d. Yes, could we both have the strawberries, please?

1. ☐   2. ☐   3. ☐   4. ☐

With a partner, practise the conversations.

Look at the menu and have conversations like those above. One of you should be a customer, the other should be a waiter or waitress.

Starters
Chicken and Mushroom Soup
Mixed Salad with Sun-dried Tomatoes
Prawn Cocktail
Mussels with Garlic and Butter

Main courses
Tuna Steak with Fresh Herbs
Roast Duck with Honey (minimum 2 people)
Fried Fish – Moroccan Style
Pasta with Cheese and Ham

Desserts
Chocolate Pudding
Baked Apples with Brandy
Fried Bananas with Ice Cream

Drinks
House Red Wine
House White Wine
Lager
Coke
Water – Still and Sparkling

7 | Sorry, but I didn't order this

Complete the sentences with the words in the box.

not boiled	not ice cream	not still
not brown	not rosé	not tomato salad
not carrots	not scrambled	not well done

1. Sorry, but I ordered red wine, ...

2. Sorry, but I wanted my steak rare, ...

3. Sorry, but I ordered sparkling water, ...

4. Sorry, but I ordered mashed potatoes, ...

5. Sorry, but I ordered white bread, ...

6. Sorry, but I ordered green salad, ...

7. Sorry, but I ordered fried eggs, ...

8. Sorry, but I ordered green beans, ...

9. Sorry, but I ordered the apple pie with cream, ...

When we correct people, we stress the incorrect and correct words. The stressed words below are in CAPITAL letters.

Sorry, but I ordered RED wine, not ROSÉ.

Sorry, but I ordered RED WINE, not BEER.

With a partner, decide which words in the sentences above should be stressed.

🎧 **Listen and check your answers. Then practise the sentences.**

Complete the collocations with six nouns from the sentences above.

a. white / brown / sliced / fresh / stale ....

b. roast / fried / baked / mashed ....

c. potato / green / side / fruit ....

d. Could I have my .... medium / well done / rare, please?

e. dry white / sweet white / sparkling / the house ....

f. boiled / fried / scrambled ....

8 | Speaking

Discuss these questions with a partner.

1. How do you prefer to eat potatoes? And eggs?

2. Do you like sparkling water or do you prefer still?

3. Do you drink wine? What kind do you prefer?

4. Do you ever eat steaks? How do you like them done?

How do you get on with her? • They're identical twins. • My mum's a bit more open than my dad. • He's much fitter than I am. • We don't have much in common. • We both have older brothers. • They got divorced when I was a kid. • My sister has just got engaged. • He's moving to an old people's home. • She's a friend from church. • He died in his sleep. • She died of a heart attack. • He passed away last year. • I'm sorry to hear that. • They met in an internet chat room. • How do you two know each other? • She's one of my oldest friends. • We've just got engaged.

10 Family

Conversation

1 | Questions we ask about families

Put the words in order and make questions.

1. you / sisters / any / brothers / Have / or / got

.... ?

2. old / How / they / are

.... ?

3. do / do / your / What / parents

.... ?

4. Are / married / you

.... ?

5. any / you / kids / got / Have

.... ?

6. they / What / like / are?

.... ?

7. with / you / Do / them / get / on

.... ?

8. grandparents / Are / still / your / alive

.... ?

9. a / got / Have / you / girlfriend/boyfriend

.... ?

🎧 **Listen and check your answers. Then practise the questions.**

Spend two minutes trying to memorise as many of the questions as you can.

Now close your book and ask a partner the questions.

2 | Talking about your family

🎧 **Listen to the first part of a conversation between two friends – Mary and Stella. They are talking about someone in Stella's family. The first time you listen, note anything you hear about this person.**

Compare what you heard with a partner. Listen again if you need to.

With a partner, use the questions and answers you heard to role play the conversation between Mary and Stella. At the end of the role play, one of you should say 'Anyway, what about you? Have you got any brothers or sisters?' Talk about your own family and continue the conversation for as long as you can.

🎧 **Now listen to the rest of the conversation and complete it.**

M: Yes, I've got two older brothers and a (1) ....

S: You're a twin. Wow. Do you look very similar?

M: I don't think so. We're not identical twins, if that's what you mean. Alison's a bit (2) .... me and her hair is darker. But yes, people are always confusing us. People she's met sometimes come up to me and say hello and start talking to me, and I've got no idea who they are.

S: Right. That must be quite annoying.

M: It's OK. I'm used to it. It can actually be quite amusing!

S: So (3) .... ? I mean, have you got similar personalities as well?

M: Not really. She's a lot (4) .... me. It's usually me who does the talking when we go out and she's a more serious person than I am. For example, she's very hard-working. Her job's really important to her. She doesn't go out very much. I guess I'm (5) .... , but she's my twin, so we're always going to be (6) ....

3 | Speaking

Discuss these questions with a partner.

1. Do you know any twins? Do they look very similar?
2. Do you know any identical twins? Can you tell them apart?
3. What do you think are the good things about being a twin? And the bad things?

4 | Using grammar: comparatives

When we describe people in our families, we often use comparatives. We make comparatives using adjective + -er or more + adjective:

- Mary's a bit taller than me.
- I'm more relaxed.

Do you know when we add -er and when we use more? Compare your ideas with a partner.

Now read the explanation in the box to see if you were right.

- Words of one syllable normally take -er: shorter, longer.
- Words of three syllables take more: more interesting, more beautiful.
- Words of two syllables normally take more: more boring, more famous. If the second syllable ends in -y, then the spelling becomes -ier: sillier, funnier.
- However, with many words of two syllables, usage varies. It would be nice if the rules were clear, but, for example, some native speakers say commoner and others say more common. Most people say quieter, not more quiet.
- In normal spoken English, we usually use the weak form of than: /ðən/.

Complete the sentences with comparatives.

1. I get on better with my dad than my mum. He's .... He lets me do what I want. (relaxed)

2. I find my mum .... to talk to than my dad. She's just generally .... than he is. He never really talks about his feelings. (easy, open)

3. My brother is ten years .... than me. He's a lot .... than I am. He's only really interested in work. (old, serious)

4. My sister is actually a bit .... than me, but she looks .... (young, old)

5. My mum is a lot .... than my dad. He never stops talking! (quiet)

6. My sister and I both really like sport, but she's a lot .... She goes running every day! (fit)

7. I don't like my cousin very much, but he's .... than his girlfriend! She's really horrible! (nice)

8. My brother is very hard-working. I'm a lot .... than he is. (lazy)

Are any of the eight sentences above true for you? Tell a partner. Can you change any of the other sentences to make them true?

Now change partners and find out about the people in their family.

Real English: a bit / a lot / much older

We often add a bit to comparatives to show there is a small difference. We can add a lot or much to show there is a big difference. Here are some examples:

He's a bit older than me. I think I'm five months younger.
She's a lot older than him. She's 45 and I think he's only 30 or 31.
I'm much taller than my dad. He's one metre fifty-four and I'm one metre ninety!

5 | Using grammar: *better / worse*

Good and bad have irregular comparative forms. These are better (good) and worse (bad).

What do you think? Complete the sentences with better or worse.

1. My English is .... than it was before I started this course.

2. My country is a .... place to live than the United States.

3. This book is .... than the last one I used.

4. The world is a .... place to live in now than it was ten years ago.

5. Modern music is .... than older music.

6. I am .... -looking than I was five years ago.

Tell a partner what you have written and why.

For more information on using comparatives, see G20.

Reading

1 | Using vocabulary: *a lot in common*

When we know someone well and we like them, it is often because we have a lot in common. This means we like the same kind of things; we come from the same kind of background; we have had the same kind of experiences in life. We often show we have things in common by saying we both like something (if you are talking about two people) or we all like something (if you are talking about three or more).

Think of your best friend or someone you get on really well with. What things do you have in common? Make as many true sentences as you can using these sentence starters.

1. We both love …
2. We both hate …
3. We're both from …
4. We're both …
5. We've both got …
6. We've both been to …
7. We're both good at …
8. We're both bad at …

Now tell a partner about your friend.

2 | Further practice

Ask a new partner questions to try to find eight things you have in common.

3 | Before you read

∩ Read this short text and find out what the two people have in common.

Jerry Taylor has the same surname as the famous Hollywood actress Elizabeth Taylor, but that's not the only thing they have in common. They're both in their seventies. They were both born in England and they both then moved to America. They've also both been married eight times. They may be extreme examples, but in the West, more and more people are getting married and divorced not just once, but two or three times. Many political and religious leaders are worried about this growing trend. I just wanted to discover why this happens and what goes wrong. I went to interview Jerry to find out.

4 | Speaking

Discuss these questions with a partner.

1. Do you know anyone who's been married more than once? Who? What happened?
2. Do you think it's better to stay married if you start having lots of arguments – or get divorced?

5 | Reading

∩ Read the interview with Jerry and find out why his marriages failed.

Eighth time lucky!

Q: So what's the longest you've been married?

Jerry: That was my third marriage – to Lisa-Marie – and it lasted six years. Sadly, she died suddenly of a heart attack. She was only 40. Nobody knows why it happened. She didn't smoke or drink. She went out shopping one day and never came back. It was terrible. She was the love of my life. In some ways, we didn't have that much in common. She was ten years older than me. She was a teacher, but she was quiet and kind. She didn't get angry about any of my bad habits. My shortest marriage was my fifth one – that only lasted six days.

Q: Six days! Why was it so short?

Jerry: Martha, my fourth wife, had just left me for another man and I was feeling really bad, so I went on holiday. One day, I was having a meal on my own in the hotel restaurant. A single woman was sitting at the next table. We started chatting and she joined me at my table. Her name was Rita. She was really good-looking and I couldn't believe she was interested in an old guy like me. It turned out that her husband had just died. We fell in love and got married two days later! The manager of the hotel came to our wedding. We had a big party with all the other guests. I bought her the most expensive diamond ring I could find. It cost me $50,000! Of course, we were booked on different flights home. Mine was leaving at nine in the morning, hers left at eleven. When I met her flight in Los Angeles, there was no sign of her! She just disappeared. I never heard from her again – and she didn't send the ring back!

Q: So what went wrong with all your other marriages?

Jerry: Well, the first time, I was just too young. I was only 20. My girlfriend, Mary, got pregnant. She was 19 and in those days, first you got married and then you had the baby. The marriage lasted about a year. After the baby was born, she didn't really want me around the house. All my other wives told me I'm a difficult person to live with. You see, I like to keep things clean and tidy. Some of them didn't have the same high standards as me. Little things make me really annoyed. For example, some of my wives didn't fold the towels the way I like, or they moved my things around. Both Donna, my sixth wife, and Sheryl – she was the seventh – left me because they said I was crazy. The other thing is, I'm a really big fan of Elvis. I love him! I have a big collection of records and Elvis bits and pieces, and some of them hated that. When Laura, my second wife, left me, because she found out I was having an affair with Lisa-Marie, she said she was happy she was going because she would never have to listen to another Elvis song in her life! I just couldn't believe it!

Q: So, why do you keep getting married again?

Jerry: I guess I just don't like living on my own. And I still believe in finding Mrs Right. And maybe this time I have. I met Kimberly in Graceland, the home of Elvis. She loves Elvis too. And she's beautiful.

Q: How long have you been married now?

Jerry: Nine weeks and it's beautiful.

6 | After you read

Can you remember why Jerry's marriages ended? Complete the sentences. Don't look back at the interview.

1. Mary didn't want Jerry to be .... the house after the baby was ....
2. Laura .... out Jerry was having an .... with Lisa-Marie.
3. Lisa-Marie died of ....
4. Martha .... Jerry .... another man.
5. Rita just .... a few days after the wedding.
6. Donna thought Jerry was .... and much too tidy.
7. Sheryl also thought Jerry was .... and much too tidy!

Read the interview again and check your answers.

7 | Speaking

Whose fault do you think each divorce was? Why? Tick the statements which describe how you feel about Jerry.

a. I feel sorry for him.
b. He sounds horrible.
c. He sounds like a nice man.
d. He sounds quite interesting.
e. He sounds a bit crazy.
f. He sounds a bit sad.
g. I understand why Rita didn't stay with him.
h. I don't understand why Rita left him.

Explain your choices to a partner.

8 | Using vocabulary: collocations

Look at the verbs in these sentences. Delete the words that don't go with the verbs.

1. I was born in Nigeria / in a little village near Rome / in 1968 / at home / a baby this year.
2. I grew up in Canada / in London / in the country / by my grandparents / by the sea.
3. I moved house / to Sao Paolo / in with my girlfriend / country / to Australia when I was 20.
4. She got a baby / married / divorced / pregnant / engaged.
5. I live on my own / with my parents / in a flat / with two friends / in a hotel for the weekend.
6. I went to university / work / home / to the cinema / crazy.

Use the verbs above to say things that are true about yourself and your family.

Complete the collocations with the verbs in the box.

buy   change   get   leave   move

a. .... house / into an old people's home
b. .... schools / jobs / your career
c. .... my first car / my first flat / my first house
d. .... primary school / school / home
e. .... my first job / my first boyfriend / married / divorced

How old do you think most people are when they do the things above? Which ones have you done already? Which ones are you planning to do sometime soon?

Listening

1 | Using vocabulary: *How do you know her?*

Complete the answers to the question above with the words in the box.

church	my old job	the tennis club	work
Germany	school	university	

1. She's a friend from .... We both did our degrees in history.

2. She's a friend from .... I usually play her every Saturday morning.

3. She's a friend from .... She's in the same office as me.

4. She's a friend from .... She's one of my oldest friends. I've known her since I was twelve!

5. She's a friend from .... We both used to work for Hitachi.

6. She's a friend from .... She's come over here to stay with me for a week.

7. She's a friend from .... We usually sit next to each other every Sunday.

Write down the names of five different friends. Give these names to a partner. Your partner will ask you How do you know him / her? Try to use some of the expressions above in your answers.

2 | While you listen

🎧 **Listen to the conversation between two women – Beth and Salma. They are talking about Mark, a friend of theirs. As you listen, decide how each of them knows Mark.**

3 | Comprehension check

Discuss these questions with a partner. Can you remember the answers?

1. How long have Beth and Mark been going out?
2. What does Mark do for a living?
3. How do Beth's parents feel about Mark?
4. How did Beth's grandmother die?
5. Did Beth get on well with her?

Now listen again and check your answers.

4 | Speaking

Discuss these questions with a partner.

1. Why do you think Beth's parents are anti-police?

2. Do you think Beth is right not to tell her parents about Mark yet? Why / why not?

Complete this sentence.

My parents wouldn't like it if I went out with ... .

5 | Keyword: *die*

Beth said that her grandmother died in her sleep.

Match the sentence beginnings with the endings.

1. She died of ... . ⬜ ⬜ ⬜ ⬜ ⬜

2. She died in ... . ⬜ ⬜ ⬜ ⬜ ⬜

a. a skiing accident

b. a plane crash

c. old age

d. her sleep

e. a heart attack

f. cancer

g. a car crash

h. a drug overdose

i. AIDS

j. the war

Can you think of any famous people who have died in the ways above?

Real English:
He passed away last year.

This is a nicer way of saying He died last year. Usually, if someone tells us this, we respond by saying Oh. I'm sorry to hear that.

6 | Using vocabulary: the internet

In the conversation you heard, Beth said she met Mark in an internet chat room. Would you date someone you met like this? Why / why not?

Check you understand all the words in these questions.

1. Do you use the internet much?

2. How many e-mails do you usually receive every day? How often do you check your e-mail?

3. How many e-mails do you usually send every day?

4. Do you have any favourite web sites?

5. Do you ever go to chat rooms? What name do you use?

6. Do you ever download music / pictures / articles from the internet?

7. Do you know anyone who has set up a web page?

8. Are you a member of any on-line news groups?

9. Do you ever buy things on-line? What?

10. Do you ever book tickets on-line?

Now ask a partner the questions.

Do you know where she lives? • Turn left at the crossroads. • When you come to the roundabout, go straight on. • It's miles away. • We'd better get the bus. • It'll be quicker by train. • I've got no sense of direction! • I couldn't find a parking space. • They've introduced a £5 charge. • They want to privatise the railways. • The buses are all state-run. • It'll be more expensive during peak hours. • It'll be cheaper if you book in advance. • Does that include insurance? • I got off at the wrong stop. • Excuse me!

11 Getting around

Conversation

1 | Using vocabulary: around town

Look at the photos. Which of the things in the box can you see?

a big monument	a crossroads	a sign
a bridge	a mosque	a sports stadium
a church	a park	a subway
a crossing	a roundabout	traffic lights

Have you got all of these things in the place where you live? What are the best-known landmarks in your city – places everyone knows how to get to?

2 | Asking for directions (1)

🎧 **Listen to a tourist asking for directions to a place called The Gagosian. As you listen, try to answer these questions.**

1. What sort of place is The Gagosian?
2. Where is it?

Which of the expressions did the speakers use?

1. Excuse me, could you help me?
2. I'm looking for a gallery called The Gagosian.
3. Do you know if this is the way to The Gagosian?
4. I'm sorry. I'm not from round here myself.
5. I don't really know the area.
6. Ask this lady here.
7. It's down there somewhere.
8. It's just past the bridge on the right.
9. Follow the signs to the city centre.
10. Just keep going straight on down this road until you get to some traffic lights. Then turn right.
11. It's along that road on your left. You can't miss it.
12. Ask someone else when you get there.

Listen to the conversation again and check your answers – or read the tapescript.

Translate the sentences into your own language.

3 | Pronunciation: sentence stress

Look at the sentences in Activity 2 again. <u>Underline</u> the sounds you think are stressed in normal speech. For example:

1. Ex<u>cuse</u> me, could you <u>help</u> me?
2. I'm <u>look</u>ing for a <u>gall</u>ery called The Gag<u>os</u>ian.

🎧 **Compare your ideas with a partner. Then listen and check your answers.**

4 | Practice

With a partner, ask and answer questions about the places on the map. Use these expressions in your questions.

- Do you know if this is the way to ... ?
- Could you help me? I'm looking for ... .

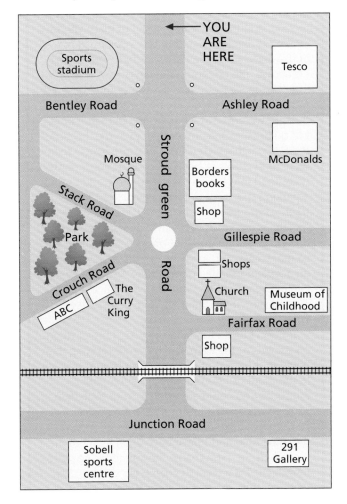

5 | Asking for directions (2)

🎧 **Listen to the tourist having another conversation. As you listen, try and answer these questions.**

1. What's the problem?
2. What does the tourist have to do?

Real English: miles

Most people in Britain use miles to talk about distance. A mile is almost two kilometres.

It's two miles to the centre of town.
The speed limit in towns is 30 miles per hour.

People often use the word miles to mean a very long way.

I live miles away from where I work.
It's miles to walk. Let's take a taxi.
You can see for miles from my flat. It's on the 16th floor of a 20-storey building.

6 | Speaking

Discuss these questions with a partner.

1. Have you got a good / bad sense of direction?
2. Have you ever got lost? On the way to where? How long did it take you to get there in the end?

7 | Using grammar: indirect questions

We often begin questions with Do you know ... ? It sounds more polite – especially if it is a difficult question and the other person might not know the answer. Notice the word order in these indirect questions.

- Is this the way to The Gagosian?
  Do you know if this is the way to The Gagosian?
- Does he work there in the evenings?
  Do you know if he works there in the evenings?
- Where does he live?
  Do you know where he lives?
- Which bus do I need to take to go to the town centre?
  Do you know which bus I need to take to go to the town centre?

Write these questions as indirect questions.

1. Is there a post office near here?
   Do you know .... ?
2. Has he got any brothers or sisters?
   Do you know .... ?
3. Is she coming tonight?
   Do you know .... ?
4. Does she live near here?
   Do you know .... ?
5. How old is he?
   Do you know .... ?
6. Where's he from?
   Do you know .... ?
7. What does she do for a living?
   Do you know .... ?
8. Where are the toilets?
   Do you know .... ?

8 | Practice

Ask a partner questions about other people in the class. For example:

A: Do you know if Javier is married?
B: Yes, he is. I've met his wife actually. She's really nice.
A: Do you know where Natalia works?
B: I don't know. I've never heard her talk about her job.

> ▶ For more information on using indirect questions, see G21.

Reading

1 | Using vocabulary: *How long does it take you to get to work?*

Complete the answers to the question above with the words in the box.

close	late	trains
cycle	traffic	underground

1. It takes me 20 minutes on a good day, when there's not much ....

2. It takes me about 40 minutes. I have to change .... twice.

3. I .... most days. It takes about half an hour.

4. It only takes me five minutes. I can walk it. I live very ....

5. It usually takes me about 20 minutes, but the bus isn't very reliable. It often comes ....

6. It takes me half an hour if there are no problems on the ....

Now ask some other students How long does it take you to get to work? Try to use some of the expressions above in your answers.

2 | Before you read

With a partner, make a list of the good and bad things about:

1. cycling to work.
2. driving to work.
3. using public transport to get to work.

Compare your list with another pair of students. Do you agree with all of their ideas? Which do you think is the best way to get to work? Why?

3 | While you read

⋒ **Read this text about getting to work and see if it mentions the things you thought of.**

It drives me mad!

I share a flat with a friend from work – Kate. She's a nice woman and we get on well, but there is one thing we always argue about: cars! She loves her car. She goes everywhere in it. She's even given it a name – she calls it Jenny! Every day Kate drives to work and I cycle. Kate thinks I'm mad. She says cycling is dangerous and dirty – you get all hot and sweaty – and she thinks it's hard and boring. Of course, the one thing she never says is it's slow. That's because every day she leaves the house 20 minutes before I do on my bike. Most days, though, we arrive at work around the same time, but quite often she arrives later than me, because the traffic lights weren't working or because there were road works or because of a car crash on the main road into town or because she couldn't find a parking space. I can always cycle past these traffic jams and problems, so it takes me more or less the same time every day. I guess it can be a bit dangerous sometimes, but only because there are so many cars, and anyway, I've never actually had an accident or fallen off my bike. And of course, cycling keeps me fit, which is why I'm still a size 10 and she's a 14, although Kate doesn't like it when I say this!

If I don't travel to places by bike, I prefer to go on the bus or the train. It's just more relaxing than going in the car. In the car, all you can do is listen to the radio or listen to music, but on public transport, you can read, listen to your Walkman, write letters, watch lots of different kinds of people, make new friends or just sleep! Anyway, the thing Kate and I have been arguing about most recently is the new charge the council is going to introduce. They want to charge car drivers £5 a day to go into the town centre. That's £25 a week if you work there! They say this will stop people making journeys that they don't really need to make. It will make the streets safer, it'll make the city safer to walk in and it will cut pollution. Also, the council have promised to spend the money they make on improving public transport. I think it's a great idea. Kate, of course, is really angry about it. She calls it robbery and has said she's not going to pay it!

4 | Vocabulary focus

Match these verbs from the text with the nouns they collocate with.

1. listen to ☐   a. public transport
2. fall off ☐   b. your Walkman
3. find ☐   c. my bike
4. improve ☐   d. a parking space

Now match these verbs with the nouns they collocate with.

5. go on ☐   e. at work
6. share ☐   f. the bus
7. cut ☐   g. a flat
8. arrive ☐   h. pollution

Can you remember what the writer said about the eight things above? Compare what you remember with a partner.

5 | Speaking

Discuss these questions with a partner.

1. What's the traffic like in your town or city?
2. Is there much pollution in your town or city?
3. Do you think introducing a £5 charge for drivers would help the situation? Why / why not?
4. Can you think of any other ways to make things better?

6 | Using grammar: comparatives

We often use comparatives when explaining decisions. For example:

A: Do you want to write him a quick e-mail?

B: No, I'll just phone him. It'll be quicker.

A: We should phone Julian before we go out.

B: No, let's wait until after six. It'll be cheaper then.

Complete the answers with It'll be + comparative.

1. How shall we get there?
   a. Let's get the bus. ....
      (cheap)
   b. Let's get a taxi. ....
      (quick)
   c. Let's walk. .... and it'll
      probably be as quick as the bus. (nice)

2. Do you want to go away this weekend?
   a. No, let's stay here. ....
      (relaxing)
   b. Yes. .... than sitting
      around here, doing nothing. (exciting)
   c. Yes. .... than watching
      football all day Saturday! (good)

3. Where do you want to go on holiday in the summer?
   a. Let's just go and see your family.
      .... (easy)
   b. Let's go to England. ....
      than here at that time of year. (cool)
   c. Let's wait till winter. ....
      and it won't be as crowded. (cheap)

Now respond to these questions using It'll + comparative.

1. A: Do you want to get the train or shall we fly?
   B: Let's ....

2. A: Do you want to go out for dinner tonight or shall we cook something?
   B: Let's ....

3. A: Do you want to go to the cinema later or shall we just stay in and watch TV?
   B: Let's ....

Listening

1 | Trains!

Discuss these questions.

1. Do you like travelling by train?

2. Have you taken the train in any different countries?
    From where to where? What was it like?

Read the text.

British people find buying a train ticket very difficult these days. Since the railways were privatised, the number of different prices has grown and grown. If you try to buy a ticket on-line from London to Manchester, they ask you what kind of ticket you want and give you sixty-four options. SIXTY-FOUR! And the prices can vary from £10 to £175! Prices change if you travel on peak days (Fridays and holidays) or if you travel back on certain days. Generally, if you get a day return – i.e. go and come back on the same day – it's cheaper than getting a single, although it depends if you travel at peak hours. It also makes a difference if you book in advance. Book two or more weeks in advance and it's half the price it is if you book only one week before. Buy your ticket on the day and it can be twice as expensive again! It's mad!

Discuss these questions with a partner.

1. Are trains in your country privatised or state-run?

2. How do you feel about that?

3. Are there different prices if:

    a. you travel at peak hours or off peak?

    b. you travel on particular days?

    c. you book in advance?

    d. you're a particular age?

    e. you travel in a group?

    f. you come back the same day?

2 | Before you listen

Look at the photos. Match the things people say when travelling with the photos.

1. Could you tell me which stop I have to get off at?

2. It's peak hour so it'll be £175.

3. What class of vehicle would you like?

4. Is this the right platform for Leeds?

5. Does that include insurance?

6. What day are you returning?

3 | Role play

With a partner, choose situations from two of the photos. Role play the conversations you think the people are having. If you need to, spend two minutes planning what you will say.

4 | While you listen

🎧 Listen to four short conversations. Match the conversation with the photos in Activity 2.

1. ☐   2. ☐   3. ☐   4. ☐

There are problems in conversations 1, 2 and 3. What are they? Listen again if you need to.

Now look at the tapescript and <u>underline</u> five new expressions you want to try to remember. Tell a partner what you have underlined.

With your partner, role play the conversations from Activity 3 again. Try to use some of the new expressions from the tapescript.

Real English: *sir / madam / mate / love*

Sometimes shop assistants, waiters and other people who serve customers will call a man sir and a woman madam – if it's an expensive place or they want to be formal. If it's a cheaper place or they're being friendly, they will call a man mate and a woman love.

Can I help you, sir?   *Yes, mate.*
Can I help you, madam?   *Yes, love.*

Do you have any equivalent words in your language? Do you like them?

5 | Key words: *right* and *wrong*

Complete the conversations with right or wrong.

1. A: Is this the .... platform for Opera?
    B: No, you're on the .... side. You need to go over there.

2. A: There you are! I've been waiting for ages!
    B: Yes, sorry. I took the bus, but I got off at the .... stop. I've had to walk about two miles!
    A: Oh right. Well, never mind. You're here now.

3. A: What happened to you last night? I was waiting for ages.
    B: Yes, I'm really sorry. I tried to ring you to say I couldn't come, but I had the .... number. You'd better give it to me again.

4. A: Are you sure we're going in the .... direction? I don't remember coming this way.
    B: Yes, definitely. I've been here before.

5. A: Is this the .... answer?
    B: No, you've used the .... form. It should be 'doing' not 'to do'.

6. A: There's something .... with your Walkman. It's not playing.
    B: Let me have a look at it. I've just changed the batteries. Maybe I put them in the .... way round.

7. A: So how did you get your job at the TV station?
    B: I was just lucky. I was just in the .... place at the .... time.

8. A: Hello, could you help me? I bought this shirt for a friend, but it's the .... size. Can I change it?
    B: Of course. Have you got the receipt?

Now <u>underline</u> the collocations using right and wrong.

6 | Speaking

Discuss these questions with a partner.

1. Have you ever got on the wrong train or bus? When? What happened?

2. Have you ever had to take something back to a shop because there was something wrong with it? What was wrong with it?

3. When was the last time you called the wrong number by mistake?

When does that exhibition finish? • The concert starts at 8.30. • Was it any good? • Do you go to the theatre a lot? • No, hardly ever. • I can't stand basketball! • Who do you support? • It was one of the best films I've ever seen. • I'm the youngest player in the team. • I'm thinking of taking aerobics classes. • I'd like to learn how to use Photoshop. • I'd like to improve my reading and writing. • I learned how to surf last year. • The course lasts for twelve weeks. • I go at least twice a week. • He's a bad loser. • I'm useless at cooking.

12 Free time

Conversation

1 Speaking

Check you understand all the words in these questions.

1. When was the last time you went to see a play?
2. When was the last time you went to see a film?
3. When was the last time you went to see a musical?
4. When was the last time you went to see an exhibition?
5. When was the last time you went to a restaurant?
6. When was the last time you went to a concert?

Now ask a partner the questions.

What other things do you do in your free time?

2 Talking about your free time

⌒ **Listen to this conversation between two new friends – Ed and Frances. The first time you listen, find out what Frances does in her free time. Don't look at the conversation while you listen.**

Listen again and complete the conversation.

E: So what did you do last night?

F: Oh I went to see this new play, *Hello You*, at The Playhouse in town.

E: Oh right. (1) .... ?

F: Yes, it was OK. I've seen better things.

E: Oh, so do you go to the theatre (2) .... ?

F: Yes, quite often, maybe once or twice a month.

E: Wow! That's quite a lot. I (3) .... go. I prefer to go to the cinema or just go out with friends.

F: Yes, I've always really liked the theatre. I actually go to a drama club and sing with a group of people as well.

E: Really? So what (4) .... do you sing?

F: Lots of things really, but mainly musicals – *West Side Story*, *Chicago*, things like that.

E: That's great. So (5) .... ? I mean, do you sing solo or what?

F: No. I'm OK, but I'm not (6) .... I just like singing.

E: Oh, that's great.

F: What about you? What do you do (7) .... ? Have you got any special hobbies?

3 Vocabulary focus

Look at these expressions from the conversation in Activity 2. Translate them into your language. DON'T use a dictionary. Ask your teacher to explain any expressions you don't understand.

1. So what did you do last night?
2. Oh right. Was it any good?
3. So do you go to the theatre a lot?
4. I hardly ever go.
5. I've always liked the theatre.
6. What kind of things do you sing?
7. So are you any good?
8. What about you?
9. I'm not that good.

Compare your ideas with a partner who speaks the same language as you.

4 Role play

Close your book. With a partner, role play the conversation between Ed and Frances. Don't worry if you can't remember their exact words. At the end of the role play, one of you should say 'What about you? What do you do in your free time? Have you got any special hobbies?' Talk about your own hobbies and continue the conversation so that it is true for you.

5 | Pronunciation: adding information

We often add the name of the thing we are talking about in the middle of the sentence. For example:

- I went to see this new play, *Hello You*, at The Playhouse in town.
- I went to see this new film, *The Trapper*, with a friend of mine.

This sounds more natural than these shorter sentences.

- I went to see a new play. It was called *Hello You*. It was on at The Playhouse in town.
- I went to see a new film. It was called *The Trapper*. I went with a friend of mine.

Before and after we add this extra information, we usually pause.

I WENT to SEE this new FILM   The TRAPper   with a FRIEND of mine.

⌒ **Listen and practise these sentences.**

a. I went to see this exhibition, *Art in Time*, at the National Gallery.

b. I stayed in and watched this programme, *Wild at Sea*, about dolphins.

c. I stayed in. I'm reading this book, *The Yakuza*, about the Japanese mafia.

d. I went to this new restaurant, Tito's, in Market Street.

e. We went on a day trip to this place, Leeds Castle, with the school.

f. I went to my karate class at this sports centre, The Sobell, near my house.

Complete the conversations with the sentences above.

1. A: .... ?
    B: Oh yes? Is it any good?
    A: Yes, it's great. It's really interesting. I love anything about crime.

2. A: .... ?
    B: Oh yes? I know the one. Was it any good?
    A: Yes, it was great. The food was fantastic and it's quite cheap.

3. A: .... ?
    B: Oh yes? Are you any good?
    A: No, not really. I'm just a yellow belt.

4. .... ?
    B: Oh yes? Was it any good?
    A: It was OK. I like animal documentaries, but I've seen better things.

5. A: .... ?
    B: Oh yes? I've seen the posters for it. Was it any good?
    A: It was OK, I suppose, but it wasn't that good.

6. A: .... ?
    B: Oh yes? I wanted to go on that. Was it any good?
    A: Yes, it was great. It was really impressive and the gardens were beautiful. We had a great time.

6 | Practice

Choose some of these sentence starters. Complete the sentences with names or titles so that they are true for you.

a. I went to see this film, ...

b. I went to see this exhibition, ...

c. I went to see this play, ...

d. I went to see this band, ...

e. I went to this restaurant, ...

f. I stayed in. I'm reading this book, ...

g. I stayed in and watched this programme, ...

h. I stayed in and played this computer game, ...

With a partner, have conversations like those in Activity 5. Begin like this:

- What did you do last night / at the weekend?

7 | Using grammar: expressions of frequency

When we answer questions about how often we do things, we can reply like this:

- Yes, all the time – I usually go at least three times a week.
- Yes, quite a lot – maybe once every two or three weeks.
- No, not that much – maybe once or twice a year.
- No, hardly ever – I can't remember the last time I went.

Complete these sentences with ONE word in each space. Can you do this without looking at the examples above?

1. A: Do you read a lot?
    B: Yes, all the .... I usually read .... least two or three books .... week.

2. A: Do you go out a lot?
    B: No, not that .... – maybe once .... two weeks.

3. A: Do you go to the cinema a lot?
    B: No, ... ever. I don't really like watching films.

4. A: Do you eat out a lot?
    B: No, not .... much – .... once a month. I prefer to cook at home.

5. A: Do you watch TV a lot?
    B: Yes, ... the time. I .... watch at .... two or three hours a ....

6. A: Do you go to a lot of art exhibitions?
    B: No, hardly .... I can't .... the last .... I went.

Now ask a partner the questions.

▶ For more information on using expressions of frequency, see G22.

Reading

1 | Using vocabulary: team sports

Match these team sports with the photos.

1. rugby

2. ice hockey

3. volleyball

4. baseball

5. football

6. basketball

Make sentences that are true for you.

- I really like watching ... . It's really exciting!
- I really like playing ... .
- I don't really like watching ... , but I like playing it.
- I don't really play ... very much, but I like watching it.
- I can't stand ... . It's so boring!

Tell a partner about your likes and dislikes.

Real English: football

In American English, football is called soccer.

2 | Typical questions

Look at these questions which fans of team sports often get asked. Complete the questions with the words in the box.

favourite	see	team
rivals	support	why

1. Do you .... anyone?

2. .... do you support them?

3. Who's your .... player?

4. How're your .... doing at the moment?

5. Who're their biggest .... ?

6. Do you ever go and .... them?

Find a new partner who follows a team sport. Ask your partner the questions.

3 | While you read

🎧 **Read the article by an English football fan. Then discuss with a partner how the writer would answer the questions in Activity 2.**

THE OTHER TEAM IN MANCHESTER

I know this probably sounds strange, but I can't stand Manchester United! I hate their manager, and I hate their players, who get paid too much and think they're the best. I hate their TV station. I hate their souvenir shop and I really really hate their fans! You see, I've got nothing in common with 98% of their fans, because – unlike them – I was born in Manchester, I know a lot about football AND I've been to Manchester United's ground, Old Trafford. I particularly hate their fans around the world who I've met when I've been abroad and who say to me, 'Oh, you come from Manchester. Do you like football? I love Manchester football team very much!' The thing is, you see, I support the other team in Manchester – Manchester CITY, not United. I always have done, and I always will. I'll be a City fan until I die!

I grew up in Moss Side, Manchester in the 1950s, and my dad supported Manchester City, so I did too. When I was growing up, he always used to say, 'You can choose your friends, but you can't choose your football team.' It's part of your family history, part of who you are. The new Manchester United fans, who first got interested in them when they won the Treble – the Champions League, the FA Cup and the Premiership – in 1999 will never understand this! They only support them because they win things! Supporting a football club is about more than that, though. It's about hope and belief! Even when everything is going wrong and your team has just gone down to the Second or Third Division or you've lost a big match against your local rivals, you have to believe that things will get better.

We were a huge club when I was a kid – and we will be again! Nothing lasts forever, and one day Manchester United will go down to the Second Division again and we will win the League again. Then the rest of the world will know how big Manchester City really are! Dreams like this have helped me through the bad times in my life – like after we lost the Cup Final and then my first husband left me. Football has helped me learn how to be a good loser. You have to be able to laugh at life, don't you?

Anyway, I've got a new boyfriend now, and I love him almost as much as I love Manchester City. I take him to all of the matches, and he says he enjoys some of them. He's perfect for me. If we ever get married, I'm going to wear my 1968 League Champion shirt to the wedding. It's got the name of the best City player ever on the back – Mike 'Buzzer' Summerbee. I'd ask Kevin to dress in a light blue suit as well. He'd look very handsome in it, I'm sure.

Best and worst are irregular superlatives. The way we normally make superlatives is very similar to the way we make comparatives. To make superlatives, we use the + adjective + -est or the most + adjective. For example:

- He's one of the tallest people I've ever seen!
- She's one of the most relaxed people I know.

Do you know when we add -est and when we use the most? Compare your ideas with a partner.

Now read the explanation in the box to see if you were right.

- Nearly all adjectives of one syllable take -est: the cheapest restaurant.
- As with comparatives, words of three syllables take the most: the most expensive restaurant.
- Words with two syllables usually take the most, unless they end in -y. Then, we remove the -y and add -iest: the silliest person, the most common dish (or the commonest).

Complete the sentences with superlatives.

1. Harry is one of the .... people I know. He runs three or four miles every single day! (fit)
2. I think she was the .... player ever to play at Wimbledon. She was only 14 or 15. (young)
3. He's one of the .... people I've ever met! He never does any activity at all! (lazy)
4. We played Liechtenstein. It was one of the .... games we've ever had! We beat them 12–1. (easy)
5. She's one of the .... people I've ever met. She never worries about anything! (relaxed)
6. I'm reading Mountains of the Mind at the moment. It's the .... thing I've read for ages. (interesting)
7. We spent three days in Machu Pichu. I think it's the .... place I've ever been to. (beautiful)

For more information on using superlatives, see G23.

4 Speaking

Discuss these questions with a partner.

1. Does the woman who wrote this article remind you of anybody you know? In what way?
2. Would you like to go out with someone like this woman? Why / why not?
3. Did you agree with anything she said? What? Why?
4. Do you think the writer is right to say she 'hates' Manchester United's manager, players and fans?

Choose one expression from the article that you would like to know more about. Ask your teacher how to use it.

5 Using grammar: superlatives

The writer said that Mike Summerbee is 'the best City player ever'. Complete the sentences with best or worst.

1. She's one of the .... players I've ever seen. She's brilliant!
2. He's one of the .... players I've ever seen. He's useless!
3. It was one of the .... places I've ever been to. It was awful!
4. It was one of the .... places I've ever been to. It was really beautiful.
5. It was one of the .... things I've ever eaten. It was disgusting!
6. It was one of the .... things I've ever eaten. It was delicious!

Listen and check your answers. Then practise saying the sentences.

Now choose four of the sentences above and use them to tell a partner about things which are true for you. For example:

- Zinedine Zidane is one of the best players I've ever seen in my life. He's brilliant! He plays for France. He helped them win the World Cup in 1998.

6 Practice

Discuss these questions with a partner.

1. Who's the fittest person you know? How do they stay so fit?
2. Who's the laziest person you know?
3. Who's the tallest person you know? How tall are they?
4. Who's the oldest person you know? How old are they?
5. Who are you closest to in your family? Why?

Listening

1 | Using vocabulary: *I'm thinking of*

Match the sentences with the follow-up comments.

1. I'm thinking of doing a photography course.
2. I'm thinking of doing a cookery course.
3. I'm thinking of doing an English course.
4. I'm thinking of doing a computer course.
5. I'm thinking of taking aerobics classes.
6. I'm thinking of having piano lessons.

a. I'd like to learn how to set up my own website.
b. I'd like to learn how to have basic conversations when I go on holiday there.
c. I'd like to learn how to develop my own pictures.
d. I'd like to learn how to do Thai and Chinese dishes.
e. I'd like to learn how to play my favourite songs.
f. I'd like to get a bit fitter.

Spend two minutes trying to memorise as many follow-up comments as you can.

Now close your book. Your partner will read out the sentences. How many follow-up comments can you remember?

Do any of these courses sound good to you? Why?

Are you thinking of doing a course in the future?

2 | While you listen

🎧 **Listen to the conversation between an English man, Mark, and an Italian friend of his, Luigi. Find out what kind of course Luigi is thinking of doing, and why.**

3 | Know how to

Mark said: 'they teach you how to develop pictures'. In English, we also say know how to and learn how to.

Complete the sentences with how to and the verbs in the box.

boil	fight	make	serve
do	get	put up	surf

1. I learnt .... while I was on holiday in Hawaii and now I go every weekend.
2. I didn't really know .... there, so I ended up getting lost.
3. I wanted to know .... the picture bigger on the photocopier, but no-one knew .... it!
4. I love playing tennis, but I'd like to get a coach and learn .... properly.
5. He's absolutely useless in the kitchen. He doesn't even know .... an egg!
6. When I went camping last year, I didn't know .... the tent, so I had to ask some other campers to help me.
7. I had to learn .... when I was very young, because I was the youngest of nine boys!

Look at this sentence starter. Think of three endings that are true for you.

• I'd like to learn how to ...

Tell some other students in the class what you have written. Ask each other Can you teach me how to do it?

4 | Before you listen

You are going to listen to Mark telephoning St. Peter's College to find out more about the photography course Luigi wants to do. Before you listen, think of four questions Mark might ask.

5 | While you listen

🎧 Listen to the conversation. Do you hear the answers to the questions you thought of? What else do you learn about the course? Compare what you hear with a partner.

6 | Vocabulary

Complete the sentences with words from the conversation.

1. Hello, St. Peter's College. How can I .... you?
2. I'm phoning to .... about the evening photography classes you run.
3. Do you need to have any .... experience?
4. I'll .... you .... to someone who knows more about it.
5. We take .... beginners.
6. Does the price for the course .... all the materials?
7. The course .... for ten weeks.
8. We've actually only got two or three .... left.

Listen to the conversation again and check your answers.

> ## Real English: arrive
>
> In normal spoken English, it's common to say get into (a town or city) instead of arrive. Here are some examples:
>
> *I should get into Rome at about eleven.*
> *What time does your train get into Paris?*
> *I don't get into Narita airport until half past one in the morning.*

7 | Using grammar: present simple for the future

In the telephone conversation, you heard:

- The course starts next week on Tuesday.
- The course lasts for ten weeks.

We use the present simple to talk about things in the future that are part of a timetable – train times, course dates, flights, the times that films start and finish, etc.

Complete these sentences about the future with the present simple.

1. The flight .... at 7.30 tomorrow morning, so we'll need to get a taxi to the airport. (leave)
2. And what time .... in Rome next Monday? (you / arrive)
3. The film .... at nine tonight, so shall we meet at half past eight? (start)
4. What time .... tomorrow? (the match / start)
5. When .... at the main station? (your train / arrive)
6. The course .... eight weeks, so I'll be really busy until it ends. (last)
7. When .... ? (that exhibition at the Town Hall / end)
8. What time .... ? (the next coach / leave)

8 | Role play

Work with a partner.

Student A: You work at St. Peter's College. Read the information on page 176. Then decide what language you will use. Activities 6 and 7 will help you.

Student B: You are interested in doing either a course called Elementary Cooking or another called Chinese Cookery. You are going to phone the college that offers these courses. Spend three minutes deciding what questions you want to ask. Activities 6 and 7 will help you.

Role play the conversation. You can begin like this:

A: Hello, St. Peter's College. How can I help you?

B: Oh hello, I'm phoning to enquire about the ...

When you have finished the telephone conversation, change roles and have a second conversation. Student B should read the information on page 176; Student A should phone to ask about the other course.

1 | Act or draw

Work in pairs. Take turns to choose five of the words or expressions in the box. Don't tell your partner which ones you have chosen! Without speaking, draw or act out the words for your partner to guess. Your partner has one minute to guess the words you have chosen.

a crossing	fall over	serve (in tennis)
a crossroads	feel dizzy	sliced
a queue	get lost	sparkling water
a roundabout	pollution	tear something
a traffic jam	put up a tent	the wrong way round
basketball	rugby	throw it in the bin
develop photos	serve (in a restaurant)	volleyball

Were there any words you didn't know?

2 | Grammar

Choose the correct or more natural alternative.

1. He's one of the fittest / the most fit people I know.

2. A: Hurry up. We're going to miss the bus.
   B: Oh, let's just get a taxi. It'll be easier / more easy with all these bags!

3. A: Do you know where is the Grand Hotel? / where the Grand Hotel is?
   B: No, I'm sorry. I've never heard of it.

4. My plane gets into / will get into Frankfurt at six and my connecting flight leaves / will leave at nine, so I've got a three-hour wait.

5. A: I'm afraid the fish is off.
   B: Oh right. Well, in that case, I have / I'll have the beef.

6. I didn't really hurt myself, but I tore / teared my trousers when I fell down / felt down.

7. Could you get some coffee when you go out? We haven't got some / any left.

8. We're thinking of doing business in China next year. I think I like / I'd like to learn Chinese.

3 | Opposites

These pairs of sentences have opposite meanings. Use the words in the box to complete the sentences.

alive	miles away	stale	well done
hard-working	off peak	tiny	worse
in advance	overcharged		

1. I bought the tickets on the day.
   I bought them well ....

2. It was expensive. It was peak hour.
   It was cheap. It was ....

3. They undercharged us, so we left quickly before they realised.
   They .... us, so we complained.

4. I like meat rare.
   I like meat ....

5. The bread was lovely and fresh.
   The bread was horrible and ....

6. My sister is very lazy.
   My sister is really ....

7. It's quite near here.
   It's .... from here.

8. My grandfather on my mum's side is dead.
   My grandfather on my dad's side is still ....

9. They give you huge portions in that restaurant.
   They give you .... portions in that restaurant.

Compare your answers with a partner and explain your choices.

4 | Questions and answers

Match the questions with the answers.

1. Have you got any brothers or sisters?
2. What does your sister do?
3. How do you get on with your sister?
4. How do you know Alison?
5. Do you see your sister much?

a. She's a friend from university.
b. Yes, one older sister.
c. She's still at university. She's doing media studies.
d. Not at the moment. She's been in Australia for the last six months!
e. Really well, most of the time. We're quite close.

Now match these questions with the answers.

6. What did you do last night?
7. Was it any good?
8. Do you like golf?
9. Are you any good?
10. Would you like some more coffee?

f. No, I'm absolutely useless.
g. No, it was rubbish.
h. No, thanks. I won't be able to sleep.
i. It's OK. I sometimes play with friends.
j. I went to see a concert.

In pairs, ask each other the questions above. This time give different answers.

5 | What can you remember

With a partner, write down as much as you can remember about the people you read about in the texts in Unit 10 and Unit 12.

Unit 10: Eighth time lucky

a. His longest marriage
b. His shortest marriage
c. His most recent marriage
d. The others

Unit 12: The other team in Manchester

a. The problem with Manchester United
b. Why she supports Manchester City
c. The future for her and Manchester City

Now work with another pair of students and compare what you can remember. Who remembered more?

Which person do you think you would like the most / least? Why?

6 | Verb collocations

Complete the collocations with the verbs in the box.

| follow hurt make set up throw |

1. .... the rubbish away / it out
2. .... my back / myself
3. .... a web-page / a business
4. .... the signs / the instructions
5. .... the town safer at night / something bigger

Now complete these collocations with the verbs in the box.

| cost cut introduce last put |

6. .... pollution / taxes
7. .... for ten weeks / for years
8. .... three pounds / millions of euros
9. .... the tent up / you through to the manager
10. .... us to his friends / a new law

Work in pairs. Spend one minute memorising the words above that collocate with the verbs. Then take turns to close your book. Your partner will read out the verbs. Can you remember both collocations?

With your partner, try to think of one more collocation for each verb.

7 | Look back and check

Work in pairs. Choose one of these activities.

a. **Look back at the conversation in Unit 9 on page 64. How much of the conversation can you remember? Have the conversation together.**

b. **Look back at the expressions for giving directions which you translated in Activity 2 on page 76. Close your book and test yourself. How many of the expressions can you remember?**

Write the names of some places you know in your town. Ask other people in the class for directions.

8 | Expressions

Complete the expressions with the words in the box.

common	finish	mixed	seen	sweet
eye	hear	round	split	thing

1. Can you try and catch the waiter's .... ?
2. Shall we just .... the bill?
3. I don't really like anything ....
4. I couldn't eat another ....
5. It was a disaster from start to ....
6. I'm sorry, but you've .... up our order.
7. We don't have much in ....
8. I'm sorry to .... that.
9. I'm sorry. I'm not from .... here myself.
10. It's one of the best things I've ....

Now discuss these questions with a partner.

1. Do you usually split the bill when you eat out in a restaurant?
2. Can you think of anything that was a disaster?
3. What's the best film you've ever seen?

9 | Vocabulary quiz

Discuss these questions in groups of three.

1. Is the food from your country usually spicy?
2. If you're on a diet, are you trying to lose or put on weight?
3. Who do you give a tip to? How much do you usually give?
4. Can you think of three ways you can cook eggs?
5. What's the difference between a play, a musical and an opera?
6. Shop assistants sometimes call men sir. What do they call women?
7. Do people die through old age or die of old age?
8. Can you think of something which causes a traffic jam?
9. If a bus service is reliable, do the buses come on time or are they often delayed?
10. Can you think of three things that can be wrong?
11. If public transport has improved, has it got better or worse?
12. What's the difference between we both like it and we all like it?
13. Can you think of two things you download from the internet?
14. Do Chelsea win Lazio or beat them?
15. If you have some previous experience, are you a complete beginner?
16. Can you think of two verbs that go with e-mail?

Pronunciation

1 | Contrastive stress

🎧 **Listen to these conversations.**

A: When's your wife going to Russia?
B: <u>She's</u> not. <u>I</u> am. Next <u>Friday</u>.

A: I saw your new car outside.
B: It's not <u>mine</u>. It's <u>Ian's</u>.

We don't usually stress words like I / he / my / your / his. However, when someone says something wrong, we usually stress the thing which was wrong and the thing which is right.

Complete these conversations with the words in the box.

he   mine   my   them   your   yours

1. A: My friend Anna's coming to visit.
    B: She's not .... friend. She's mine.

2. A: You forgot your book.
    B: It's not mine, it's ....

3. A: It's Anna's, isn't it?
    B: No, it's not hers. It's ....

4. A: This is all your fault.
    B: It's not .... fault. It's his.

5. A: Did you lot make this mess?
    B: No, it wasn't us. It was ....

6. A: When did you do it?
    B: I didn't do it. .... did!

🎧 **Listen and check your answers. Then practise the conversations with a partner.**

Work with a partner. Underline the stresses in these sentences.

a. It's not you. It's me.
b. It's not yours. It's mine.
c. It wasn't me. It was him.

In what situations could someone say the sentences above?

2 | Consonant sounds: /l/ and /r/

🎧 **Look at the pictures. They show how we make these sounds. Notice that the tongue doesn't touch the roof of the mouth when you say /r/. Listen and practise the sounds.**

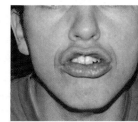
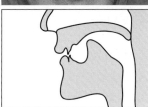

/l/   /r/

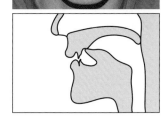

Now say these words.

roundabout

my local team

a rival team

look on-line

the wrong direction

a delicious lunch

serious pollution

a reliable service

3 | Difficult sounds: consonant clusters

Many words in English start with a combination of a consonant plus /r/ or /l/. When you try and say these words, start by forming the lips and mouth to say the /r/ or the /l/. Then say the word. Practise saying these words.

crash

sleep

traffic

platform

friend

Now try and say these tongue twisters.

- Drive slowly, please.
- I was on the wrong platform and got on the wrong train.
- I love sparkling drinks, but my friend from Brazil prefers still.
- The local government recently introduced a new law.
- Try not to slip on the slippery surface.
- Break the eggs and scramble them.

Who can say this tongue-twister ten times without making a mistake?

a red lorry and a yellow lorry

Try to write your own sentences using as many consonant clusters as you can. Read your sentences out to the class.

Who had the most clusters? Which was the funniest sentence?

The hotel was really posh. • We rented a villa in the south of Spain. • I'd like a twin room for two nights. • I'll carry those for you, if you want. • If you wait a minute, I'll check on the computer. • Do you have internet access? • It had satellite TV. • We stayed in a little wooden hut in the jungle. • There were hardly any people there. • Our room looked out over the beach. • I just need to comb my hair. • I don't mind, as long as you're quick. • What's the expiry date? • There's a great view. You can see for miles. • I'll give you a spare key.

Conversation

1 | Using vocabulary: places to stay

When was the last time you went on holiday or went away for the weekend? Where did you stay?

Match the first two lines of the conversations with A's follow-up comments.

1. A: We stayed in a little campsite by a big lake.
   B: Oh, that sounds nice.

2. A: We stayed with some friends who've got a flat there.
   B: Oh, that sounds nice.

3. A: We stayed in this big five-star hotel.
   B: Oh, that sounds great.

4. A: We stayed in a little bed and breakfast on the seafront.
   B: Oh, that sounds nice.

5. A: We rented a villa up in the mountains.
   B: Oh, that sounds nice.

a. Yes, it was. Our room looked out over the beach.

b. Yes, it was. It's the poshest place I've ever been to.

c. Yes, it was. You could hire boats and go fishing.

d. Yes, it was, but we had to sleep on their sofa.

e. Yes, it was. You could see for miles from up there.

Tell a partner about the last time you went on holiday or went away for the weekend. Try to continue the conversation for as long as you can.

2 | Booking a room in a hotel

You are going to listen to a conversation between a hotel receptionist and Anton, a customer. Before you listen, try to complete the conversation with these questions.

a. Is that with an en-suite bathroom?

b. So you'd like one twin room for five nights arriving the 19th and departing the 24th?

c. So how much would two singles be?

d. What kind of card are you paying with?

e. And what kind of room would you like?

f. And what's the expiry date?

g. And the number?

h. And your name as it appears on the card?

i. And what if we shared a twin room?

j. When exactly would you be arriving?

⌒ Now listen to the conversation. Were you right?

R: Hello. The Old Ship Hotel. How can I help you?

A: Oh, hello. I'd like to book a room for next month.

R: Of course. (1) ....

A: The 19th and we're leaving on the 24th.

R: So that's five nights. (2) ....

A: Well, there are actually two of us. (3) ....
....

R: That would be £60 each per night.

A: Right. (4) ....

R: That would be £95 for the room per night.

A: (5) ....

R: Yes, of course. All rooms are en-suite and have all the normal facilities.

A: OK. Well, in that case, I'd like two singles, if possible.

R: Let me just check if we have those available. ... No, I'm sorry. We only have one single room available for those days.

A: Oh right. Well, never mind. We can share.

R: (6) ....

A: That's right.

R: That'll be £475. We'll need to take your credit card details to make the booking.

A: Yes, sure.

R: (7) ....

A: Visa.

R: OK. (8) ....

A: 5362 3870 6429 8479.

R: That's fine. (9) ....

A: 06 / 09.

R: OK. (10)..

A: Anton Yurick. That's Y-U-R-I-C-K.

R: Great. So that's all booked for you, Mr Yurick.

Reception

do not disturb

3 | Role play

Work with a partner.

Student A: You are going to phone a hotel to book a room. Decide what kind of room you would like, when you want it and how much you can afford to pay.

Student B: You are a hotel receptionist. Read the information on page 176. During the telephone conversation, you should invent a problem with Student A's booking. For example, there are no single rooms available or the caller's credit card is rejected.

Spend five minutes preparing what you are going to say. Look back at the conversation for help if you need to. Then role play the conversation.

4 | Using grammar: first conditionals

🎧 **Listen to the second part of the conversation and find out what else Anton Yurick asks.**

Have you ever applied for a visa? When? Was it difficult?

Can you complete these sentences from the conversation? Put the verbs into the correct form.

1. If you .... (fax) us with your request, we .... (fax) you back a letter by tomorrow.
2. If you .... (wait) a second, I .... (get) a pen.

Listen to the second part of the conversation again if you need to.

If-sentences like these are called first conditionals. We often use them when we offer or promise to do something, or warn somebody about something. The If part of the sentence is usually in the present tense. The second part of the sentence usually uses will + verb. You will also see similar sentences which use can, might and going to + verb. Here are some examples:

- If it happens again, I'll phone the police.
- If the weather's nice tomorrow, we might take the kids up to the park.
- If you send me the money today, I can post the books to you tomorrow.
- If I pass all my exams, I'm going to go to university in the autumn.

<u>**Underline**</u> **the verbs in the above examples.**

Complete the conversations. Use the present simple or will + verb.

1. A: Right, I've got to go, or I'll be late for work.
   B: If you .... a moment, I .... you to the station. I just need to brush my teeth. (wait, drive)
   A: Oh OK, great. Thanks.

2. A: Hello, could you help me? I've lost my wallet. Has anyone handed it in?
   B: If you .... there, I .... and see. (wait, go).
   A: OK, thanks.

3. A: I'm not sure what time I'm arriving yet.
   B: That's no problem. If you .... me when you get to the station, I .... and pick you up in the car. (call, come)
   A: OK, great.

4. A: I've got to go to the Embassy to get my visa today.
   B: I .... with you if you .... You'll have someone to talk to while you wait. (come, like).
   A: Thanks. If you .... sure you don't mind, that .... really nice. (be, be)

5. A: I'm almost ready. I just need to go to the toilet and then put these bags in the car.
   B: I .... your bags down if you .... (take, like)
   A: Are you sure? They're quite heavy.

6. A: Excuse me, can I speak to the manager?
   B: I'm afraid he's not here at the moment, but if you .... your details, I .... him to call you when he gets back. (leave, ask)

7. A: Have you booked the hotel yet?
   B: No, I .... it this afternoon if I .... (do, not forget)
   A: Well, try to remember. There .... any rooms left if we .... one soon. (not be, not book)

🎧 **Listen and practise the first conditionals.**

5 | Practice

Tell a partner what you think you'll do.

1. I'm not sure what I'll do on Saturday, but if the weather's nice, I'll probably …
2. I'm not sure what I'll do in the summer, but if I go on holiday, I'll probably …
3. I'm not sure what I'll do tonight, but if I'm not too tired, I'll probably …
4. I'm not sure what I'll do after this course, but if I've got enough money, I'll probably …

▶ For more information on using first conditionals, see G24.

Reading

1 Using vocabulary: hotels

Check you understand all the words in the box.

> a bar or a mini-bar
>
> a gym
>
> a swimming pool
>
> air conditioning
>
> amazing views
>
> central heating
>
> internet access
>
> room service
>
> satellite or cable TV
>
> somewhere you can leave the children

Make sentences that are true for you. Use all the words in the box.

- When I stay somewhere, I like it to have ...
- When I stay somewhere, I don't care if it has ... or not.

Tell a partner about your choices. Try to explain how you made your decisions.

2 Before you read

Look at the photos. Decide which place you would most like to stay in. Explain your decision to a partner. You can start like this:

- I think this looks like the nicest place to stay because ...

3 While you read

🎧 **Now read what five people said about the places in the photos. Match the people and the places. Does anything the people say make you change your mind about which is the nicest place to stay in?**

The best place I've ever stayed

Katherine

The best place I've ever stayed was a little wooden hut in the rain forests of Borneo, looking out over the mountains. There were lots of mosquitoes there and I woke up covered in bites, but the really great thing was that the following day, we climbed the highest mountain in South-east Asia – Mount Kinabalu. I spent my eighteenth birthday there and my cake was a piece of bread covered in little bits of chocolate! It was wonderful.

James

The best place I've ever stayed is a small Greek island called Serifos. It's really quiet. There is no airport. There are hardly any hotels and most people who go there rent a room from a local family. When I go there, I always stay with the same family. They are lovely and give me home-made bread and cakes, and even eggs! There are some wonderful beaches with hardly any people on them and the house I stay in looks out over the sea. When you're there, you can forget about the rest of the world, eat well and just relax.

Harry

The best place I've ever stayed in is the Miyamoto hotel in Tokyo. It's in a district which is a great mixture of modern buildings, restaurants, old squares, bookshops and museums. The hotel has one of those foyers that seem to go up to the sky, and about seven or eight restaurants, but what I really like about it is the open-air swimming pool on the ninth floor. Swimming about up there and looking out over Tokyo is amazing. I stayed at the hotel in August, though, which was maybe a mistake. Going back into the air-conditioned hotel in the afternoon from the hot streets was a real shock because it was so cold!

Diana

The best place I've ever stayed was a 1920s hotel in France. It was a lovely building with a big fountain in lovely gardens, but what I really remember about it is that it's where my husband asked me to marry him! While I was having a shower, I think he phoned room service and organised it. They brought breakfast up, and all the hot food was covered with metal lids. I sat down expecting a nice breakfast. I lifted up one metal lid, and there was toast. I lifted up a second, and there were some eggs. I lifted up a third lid and there was the ring! I started crying immediately. It was so romantic!

Alan

One of the best places I've ever stayed in was my friend Joel's parents' house in Maine. I've been there for the last two Thanksgiving holidays and I've had a wonderful time. They have a beautiful house on the beach looking out over the Atlantic Ocean. They designed the house themselves and the rooms have amazing light, especially during the morning and at sunset. They have a great dog called Kaja that my girlfriend really loved!

4 | Using vocabulary: *hardly*

James loves Serifos because there are hardly any people on the beaches there. This means the beaches are almost empty. Complete the sentences with the words in the box.

cars	experience	people	shops
crime	money	pollution	

1. It's a very safe city. There's hardly any .... there. You can walk around in the middle of the night, no problem.

2. It was a really cheap place to stay. There are hardly any .... there, so I spent hardly anything all week!

3. It was really relaxing. There were hardly any .... staying there. I didn't even talk to anyone for three days!

4. It's a very clean place. There are hardly any .... there, so there's hardly any .... It's lovely.

5. I'd love to come out with you tomorrow, but I've got hardly any .... I've only got £50 until I get paid.

6. I don't think I'll get the job. I've got hardly any .... I've only done three weeks' work in a bank before!

Complete these sentences with anyone or anything.

7. It was a really boring party. There was hardly .... there.

8. It's a really cheap place to stay. It cost us hardly .... the last time we went.

9. It was a lovely break. We did hardly .... for the three days we were there!

10. It's not a very popular place to stay. Hardly .... ever goes there.

Discuss these questions with a partner.

1. Have you ever been anywhere where there was hardly any crime / pollution / cars / noise?

2. Have you ever been anywhere where hardly anyone ever goes?

5 | Using vocabulary: describing places

If there are good views of a city from a place, the place looks out over the city. Choose four of these descriptions and draw pictures to show the view in each one. Show your pictures to a partner. Can they guess which of the descriptions you chose?

1. It's lovely. It looks out over the mountains.

2. It's lovely. It looks out over a lake.

3. It's lovely. It looks out over the rice fields.

4. It's lovely. It looks out over a square.

5. It's lovely. It looks out over the ocean.

6. It's lovely. It looks out over the harbour.

7. It's nothing special. It looks out over a street.

8. It's not very nice. It looks out over a building site.

Discuss these questions.

1. Have you ever stayed in any places like those in the above descriptions? Where? When?

2. What does your house or flat look out over?

3. Where's your favourite view?

Listening

1 Are you ready?

Discuss these questions with some other students.

How long does it take you to get ready:

1. when you go to work or school in the morning?

2. when you go out to meet friends?

3. when you go on holiday?

4. if you go out on a date?

Who takes the longest time? Who takes the shortest? Why?

Match the activities with the conversations. There are four activities for each conversation.

1. comb my hair ☐

2. put on some lipstick ☐

3. make a very quick phone call ☐

4. iron this shirt ☐

5. finish some work before we go out ☐

6. have a shower and get changed ☐

7. go to the toilet ☐

8. go to the bank and get some money out ☐

a. A: Are you ready?
   B: Almost. I just need to ... . I'll be two seconds.
   A: OK.

b. A: Are you ready?
   B: Not really. I need to ... . I'll try to be quick.
   A: No problem. Take your time. I can wait.

Close your book. In pairs, take turns to ask the question Are you ready? Try to give a different reply each time. The person who cannot think of a new reason for not being ready is the loser.

2 While you listen

⌒ **Listen to the conversation between Kasia and her friend Jeremy. She is staying at his house for a week. Kasia is going to go out and meet a friend, Tom, later. As you listen, try to answer these questions.**

1. What does Kasia still need to do to get ready?

2. What's her relationship with Tom?

3 | Comprehension

Correct the mistakes in these extracts from the conversation.

1. J: Have you had a good day?
   K: Yes, great thanks. I spent most of the day shopping.

2. K: Can I do anything to help?
   J: You could clear the table, if you like.

3. K: Have you got a hair dryer I could use?
   J: Yes sure. It's on the shelf in the back room.

4. J: Are you going anywhere nice?
   K: Yes, we're going to a really posh restaurant.

5. J: Make sure you come back before midnight.

6. J: Make sure you turn on the burglar alarm before you go to bed.

Compare your ideas with a partner. Do you agree about the mistakes? Listen again if you need to.

4 | Speaking

Discuss these questions with a partner. Give reasons for your answers.

1. If you were a guest in someone's house, which of the following would you be happy to do?
   a. go out in the evening with someone else
   b. ask for a spare key
   c. use their telephone without asking
   d. ask to make food for yourself
   e. bring them a present
   f. watch TV

2. If you had someone to stay in your house, would you:
   a. let them use your computer to surf the net?
   b. give them a key, and let them come and go as they please?
   c. let them use your car?
   d. go to bed before they did?
   e. ask them to help you make the dinner?
   f. expect them to give you a present?

3. Are there any other things you would never do in these situations?

5 | Using grammar: asking for permission

We often use as long as in answers to questions asking for permission. It means 'you can do it, but only if you do or don't do something else'. For example:

A: Is it OK if I turn the TV over?

B: Yes, of course, as long as I can watch the news at ten.

A: Do you mind if I make myself some tea?

B: No, of course not, as long as you make me a cup as well!

Remember when we reply positively to Do you mind ... ? requests, we start by saying No.

Match the requests with the replies.

1. Is it OK if I have a shower now?
2. Is it OK if I put this stuff in with your washing?
3. Is it OK if I use the telephone?
4. Is it OK if I have some milk?
5. Do you mind if a friend of mine comes over this evening?
6. Do you mind if I come back late this evening?
7. Do you mind if I put some music on?
8. Do you mind if I just check my e-mail on your computer?

a. Yes, of course, as long as you leave some for my coffee.

b. No, of course not, as long as you're quick. I need to finish some work on it.

c. No, not at all, as long as it's not too loud.

d. Yes, as long as you're quick. I want to have one as well before I go out.

e. No, of course not, as long as they don't stay too late.

f. No, not at all, as long as you don't wake the baby up when you come in.

g. Yes, of course, as long as they're all dark things.

h. Yes, of course, as long as you're quick. I'm expecting a call.

🎧 **Listen and check your answers.**

Notice that when we say as long as we use the weak form of as and link the words together so it sounds like /əzlɒŋəz/.

6 | Practice

Think of different replies with as long as to the requests in Activity 5. For example:

A: Is it OK if I have a shower now?

B: Yes, sure, as long as you're finished by half past seven.

With a partner, make the requests and reply. Use your new replies.

> ▶ For more information on using *as long as*, see G25.

7 | Role play

Work with a partner. One of you is at home and the other is a friend who has come to stay. You are having breakfast together and deciding what you are going to do today. Write your conversation. Try to include some of the language on these pages. You can start like this:

A: So what do you want to do today?

B: I don't know. How about going for a picnic in the park?

When you have finished writing your conversation, act it out for another pair.

I got badly sunburnt. • It's such an interesting place. • I went there a few years ago on business. • I'd like to go to Mali one day. • I'd really like to try snow-boarding. • It's supposed to be amazing. • They're on strike at the moment. • What are the hours like? • And what's the money like? • I just had a quiet night in. • I'm just going to have a quick shower. • I had a day off. • What's the flat she's moving into like? • It's dreadful! • The atmosphere was incredible! • I'm quite jealous. I'm starving.

14 What was it like?

Conversation

1 | Speaking

Do you think the people in the photos are having a good time or a bad time?

Think of three reasons why you would have a great time on holiday and three reasons why you would have a terrible time.

Now ask a partner these questions.

1. When did you last go on holiday?

2. Where did you go?

3. What was your holiday like? Did you have a good time or a bad time?

2 | What was your holiday like?

🎧 **Listen to this conversation between two people – Mary and her friend Tom. As you listen to the first part of the conversation, decide how Tom would answer the questions in Activity 1. Don't look at the conversation while you listen.**

Listen again and complete the conversation.

M: Hello, Tom. Are you all right? I haven't seen you (1) ....

T: Yes, I'm fine. I was in the States all last week visiting a friend of mine. (2) .... I'd told you about it.

M: No, I don't think so. So (3) .... did you go?

T: Most of the time I was in Boston where my friend lives, but I went up to New York for (4) ....

M: Right. So what (5) .... ?

T: It was great. New York was amazing. It's just such a (6) .... , there's a real mixture of people, and the food's great.

M: Yes? What about Boston? What was that like?

T: Oh, it's nice. It's quite an interesting place. I didn't (7) .... there – mainly just spent time with my friend – but it was good. I met a lot of his friends and they were really nice (8) ....

M: Sounds great. I'm quite jealous.

T: Have you ever been to the States?

M: Yes, I went there about (9) .... , but I went to the West Coast.

Read the conversation with a partner. Continue the conversation using your own ideas for as long as you can. Don't worry if you don't know anything about the West Coast of America! Use your imagination to describe what you think California is like.

🎧 **Now listen to the second part of the conversation and find out how Tom and Mary actually continued the conversation.**

Translate these expressions into your language. DON'T use a dictionary. Ask your teacher if you need help. Compare your ideas with a partner who speaks the same language as you.

1. I haven't seen you for a while.

2. I thought I'd told you about it.

3. Most of the time I was in Boston.

4. There's a real mixture of people.

5. I'm quite jealous.

6. We spent a week travelling around the country.

7. It's supposed to be brilliant.

8. It rained nearly the whole time we were there.

9. What a shame!

Now close your book. Your partner will say the translations. Can you remember the expressions in English?

Listen to the whole conversation one more time. Then try to repeat the conversation without looking at your book.

3 | Using grammar: present perfect questions

Look at these two questions.

- Have you been to Disneyworld?
- Have you ever been to Disneyworld?

The meaning is very similar. In the second question, the idea is 'ever in your life before'.

When we reply to questions beginning Have you (ever), we don't usually just reply Yes, I have or No, I haven't. We usually say Yes or No and add a comment or a question. For example:

A: Have you ever been to Italy?
B: Yes, I went to Rome a couple of years ago.

A: Have you been to that new restaurant in Jennings Street?
B: No, not yet. Have you?

Put the words in order and make replies to the question Have you ever been there?

1. I'd / but / to / like
   No, ...

2. like / it / what's
   No, ... ?

3. never / I've / wanted / really / to
   No, ...

4. Washington / I / to / last / went / year
   Yes, ...

5. ago / went / three / there / years / I
   Yes, ...

6. last / there / I / holiday / year / on / went
   Yes, ...

7. there / I / not / on / went / business / ago / long
   Yes, ...

8. went / I / there / a / years / to / a / visit / few / friend / of / ago / mine
   Yes, ...

9. I'm / but / actually / summer / there / in / the / going
   No, ...

10. going / next / I'm / but / thinking / year / of / there
    No, ...

4 | Practice

In groups, ask questions with Have you ever ... ? to find out:

1. who's been to the most countries.
2. who's been to the most places in your country.
3. who's been to the most restaurants in your town.

Make sure you add a comment or a question in your replies, as in Activity 3.

For more information on using present perfect questions, see G26.

5 | I'd like to

We often say why we would like to do something or why we've never wanted to do something:

- I'd like to go to that fish restaurant by the beach. The food's supposed to be great.
- I'd like to go to China one day. I'm really interested in Chinese culture.
- I've never wanted to go to Australia. It's too far away and I don't like flying.
- I've never wanted to try skiing. I don't really like that kind of thing. I'm scared of breaking my leg!

These sentences are about things you have not done yet, but would like to do sometime in the future. Complete the sentences so that they are true for you.

1. I'd like to go to .... one day. It's supposed to be amazing.

2. I'd like to go to .... The food's supposed to be great.

3. I'd like to go to .... some day. I'm interested in .... culture.

4. I'd like to try .... one day. I think it would be good fun.

These sentences are about things you aren't interested in doing. Complete the sentences so that they are true for you.

5. I've never really wanted to go to .... It's supposed to be horrible.

6. I've never really wanted to go to .... It's supposed to be quite dangerous.

7. I've never really wanted to go to ....

8. I've never really wanted to try .... I don't really like that kind of thing.

Try and remember what you have written and then tell some other students. Does anyone share your ideas?

Reading

1 | While you read

Read this introduction to an article about teachers in Britain. <u>Underline</u> anything which you think is the same for teachers in your country. Then compare what you underlined with a partner.

Teachers in Britain are going on strike this week. They have decided not to work for a day because they are protesting about low pay. This is nothing new. Teachers are always complaining! They complain about the condition of their classrooms and the school buildings; they complain about students being lazy; they complain about parents not teaching their children to be polite; they complain that there are too many exams or that they have to do too much marking; they complain that holidays for teachers are too short and they complain that the terms are too long. They complain that they don't have computers. Then when they get the computers, they complain about having to use them, or that they don't work! Then they complain that people don't respect them and that people complain too much about teachers! All they ever seem to do is complain! Well, I think they should be happy that they are teachers in Britain because things are a lot better here than in some other places.

2 | Speaking

Discuss these questions with a partner.

1. Have any workers gone on strike in your country in the last few years? What about?

2. Would you ever go on strike? Why / why not?

3. Do people in your country complain much? About the weather, work, the government, banks or what?

4. What things do you complain about most?

3 | Reading

Work in groups of three. You are each going to read about a different teacher. One of you should read Text A; one of you should read Text B on page 176; one of you should read Text C on page 176.

Imagine you are the person you read about. Answer these questions.

1. Where are you from?

2. Whereabouts exactly?

3. What do you teach?

4. Do you like it?

5. What are the hours like?

6. What's the money like?

7. What do you do when you're not teaching?

Check your answers with someone who read the same text as you.

What's your life like?

Text A:
Megan lives in Coventry, a city in the centre of England.

Life is pretty good for me at the moment. I moved in with my boyfriend a few months ago, and we're planning to get married next year. We're both teachers. My boyfriend, Bryan, teaches in a primary school and I teach English in a secondary school. Teaching is OK, I suppose, but it's much harder than I expected. I decided to do it because you get lots of holidays and I thought that teachers only really work from nine till four. Actually, I work around 60 hours a week. After teaching, we have to do lots of marking and lots of paperwork – planning lessons, writing reports, things like that. I really hate that part of the job. I work in quite a difficult school, so sometimes the students shout at me and are really rude, which makes it difficult to teach. By the end of the week, I'm so tired I just usually sit in front of the TV and order a take-away pizza or something like that. I used to go out a lot before I started this job, but now I hardly ever do. We sometimes go to the cinema, but most of the time I prefer to get a video out from the local video shop and have a quiet night in. The other reason we don't go out much is that we're saving up for our wedding and then we might try to buy a flat. It's just so expensive. The wedding will probably cost us over £10,000, which is half my yearly salary. It's crazy really, but I guess it is our special day, and we want it to be perfect.

4 | Role play

In the same groups of three, imagine you are the teachers you have just read about and that you have all met on a course for teachers. Introduce yourselves and have conversations using some of the questions from Activity 3. Start like this:

A: Hi, do you mind if I join you?

B: No, of course not.

A: Hi, I'm Megan.

B: Hi, I'm Patrick. And this is Olga.

A: Oh right, Hi. Nice to meet you. So where are you two from?

Use some of these responses:

*   I know what you mean.
*   It's the same for me.
*   It's the same with my students.
*   Really? That's terrible!
*   Really? That's good!
*   Congratulations!
*   You're so lucky!

Who do you think has the best life? Who has the worst? Why?

> **Real English:** have a quiet night in
>
> If you have a quiet night in, you stay at home and relax. Maybe you go to bed early or you just watch some TV or do some reading.
>
> A: Are you going to go out later?
> B: No, I'm tired. I'm just going to have a quiet night in.

5 | Key word: *have*

Find ten expressions with the word have. Mark the end of each expression using /.

```
Ihadareallynicetimewehadareally
terribletimeIhadsomethingtoeatI
didn'thaveanybreakfasthavea
quickshowerIhadthedayoffIhada
meetinghavedinnerI'vejusthadan
argumenthaveyouhadanylunch
```

🎧 **Listen to the ten expressions and check your answers. Practise saying each expression. Make sure you stress the words which carry the main meaning. Remember that this isn't usually a verb.**

Now complete the conversations with the expressions.

1. A: Are you hungry?
    B: Yes, I'm starving. .... this morning.

2. A: What was the party like last night?
    B: It was great. .... It's a shame you couldn't come.

3. A: .... ? I can make you a sandwich, if you like.
    B: No, it's all right. I'm fine. .... just before I got here.

4. A: Are you all right? I didn't see you yesterday.
    B: Yes, I'm fine. I just felt really tired yesterday, so .... and just stayed at home and relaxed. I feel much better now.

5. A: Are you OK? You look a bit upset.
    B: I'll be OK in a moment. .... with my boyfriend. He can be so stupid sometimes.

6. A: How was your holiday?
    B: Oh, don't ask! .... Everything that could possibly go wrong went wrong!

7. A: Sorry I wasn't at the class on Tuesday. .... at work and it went on till eight.
    B: Don't worry. Maybe you could ask Yumiko to show you what we did.

8. A: Do you want to go and .... now?
    B: No, I just want to. .... and unpack first.

6 | Speaking

Discuss these questions with a partner.

1. At lunchtime, do you usually have a big meal or a quick snack?

2. If you want to go and have something to eat in the evening, where do you normally go?

3. Do you have meetings at work or school? What about? What are they like?

4. When was the last time you had a great time? What did you do? Who with? Where were you?

5. When did you last have a day off work or school? Why?

6. Do you ever have arguments or do you try to avoid them? Who did you last have one with? Why?

7. Do you prefer to have showers or baths? Why?

Listening

1 | Before you listen

Match the questions with the photos.

a.   What's your brother like?

b.   What's your new flat like?

c.   What was the concert like?

d.   What was Italy like?

e.   What's the area you live in like?

f.   What's that course you're doing like?

g.   What was that film you saw the other day like?

h.   What's the food in that Moroccan restaurant like?

Have eight short conversations with a partner. Use the questions and the ideas in the photos. For example:

A: What's your brother like?

B: He's great. We get on really well.

2 | While you listen

🎧 **Listen to eight people answering the questions in Activity 1. Decide which of the questions each person is answering.**

1. ☐   2. ☐   3. ☐   4. ☐
5. ☐   6. ☐   7. ☐   8. ☐

With a partner, have similar conversations to those you just heard.

1

RUSSELL CROWE
MASTER AND COMMANDER
THE FAR SIDE OF THE WORLD

2

3

4

5

6

7 HALAL MEAT FRESH BANGLADESHI FISH &
TEL:0171 247 1009   FAX:0171 247

8

3 Pronunciation: the food, the wine, everything!

🎧 Listen and practise these sentences.

1. It was great! The food, the wine, everything!
2. It was wonderful! The hotel, the weather, everything!
3. It was lovely! The music, the venue, everything!
4. They're great! My colleagues, my boss, everyone!
5. It was awful! The train journey, the taxi, everything!
6. It was terrible! The hours, the money, everything!
7. It was dreadful! The acting, the story, everything!
8. It was great! The noise, the atmosphere, everything!

🎧 Write questions for the answers above. Then listen and compare your ideas. Say the answer to each question you hear.

Think of things in your life you could describe with some of the answers above. Tell a partner as much as you can about the things.

4 Using grammar: asking longer questions

Match the questions with the pairs of missing words. The first one has been done for you.

1. What was that film ... like?   *e*
2. What's that guy ... like?
3. What was that hotel ... like?
4. What was the company ... like?
5. What's the area ... like?
6. What's that restaurant ... like?
7. What was that party ... like?

a. you went to last Friday / at Robin's house
b. that does East African food / you went to yesterday
c. who lives upstairs from you / who's just started in your office
d. you booked your holiday with / you used to work for
e. you went to see the other day / on Channel 4 last night
f. you stayed in in Rome / you had your wedding reception in
g. you work in / round there

Complete the answers with Great or Awful.

1. .... ! The food, the service, everything! It's one of the best places to eat in town.
2. .... ! It was one of the best places to stay in the whole town.
3. .... ! It was one of the worst things I've seen for a long time.
4. .... ! We get on really well.
5. .... ! There are hardly any shops there and it's really really quiet. It's not much fun round there.
6. .... ! They're one of the best firms around.
7. .... ! The food, the music, everything! Honestly, we had a terrible time!

With a partner, have conversations. Your partner will ask you some of the longer questions. You should reply with the answers above. For example:

A: What was that film you went to see the other day like?
B: Awful! It was one of the worst things I've seen for a long time.

Have more conversations. This time use answers with the opposite meaning. For example:

A: What was that film you went to see the other day like?
B: Great! It's one of the best things I've seen for a long time.

5 Free practice

Work with a partner. Write four questions you would like to ask your partner.

1. What .... like?
2. What .... like?
3. What .... like?
4. What .... like?

Ask your partner the questions.

> ▶ For more information on how to ask longer questions, see G27.

6 Can you remember?

Spend one minute looking back at the conversation at the beginning of the unit.

Close your books. With a partner, try and have the same conversation. However, this time, say you went to another country – not the USA.

I can't stand martial arts movies! • Who's in it? • Where's it on? • She's a really famous TV personality. • One contestant won a million pounds last week. • I love that chat show. • My favourite soap opera's on at eight. • There's a great new sitcom on on Channel 3. • I missed the last episode. • I've got cable at home. • It's a very under-rated film. • The concert is sold out, I'm afraid. • The show's been cancelled. • I'm afraid your card has been rejected. • My bag's been stolen! • Sorry. Wrong number. • Shall we go to the 8.30 showing?

15 What's on?

Conversation

1 | Speaking

Match the films with the photos.

1. a horror film
2. a martial arts film
3. a drama
4. an action movie
5. a comedy

Discuss these questions.

1. Do you know the names of the films in the photos?
2. Have you seen any of these films? Did you enjoy them?
3. What kind of films do you like? Are there any kinds of films you really don't like?

2 | Arranging to go to the cinema

🎧 **Listen to this conversation between two friends – Ian and Jo. The first time you listen, find out what they decide to go and see, and at what time.**

Listen again and complete the conversation.

I: What are you doing tonight?

J: I've got (1) .... What about you?

I: Well, I was thinking of going to the cinema. Do you want to come with me?

J: Yes, maybe. What are you thinking of seeing?

I: (2) .... *Lands of Hope* yet? It's supposed to be really good.

J: Yes, I saw it last week. It's OK, but it's not brilliant. What else is on?

I: Well, there's a film with George Clooney.

J: Oh, yes? I don't really like him.

I: No, (3) .... And then there's this film, *City of Dreams*.

J: I haven't heard of it. (4) .... ?

I: It's a French film. It's a drama about some Algerians growing up in Paris. It's got quite a good review.

J: It sounds quite interesting. What time's it on?

I: 6.30, 8.15 and 11.20.

J: And (5) .... ?

I: The ABC.

J: OK. Well, shall we go to the 8.15 showing? I want to have (6) .... before we go.

I: Yes, OK. Shall I meet you there, then? You know where it is, don't you?

J: Yes. So I'll see you there (7) .... If I'm there first, shall I get the tickets?

I: Yes. Fine.

Now look at the tapescript and practise reading it with a partner. Remember to stress the sounds in CAPITAL LETTERS and try to say each group of words together.

3 | Using vocabulary: questions

Complete the conversations with the questions in the box.

What's it about?	Where's it on?
What's on?	Who's in it?
What time's it on?	Who's it by?

1. A: I'm thinking of going to the cinema later. Do you want to come?
    B: Yes, maybe. ....
    A: There's that new Bud Barker film, *Time and Space*.

2. A: I'm thinking of going to see this new film, *Hot Nights*, later. Do you want to come?
    B: I haven't heard of that one. ....
    A: Nobody I've heard of, apart from Kevin Cline. He was in that film, *The Ice Storm*.

3. A: I'm thinking of going to see *Ghost Town* tonight. Do you want to come?
    B: Yes, OK. ....
    A: It's on at The Showcase Cinema, so we can walk there.

4. A: I'm thinking of going to see the new Julia Roberts film later. Do you want to come?
    B: Yes, I'd love to ....
    I might not finish work till half seven tonight.
    A: That's OK. There's a showing at 9.15.

5. A: I'm thinking of going to see this new Mexican film, *La Loca*, later. Do you want to come?
    B: Yes, maybe. ....
    I haven't heard of it.
    A: It's a kind of love story between this woman who's a bit mad and a doctor.

6. A: I'm thinking of going to see *Breaking Tess* later. Do you want to come?
    B: Yes, maybe. I've seen something about that.
    .... ?
    A: Sven Larström. He's a famous Swedish director. His films are supposed to be brilliant.

4 | Practice

We often respond to descriptions of films and other things by saying That sounds + adjective. For example:

- That sounds fine.
- That sounds good.
- That sounds interesting.
- That sounds great.
- That sounds a bit boring.
- That sounds very serious.

With a partner, practise the conversations in Activity 3. Use That sounds + adjective and continue the conversations.

Real English: That sounds good

In informal spoken English you can say That sounds good! or simply Sounds good! It is quite common to miss out 'that' – especially if you're talking to a good friend. Here are some examples:

A: *Shall we meet at eight at the Odeon, then?*
B: *Sounds great!*
A: *Fancy a pizza first?*
B: *Sounds even better! Let's say seven, then.*
A: *Brilliant! See you then.*

5 | Further practice

Think of two films you'd like to see. With a partner, have conversations like those in Activity 3.

6 | Using vocabulary: describing who people are

In Activity 3, you read that Sven Larström is a famous Swedish director. Spend a few minutes thinking of your own answers to these questions.

Who's the most famous:

1. film star you can think of?
2. film director you can think of?
3. singer you can think of?
4. artist you can think of?
5. writer you can think of?
6. TV personality you can think of?
7. politician you can think of?
8. sports personality you can think of?
9. scientist or inventor you can think of?

Compare your answers with a partner. Were any of your answers the same? Who made the best choices?

Would you like to meet any of the people you have chosen? Who? Why / why not?

Now think of three famous people who the other students in the class probably WON'T know. Have conversations with some other students. For example:

A: Have you ever heard of Curtis Mayfield?
B: No, who's he?
A: He's a famous old American singer. He's dead now, though. He's brilliant.
B: Oh right.

Try and continue the conversations for as long as you can.

Reading

1 | Using vocabulary: What's on TV?

Match the sentences with the follow-up comments.

1. There's a history programme on later I'd like to watch.
2. There's a game show on later I'd like to watch.
3. There's a chat show on later I'd like to watch.
4. I'd like to watch the news later.
5. There's a cartoon series on later I'd like to watch.

a. There was a contestant on last week who won a million pounds!
b. There might be something more about that bombing in London.
c. The guy who hosts it is really funny and they have some interesting guests on sometimes.
d. It's by the same people who did *The Simpsons*. It should be really funny.
e. It's about life in the 19th century.

Now match these sentences with the follow-up comments.

6. There's a film on later I'd like to watch.
7. My favourite soap opera's on later. I have to watch it!
8. There's a nature programme on later I'd like to watch.
9. There's a new sitcom on later I'd like to watch.
10. There's a documentary on later I'd like to watch.

f. I saw an advert for it and it looked really funny.
g. Two of the main characters are getting married in the episode tonight.
h. It's a classic thriller by Alfred Hitchcock. Cary Grant's in it.
i. It's about monkeys in Madagascar.
j. It's about the rise of gun crime in the country.

Spend two minutes trying to memorise the sentences.

Close your books. Your partner will read out the follow-up comments. Can you remember what kind of TV show each comment is about?

2 | Speaking

Discuss these questions with a partner.

1. How much TV do you watch every day? How much is that in a week?
2. Have you got satellite, cable or digital TV?
3. How many national channels are there in your country?
4. Have you got a favourite channel? Which do you watch most? Why?
5. Have you got a favourite programme which is on at the moment?

3 | While you read

Read the TV Guide for Saturday night TV on the opposite page. Decide if there is anything you would like to watch:

a. between six and eight in the evening.
b. between eight and ten in the evening.
c. after ten o'clock.

Compare what you would like to watch with a partner. Try to agree on something to watch:

1. between 6 p.m. and 8 p.m.
2. between 8 p.m. and 10 p.m.
3. after 10 p.m.

Would your partner be a good person for you to watch TV with?

4 | Speaking

How does the TV guide compare to a typical Saturday night's TV in your country? Use sentences like these:

- A lot of the programmes are exactly the same.
- We don't have any programmes like (*Love at First Sight*).
- There are no (variety programmes) here.
- We don't have as much (sport) as this.
- We don't have as many (films) as this.
- We have more (American programmes) than this.
- I think our TV looks (better) than this.

Real English: over-rated

We say something is over-rated if all the reviews say it's brilliant and it wins lots of awards, but when you actually see or experience it, it's only quite good or not very good. The opposite is when lots of people hate something and you love it. Then you can say it's under-rated. Do you know anything which is over-rated or under-rated?

5 | Role play

Work in groups of three. Imagine you share a flat together. It is six o'clock in the evening and you are all feeling too tired to go out tonight. Instead, you all want to spend the evening watching TV. Tell your flatmates what you would like to watch. If they don't agree, try to persuade them! Try to use some of the language you have already studied in this unit.

Can you agree about what to watch for the whole evening?

Saturday night TV

BBC1

6.10
My Family (T)(R)
Roger is mistakenly announced as dead in the local paper.

6.40
Whatever you want
Game show in which contestants win whatever they've always dreamt of doing.

7.30
The National Lottery
With music from Beloved.

8.00
Near Death
Hospital drama continues. James finds himself in trouble over an operation that goes wrong.

8.50
Film: The Tuxedo (T)
(Kevin Donavon, 2002)
Action film starring Jackie Chan who saves the world with the help of a special computerised dinner jacket. Stupid but fun.

10.50
BBC News (T)
Plus sport and national lottery update. Followed by the weather.

11.10
Jonathan Woss
Guests this week are the footballer Michael Owen, film star Ben Affleck and the comedian Jo Brand.

12.10
Film: Evening in Leeds
(Andrew Walkley, 1995)
Dreadful sentimental drama about a man suffering from a terminal disease.

2.00 Top of the Pops (T)(R)

2.30 A Question of Sport (T)(R)

3.00 Fawlty Towers (T)(R)

3.30 News 24

BBC2

6.00
Wimbledon (T)
Continuing live coverage of day 6 of the tennis championships.

8.20
Best of The Simpsons (T)(R)
The favourite episodes from the long-running cartoon series, which were voted for by the British public.

8.50
Dad's Army (T)(R)
Classic British sitcom.

9.20
Roman Britain (T)
What did they do without TV? Fascinating programme about life in Britain over two thousand years ago. This programme looks at what people did when they weren't working – or fighting the Romans.

10.15
Today at Wimbledon (T)
John McEnroe presents highlights of the last of the third round matches.

11.00
Film: Ring
(Hideo Nakata, 1998)
A truly scary movie about a video film which causes people who watch it to die horribly.

2.05
The Learning Zone:

2.15 Languages: Brazil Inside Out

3.00 Art focus: Picasso's sculptures

3.30 History Today: China's Modern Revolution

4.30 Quantum Physics

5.30 Engineering for beginners

ITV1

6.25
Emmerdale (T)
Bob finds out about Susie's affair.

6.55
Coronation Street (T)
Double-length episode to celebrate the 10,000th episode of the Manchester-based soap.

7.55
You've been framed (T)(R)
More people send in their videos of their wives and children falling over. Why do people find this funny?

8.25
Love at First Sight (T)
Mel Sykes presents the dating game show in which contestants have just 30 seconds to choose a partner to go out with for a week and maybe the rest of their lives.

9.15
Jump!
Six more people go up in a plane and try to explain to the watching audience why they should win £250,000 and not be thrown out of the plane. You can vote on-line at www./itv/co.uk/jump!

10.20
Film: Mission Impossible 2
(John Woo, 2000)
Tom Cruise returns as the spy and John Woo directs this slick, fast action movie.

11.05
ITV Weekend News (T)
Weather

11.20
Film: Mission Impossible 2
(John Woo, 2000) Continued.

12.50
The Cable Guy
(Ben Stiller, 1996)
Under-rated black comedy starring Jim Carrey as a TV repair man who stalks his client Matthew Broderick.

2.00
CD UK (T)(R)

Channel 4

6.30
News (T)
Including sport and weather.

7.15
Cooking Out (T)(R)
Chef, Oliver James, shows us how to cook fish on a barbecue.

7.45
Friends (T)(R)
Monica and Chandler's wedding. Yet another repeat of the American sitcom.

8.15
Losing the War
After another bombing killed 20 people last month, this documentary by journalist Jon Pilgrim asks if the war on terror started by George W Bush is ever going to work.

9.30
Big Brother
In the ninth series, the reality TV game show became rather boring. Showing ten beautiful twenty-year-olds who are basically all trying to be famous doesn't make good TV, even when they want to have sex with each other. This year, the mix of people is much wider and the result is quite compulsive TV.

10.35
Film: Shakespeare in Love
(John Madden, 1998)
Multi-Oscar winning comedy about Shakespeare writing Romeo and Juliet and falling in love with Gwyneth Paltrow at the same time. Amusing but very over-rated.

12.45
International One-Day Cricket
Highlights of the game between England and South Africa.

1.35
4Music
Sounds of Ibiza (T)(R)

2.10 Phat: Soul music

3.00 The Gig: The Beatpack live at the Hollywood Bowl

3.10 Garage Rocks

Five

7.05
The Royals (T)
Dull documentary series on the royal family. This week the focus is on Prince Andrew.

7.55
Shrekal (T)
Last in the current series of the fantasy drama. Can Ark finally find the holy ring? Probably not.

8.45
Five News and Sport (T)

9.00
Law and Order
Admissions (T)
When a pregnant student is found murdered on her university campus, Briscoe and Curtis investigate.

10.00
Film: Robocop
(Paul Verhoeven, 1987)
Classic futuristic film where a cop, who is injured in an explosion, is rebuilt as half-man, half machine. The action is sometimes very violent, but there are also real moments of humour.

12.05
Film: Sex Crimes
(John Thomas, 2001)
Adult erotic thriller starring Sharon Tweed. Complete rubbish.

01.50
The Sports Zone

1.30 South American Football

3.15 Senior Tour Golf

5.00 World Surfing Championships

(T) Teletext subtitles (R) Repeat

Listening

1 | Using vocabulary: problems

Discuss these questions.

1. When was the last time you booked tickets for a show / movie / sports event?

2. When was the last time you booked train or plane tickets? Where were you going?

3. Have you ever booked tickets on the internet? What for? Was it easy?

Have you ever had any problems like the ones below? When? What happened?

1. The show was completely sold out.

2. The show was cancelled.

3. They didn't have the seats I wanted.

4. They didn't accept my credit card.

5. My credit card was rejected.

6. All the nice seats were much too expensive.

2 | While you listen

🎧 **Listen to Leroy booking tickets for a show at the box office. The first time you listen, find out which of the problems in Activity 1 he has.**

3 | Comprehension check

How much of this booking form can you complete? Compare what you remember with a partner.

Name: .... Jones
Number of tickets: ....
Row: ....
Payment: American Express
Card number: 4926– .... –6231– ....
Expiry Date: ....
Address: .... ,
        Beechwood Park,
        ....

Now listen again and check your answers.

4 | Speaking

Discuss these questions with a partner.

1. When you go to the cinema or to the theatre, where do you usually like to sit – at the front, in the middle or at the back?

2. When you fly, where do you prefer to sit – in a window seat or in an aisle seat? At the front of the plane, at the back, in the middle, over the wings, or beside an emergency exit?

3. What are the most expensive concert / cinema / plane / train tickets you've ever bought?

4. Have you ever made any telephone calls in English? When? Why?

5. How do you feel about using English on the telephone?

5 | Using grammar: passives

Look at these sentences. Which two verbs are in the passive? How do you know?

- I'm afraid the show's been cancelled.

- I've cancelled all my credit cards because I lost my wallet and now I don't have any money!

- The film was written by John Hodge, who also wrote the film *Shallow Grave*.

We use the passive to change the word order of a verb phrase so that the object of a verb can come before the verb. We sometimes do this because we don't know who the subject of the verb is:

- My bag's been stolen.
  (Someone has stolen my bag, but I don't know who.)

We also use the passive when the object of the verb is more important than the subject:

- It's a great film. It's directed by Luis Buñuel. Do you want to go and see it?
  (I want to talk about the film more than the director.)

- My boss was arrested for stealing money from the company.
  (I'm more interested in my boss than in the police!)

- My car's being repaired at the moment, so I'll have to go on the bus.
  (I'm more interested in the fact that my car has a problem at the moment.)

Passives are formed by using the verb be in the tense you want + past participle of the verb:

- The rubbish is collected every Wednesday.
- My camera is being fixed at the moment.
- The church was built in 1694.
- My bike has been stolen.

What are the tenses in the four examples above?

Decide which of these sentences are passive.

1. The book was made into a film a few years ago.
2. My flight's been delayed.
3. I just caught the train in time.
4. I've been really busy recently.
5. I'm being picked up from the airport.
6. I was caught on the bus without a ticket.
7. I was woken up at five o'clock this morning by a friend phoning me from America.
8. I woke up really late this morning.
9. I was sacked because I was late all the time.
10. John Woo's new film is coming out next week.
11. We weren't served very quickly and when we were finally served, the food wasn't very hot.
12. The show's got some really good actors in it.

Check your answers with a partner. Do you agree?

6 | Practice

Complete the sentences with the words in the box.

are made	been translated	's directed
been closed down	being repaired	wasn't cleaned
been invited	be knocked down	was rejected

1. The hotel was really horrible. Our room .... the whole time we were there.

2. Most of that company's clothes .... in China.

3. A: Do you know that lovely old cinema near our house? Well, it has ....
   B: Yes, I know. Someone told me it's going to .... and they're going to build a car park there.

4. It was really embarrassing because my credit card .... and I didn't have enough money to pay the bill.

5. A: Have you ever read any books by Antonio Gala? A lot of them have .... into English.
   B: No, sorry. I've never heard of him.

6. You can't go inside the church at the moment because the floor is ....

7. A: Are you going to Alastair and Judith's wedding?
   B: No. I haven't .... !

8. A: Do you want to go and see *Hell in the Afternoon*?
   B: Maybe. Who's in it?
   A: Nobody very famous, but it .... by Hamish McKay, so it should be good.

Did you notice that in most of the sentences, we don't say who the actions were done by? This is normal in spoken English.

> For more information on using passives, see G28.

7 | Speaking

Discuss these questions with a partner.

1. Have any famous people been arrested in your country recently? What for?

2. Do you know any books which have been made into films? Which was better, the film or the book?

3. Do you know anywhere which has been closed down or knocked down recently?

4. Have you had any flights which were delayed or cancelled? Why?

5. Have you been invited to any parties or weddings recently? Whose?

I'm going to phone in sick. • I might give you a ring over the weekend. • Do you know when he'll be back? • Do you want to leave a message? • It was really embarrassing! • I had to change my number. • She just hung up straightaway. • Let's swap numbers. • I was so annoyed I wanted to hit him! • Charlotte told me to say hello. • Brian asked me to tell you he's going to be late. • I need to recharge the battery. • I had my phone stolen. • I left it lying on the table. • Can u do it asap? • Someone broke into their house. • I was shocked.

Conversation

1 | Key word: *phone*

Complete the sentences with the words in the box.

answered	look up	phone	sell
book	make	put	spends

1. I won't be a minute. I just need to .... a couple of quick phone calls.

2. If you're not feeling very well, why don't you just .... in sick? I'm sure your boss will understand.

3. Shall we just .... the tickets over the phone?

4. We had a big argument and she got really angry, and then she .... the phone down on me.

5. Hi. Do you .... phone cards?

6. Why don't you .... her number in the phone book? It'll probably be listed.

7. She's a typical teenager! She .... hours on the phone every evening!

8. I rang him five times last night, but every time his wife .... the phone, not him.

What do you think the situation is in sentence 8?

2 | Speaking

Discuss these questions with a partner.

1. Who usually answers the phone in your house?

2. Who spends longest on the phone in your house?

3. Have you ever been so angry you put the phone down on someone? Why did you get so angry?

4. When did you last have to phone in sick?

> **Real English: give you a ring**
>
> In normal spoken English, a common way of saying phone you is give you a ring. You can also give someone a call.
>
> *Listen, I might give you a ring later.*
> *I'll give you a call tomorrow and we can talk about it then.*

3 | Answering the phone (1)

Who was the last person you phoned? Why? When was the last time you got or left a message?

🎧 **Listen to the conversation between two friends – Lara and Paola. The first time you listen, note down as much of the missing language as you can. Then work with a partner and try to write the whole sentences.**

L: Hello.

P: .... , ... Jenny .... ?

L: .... not. ....
....

P: ....
.... back?

L: She'll probably ....
....
.... message?

P: .... , ... I'll ....
....

Only listen to the conversation again when you and your partner can't work out any more of the missing language.

4 | Answering the phone (2)

Complete the conversations with the groups of words in the box.

> closed + between ten and four
> for lunch + an hour
> his day off + around half eight
> in the shower + ten minutes
> off sick + a couple of days
> on holiday + next week

1. A: Is Lindsay there?
   B: Sorry, she's just gone out ....
   A: When will she be back?
   B: She's normally back in ....

2. A: I'd like to speak to Mr. Thunders, please.
   B: I'm sorry. He's ....
   A: Oh dear. When will he be back?
   B: I'm not sure. He said he might be back in
      .... , if he's feeling better.

3. A: Hi. Is Mina there?
   B: I'm afraid not. She's away ....
      at the moment.
   A: Do you know when she'll be back?
   B: She said she'll be back ....
      sometime, I think.

4. A: I'd like to speak to John Patterson, please. Is he
      around?
   B: I'm afraid not. It's ....
   A: What time will he be in tomorrow?
   B: He usually gets here .... ,
      so you could try again after that.

5. A: Is Henri there?
   B: Yes, but he's actually .... !
      Do you want to ring back in .... ?

6. A: I'd like to speak to the box office.
   B: I'm sorry, it's .... It'll be
      open again tomorrow ....

Can you think of any other good reasons why people can't come to the phone?

5 | Grammar questions

Did you notice the two ways of starting the conversations in Activity 4?

- I'd like to speak to X, please.
- Is X there?

Which one would you use when you phone:

1. an office?
2. a friend's house?

Did you notice the different ways the people replied to When will she / he be back? Match the forms with the explanations.

1. She's normally back by seven. ☐
2. She said she'll be back by seven. ☐
3. She said she might be back by seven. ☐

a. She is not sure.
b. She is sure.
c. This is what usually happens.

6 | Practice

With other students, have telephone conversations like those in Activity 4. Take turns to ask to speak to someone. When you answer the phone, explain why this person can't come to the phone.

7 | Talking on the phone

🎧 **Listen to the conversation between Paola and Jenny when Paola phones back. As you listen, try to answer these questions.**

1. Why is Paola ringing Jenny?
2. What does Jenny offer to do?

8 | Word check

Complete these extracts from the conversation.

1. We go to the .... school to learn English.
2. She's .... me about you.
3. I was .... if you could help me.
4. Fernanda said you might be able to ....
   somewhere cheap to stay.
5. I've got a .... room.
6. It's no ....
7. In two weeks' ....
8. Do you want to give me a ring .... the time?
9. Can you .... hi to Fernanda from me?
10. Thanks for the ....

Listen again and check your answers.

With a partner, try to have the conversation between Paola and Jenny.

Now read the tapescript. How much did you remember? Practise the conversation again.

Translate the sentences above into your language. DON'T use a dictionary. Ask your teacher if you need help. Compare your ideas with a partner who speaks the same language as you.

Reading

1 | Before you read

Complete the sentences with the expressions in the box.

> It was really annoying!
>
> It was really embarrassing!
>
> It was really funny!
>
> It was really horrible!

1. Did I tell you about what happened to Liam the other day? .... He slipped on a banana skin and fell over. Everybody laughed and laughed.

2. Did I tell you about what happened to me the other day? .... There was a hole in my trousers and everybody could see my underwear. I felt really stupid.

3. Did I tell you about what happened to me at work the other week? .... My boss asked me to tell my partner he'd lost his job! I felt really bad about it, but I had to do it.

4. Did I tell you about what happened with that company I applied for a job with? .... They told me to phone back later, but when I did, there was nobody there. I was really angry about it, actually!

Can you think of any times in your life you could describe using the expressions in the box? Tell a partner as much as you can about what happened. You can begin like this:

*   Did I (ever) tell you about what happened to me ... ?
    It was really ... !

2 | While you read

With a partner, think of two possible reasons why a phone conversation could be embarrassing, funny, annoying or horrible.

🎧 **Now read about three different experiences involving telephones. Add the best word to complete the last sentence in each story.**

Telephone stories

Jiang

The other evening, I was at home in my flat and I was feeling really homesick. I was really missing my girlfriend, Hong Jie. She's back home in China and China's seven hours ahead of Ireland where I'm studying, so it was in the middle of the night there. But I thought I'd ring her anyway, because I just really needed to talk to her and tell her how much I loved her. Anyway, I phoned her on my mobile and a woman's voice answered – she sounded a bit tired – and I just started talking. 'Hi, it's me. Sorry to phone you so late, but I just had to ring you.' And then I just went on saying how much I missed her and all kinds of other personal stuff, and then suddenly the woman on the other end of the line said, 'Who is this?' I was so embarrassed I hung up straightaway. When I looked again at the number I had dialled, I realised I'd called my mum by mistake. I don't know if she recognised my voice, but she never said anything about it! It was really ....

Emilie

About a year ago, I met this guy while I was on holiday. He came from the same town as me and seemed quite nice. We got on quite well, so we swapped telephone numbers and said we would meet up when we were back in England. Anyway, we went out together one night and I didn't have a very good time. He was a bit strange with me – quite serious – and he obviously wanted to go out with me as his girlfriend. The next time he rang, I just made some excuse to say I couldn't meet him. The same day he rang again and I told him I was busy. He didn't take the hint, though, because he kept on ringing me again and again and again. I told him I wasn't interested and that he should stop calling me, but he took no notice. He started ringing and texting me ten or fifteen times a day. In the end, I had to change my number. It was really ....

Rebecca

I was on the train going to a meeting and I was trying to do some work. There was this guy sitting opposite me who spent the whole journey talking really loudly on his mobile. They were all really stupid conversations as well. I asked him to go and talk somewhere else or talk a bit more quietly, but he didn't take any notice. I didn't get any work done and by the end of the journey, I was so annoyed I wanted to hit him. It was really ....

3 | Speaking

Discuss these questions with a partner.

1. Have you ever had any experiences like the ones described in the stories?

2. How much do you use your mobile phone? Do you ever answer it when you're on a bus or train? When you're in class? While you're eating? When do you switch it off?

3. How well do you usually know somebody before you give them your number?

4. Have you ever had to change your number or your e-mail address? Why?

4 | Texting

Do you send text messages much? Do you use abbreviations? Which ones? Have you ever texted in English?

Do you understand these text messages? Discuss your ideas with a partner.

1. thx 4 the info
2. it's up 2 u
3. c u 2moro
4. it's ezi
5. can u do it asap?
6. c u 2nite
7. ruok?
8. cu l8r
9. gr8 news
10. myob!

Ask your teacher about anything you didn't understand.

5 | Word check

Complete the sentences with words from the text. Try not to look back at the text.

1. My brother phoned me .... his mobile.

2. Do you make phone calls .... at night?

3. I couldn't hear the person at the other end of the ....

4. It was a wrong number and the person .... up.

5. I .... the wrong number by mistake.

6. Most people in the class have .... telephone numbers.

Now look back at the text and check your answers.

6 | Writing

With a partner, write what you think Jiang said to his mother. You can begin like this:

*   Hi, it's me. Sorry to phone you so late, but I just had to ring you.

7 | Using vocabulary: adjectives ending with -ed or -ing

Jiang phoned his mother when he meant to phone his girlfriend. He said: 'It was really embarrassing'. He also said: 'I was so embarrassed'.

Do you know when you can use these two different forms?

There are several other adjectives in English which have two forms: an -ing form and an -ed form. We use the -ing form to describe things and the -ed form to describe our feelings. For example:

*   I've had a really tiring day.

*   The programme was really shocking.

*   I'm really tired. I've been working all day.

*   I was shocked I got the job. I really didn't expect to.

Complete the sentences with one of the words in brackets.

1. The talk was really .... I fell asleep in the middle of it. (boring / bored)

2. I'm going to San Francisco next week. I'm really .... about it. (exciting / excited)

3. I was very .... to hear what you were saying about Mexico. (interesting / interested)

4. I was so .... about it I wanted to hit him! (annoying / annoyed)

5. Madrid is a really .... place to visit. (exciting / excited)

6. It was the most .... thing that's ever happened to me. (frightening / frightened)

7. He's a very .... guy. It was great talking to him. (interesting / interested)

8. They told me they would help me, but they didn't do anything. It was really .... (annoying / annoyed)

Have you ever felt:

1. so bored you fell asleep in the middle of something?

2. so annoyed you wanted to hit someone?

3. so frightened you thought you were going to have a heart attack?

Listening

1 | Using grammar: reporting what people say

Spend one minute trying to memorise the conversation between Jenny and Paola in the tapescript at the back of the book.

Now close your book. Try to have the conversation again with a partner.

In the conversation, Paola said: 'Fernanda told me to say hello.' Paola was reporting what Fernanda said. Fernanda probably said: 'When you speak to Jenny, say hello from me.'

When we want to report what someone else said, we often use these structures:

- (Paul) told me to say thanks for everything.
- (Paul) told me to tell you he's not coming into work tomorrow.
- (Paul) told me to ask you if you could book a ticket for him as well.
- (Paul) was telling me about your new car. It sounds really good.

Complete these sentences with the correct form of say, ask or tell.

1. Alan told me to .... you he can't come tonight. He's got a meeting.
2. Alan told me to .... you he's going to be late.
3. Alan told me to .... you if you could call him.
4. Alan told me to .... hello.
5. Alan was .... me you're going to Thailand in a couple of weeks. It sounds really good.
6. Alan told me to .... good luck with the exam.
7. Alan told me to .... you if you could get some milk on the way home.
8. Alan was .... me you really like tennis. Do you want to have a game some time?
9. Alan told me to .... thanks for the tickets.
10. Alan told me to .... you not to be late. The film starts at eight.
11. Alan was .... me he's thinking of leaving his job. Has he said anything to you about it?
12. Alan was .... me about the party last night. It sounded as if you all had a really good time.

> ▶ For more information on how to report what people say, see G29.

2 | Pronunciation

🎧 **Listen to the sentences from Activity 1 and mark the main stressed words.**

Compare your answers with the tapescript and then practise saying the sentences.

3 | Practice

In the conversation, Jenny said: 'Can you say hi to Fernanda for me and thank her for the birthday card?' How do you think Paola will report this the next time she speaks to Fernanda?

Complete the sentences reporting these things Alan said. Use the structures in Activity 1.

1. A: If you see Clare later, say hello from me.
    B: By the way, Clare, Alan told .... hello.

2. A: When you see John, say good luck from me for the interview tomorrow. I'll be thinking of him.
    B: By the way, John, Alan told .... good luck with your interview tomorrow.

3. A: Did you hear that Ingrid is going to have a baby?
    B: By the way, Ingrid, Alan was telling .... to have a baby. Congratulations! When's it due?

4. A: If you see Charlie later, can you tell him to give me a ring?
    B: By the way, Charlie, Alan told .... to give him a ring.

5. A: If you see Jane later, can you ask her if she can bring something to eat with her tomorrow?
    B: By the way, Jane, Alan told .... bring something to eat tomorrow.

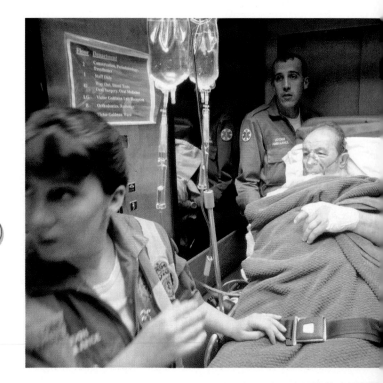

4 | Further practice

Work with a partner. Tell each other something interesting about yourself. This could be something you're going to do soon, something you did the other day or something about your family or friends.

Now report what you learned about your partner to some other students. You can start like this:

• ... was telling me he / she ...

Try to continue the conversations for as long as you can.

5 | While you listen

⌒ Listen to four conversations and decide which is the correct sentence ending.

1. Lek was explaining to Carl
   a. how his mobile phone works.
   b. why he didn't meet him yesterday.
   c. about the film he saw.

2. Kenny was telling Pat about
   a. a new coffee bar near the university.
   b. losing his address book.
   c. having his mobile phone stolen.

3. Frances and Ed were deciding
   a. where to meet Tom.
   b. whether to wait for Tom or not.
   c. whether to phone Tom or not.

4. Takashi was telling Ben about
   a. his new DVD player.
   b. his trip to Hong Kong.
   c. his new phone.

6 | Vocabulary focus

Complete the collocations from the conversations in Activity 5 with the words in the box.

| contact | leave | recharge | take |
| go | miss | sort out | try |

a. .... people
b. .... calling him
c. .... the problem
d. .... it lying on the table
e. .... photos
f. .... the battery
g. .... without him
h. .... the beginning of the film

Can you remember in which conversation you heard each collocation? Can you remember why each collocation was used?

Listen to the conversations again and check your answers.

7 | Speaking: talking about crimes

In the second conversation, Kenny said: 'I had my phone stolen'. Can you remember how this happened?

Have any of these crimes ever happened to you? Tell a partner what happened.

1. I had my bag stolen.
2. I had my phone stolen.
3. I had my passport stolen.
4. I had my car stolen.
5. I had my wallet / purse stolen.
6. Somebody tried to steal my bag.
7. Somebody tried to steal my phone.
8. Somebody tried to steal my passport.
9. Somebody broke into my house and stole some things.
10. Somebody used my credit card without me knowing.

When you listen to other students' stories, try to use these questions.

• Were you insured?
• Did you report it to the police?
• What did they say?

Review: Units 13-16

1 | Act or draw

Work in pairs. Take turns to choose five of the words or expressions in the box. Don't tell your partner which ones you have chosen! Without speaking, draw or act out the words for your partner to guess. Your partner has one minute to guess the words you have chosen.

a building site	have my card stolen
a campsite	I was really embarrassed
a twin room	lift something
be shocked	pay by credit card
central heating	put on some lipstick
covered in bites	reject my credit card
dial the number	room service
fold up something	snowboarding
get changed	swap numbers
hang up	sunburnt
have an argument	

Were there any words you didn't know?

2 | Tenses

Choose the correct alternative.

1. A: Have you ever been to Hungary?
   B: Yes, I have, actually. I've travelled / I travelled round there a few years ago.

2. A: Have you ever been to Prague?
   B: No, but I'll actually go / I'm actually going there next month with my wife. It's a surprise present for her birthday, so don't tell her about it!

3. A: Do you want to go out later?
   B: I don't think so. I'm quite tired, but if I change / I will change my mind, I call you / I'll call you.

4. A: How long will it take to repair?
   B: I can finish it / I finish it by Thursday if the parts will arrive / arrive tomorrow.

5. I'm an interpreter. I translate / I am translated for French and Swiss businessmen when they come to England.

6. I'm just ringing to say I'm going to be late. Our train has delayed / has been delayed.

7. Normally you could stay with us, but our house is being decorated / is decorating at the moment, so it's a bit difficult.

8. A: When will Joan be in the office next?
   B: Thursday. She'll normally be here / She's normally here in the morning till about one.

3 | Grammar

Complete the sentences. Write ONE word in each space.

1. A: Do you mind if I have a shower?
   B: No, of course .... – as long .... you're quick. We need to leave by half seven.

2. A: I'd love to go to Brazil. It's supposed to .... amazing.
   B: Yes, it .... I went there a couple of years .... It was great.

3. By the way, John told me to .... sorry, but he can't come tonight. He's really busy.

4. We had .... a good time in York last year that we've decided to go there again this year.

5. A: What was the hotel you stayed in .... ?
   B: It was great. The room, the food, ...

6. A: We went to this beautiful sandy beach and there was .... anyone there.
   B: It .... great. I'm quite jealous. I really need a nice holiday.

7. A: It was terrible. I .... my bag stolen while I was there.
   B: What .... shame! I hope it didn't completely spoil your holiday.

8. A: Hello, is Kevin .... ?
   B: No, I'm sorry, he's .... at the moment. He's gone shopping. He .... probably be back in an hour if you want to try then.

Compare your answers with a partner and explain your choices.

4 | Questions and answers

Match the questions with the answers.

1. Are you hungry? ▢
2. Are you ready? ▢
3. Are there any tickets left for tonight's performance? ▢
4. Is there anything good on TV tonight? ▢
5. Is Chris there? ▢

a. Not really. I need to have a shave and iron my shirt.

b. Yes, I'll just get him.

c. No. Twenty two channels and there's nothing on!

d. Yes, I'm starving!

e. I'm afraid it's completely sold out. Sorry.

Now match these questions with the answers.

6. What kind of day have you had?

7. Do you want to leave a message?

8. Did you get through?

9. Can I do anything to help?

10. Is it OK if I use your phone?

f. No, it's OK. I'll try again later.

g. OK, I suppose. I didn't do very much really.

h. Yes, thanks. You could chop these onions, if you don't mind.

i. Yeah, sure. Go ahead. You need to dial 9 first for an outside line.

j. No, it was engaged.

In pairs, ask each other the questions above. This time give different answers.

5 | What can you remember?

With a partner, write down as much as you can remember about the people you read about in the texts in Unit 14 and Unit 16.

Unit 14: What's your life like?

a. Teachers in Britain generally

b. Megan, the English teacher from Coventry

c. Patrick, the English teacher from Guinea Bissau

d. Olga, the History teacher from Latvia

Unit 16: Telephone stories

a. Jiang's embarrassing story

b. Emilie's horrible story

c. Rebecca's annoying story

Now work with another pair of students and compare what you can remember. Who remembered more?

Which text did you enjoy more? Why?

6 | Verb collocations

Complete the collocations with the verbs in the box.

answer	complain	have	lock	look out	over

1. .... the phone / a question

2. .... a good time / the day off

3. .... the door when you go out / the car

4. .... a square / a building site

5. .... about the bad weather / about students' behaviour

Now complete these collocations with the verbs in the box.

miss	sit	stay	take	watch

6. .... the beginning of the film / my train

7. .... a photo / your time

8. .... a documentary / a sitcom

9. .... in the front row / in the upper circle

10. .... in a bed and breakfast / in a camping site

Work in pairs. Spend one minute memorising the words above that collocate with the verbs. Then take turns to close your book. Your partner will read out the verbs. Can you remember both collocations?

With your partner, try to think of one more collocation for each verb.

7 | Look back and check

Work in pairs. Choose one of these activities.

a. **Look back at the conversation in Unit 13 on page 92. How many of the questions can you remember? Test your partner and then do the role play in Activity 3 again.**

b. **Look back at the questions to talk about films in Unit 15, Activity 3 on page 105. Can you remember all the questions? Test each other.**

Student A: Start the conversation by saying 'I'm thinking of going to see this new film, ... , later. Do you want to come?'

Student B: Reply with one of the questions.

Continue the conversation.

8 | Expressions

Complete the expressions with the words in the box.

ask	jealous	miles	seconds	told
hand	mean	same	shame	went

1. You can see for .... up there.
2. I know what you ....
3. I'll only be two ....
4. It's a .... you couldn't come.
5. Don't .... !
6. I thought I'd .... you about it.
7. I'll give you a .... if you like.
8. I'm quite .... of her.
9. It's the .... for me.
10. Everything that could go wrong .... wrong!

Now discuss these questions.

1. Do you know a place where you can see for miles?
2. Have you ever wanted to say I'm quite jealous? When? Why?
3. When did you last give someone a hand? What did you do?

9 | Vocabulary quiz

Discuss these questions in groups of three.

1. What do you see in a harbour?
2. What do you comb?
3. What's the opposite of being in the shade?
4. Why are buildings knocked down?
5. Is a two-star hotel posh?
6. How many people are usually in a private class?
7. What are credit card details?
8. What do you do if you have a quiet night in?
9. What do you read about in a review in a newspaper?
10. What do you have to do if your mobile is dead?
11. Where do you usually have a burglar alarm? When do you switch it on?
12. What does an author do?
13. What do you do at the box office?
14. Can you think of two things that are scary?
15. Can you think of two reasons why people go on strike?
16. Is 'Sounds great!' correct English?

Pronunciation

1 | Contrastive stress

🎧 **Listen to this conversation.**

A: Are you still OK for Tuesday?
B: <u>Tues</u>day? I thought you said <u>Thurs</u>day.
A: No, I definitely said Tuesday. I'm sure of it.

When someone says something we think is wrong, we often repeat what they have said and then try to correct it. The key words in our corrections are given extra stress. For example:

A: Whereabouts in Japan are you from?
B: Ja<u>pan</u>? I'm from Ko<u>rea</u>!

Complete the conversations with the words in the box.

eleven	foot	the main exit	train	tomorrow

1. A: Are you still coming round tonight?
   B: Tonight? I thought we said ....
   A: No, I definitely said tonight. I'm sure of it.

2. A: We're meeting on Wednesday at nine, yeah?
   B: Nine? I thought you said ....
   A: No, I definitely said nine. I'm sure of it.

3. A: So we're meeting on the platform, then, yeah?
   B: On the platform? I thought you said by
   ....
   A: No, I definitely said on the platform. I'm sure of it.

4. A: I'll pick you up in my car at six then, yeah?
   B: We're going by car? I thought you said we were going to go on ....
   A: No, I definitely said we'd take the car. I'm sure of it.

5. A: I'll meet you at the bus stop, then, yeah?
   B: At the bus stop? I thought we agreed we were going by ....
   A: No, I definitely said at the bus stop. I'm sure of it.

🎧 **Listen and check your answers. Then practise the conversations with a partner. Make sure you stress the key words.**

2 | Vowel sounds

🎧 **Look at the pictures. They show how we make these sounds. Listen and practise the sounds.**

/iː/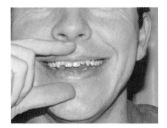

/uː/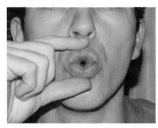

/ɔː/

/ɜː/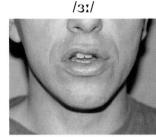

/aː/

Look at these words. They are written in phonetic script. Try and say the words, then write them down.

1. /ˈviːzə/ ....
2. /pəˈluːʃn/ ....
3. /wɜːst/ ....
4. /ˈhaːbə/ ....
5. /ˈmɔːnɪŋ/ ....
6. /ˈpaːspɔːt/ ....

Now try and say these expressions, then write them down.

7. /ðə treɪn ˈdʒɜːnɪ/ ....
8. /ʃiː ˈtiːtʃɪz griːk/ ....
9. /juːz jə kəmˈpjuːtə/ ....
10. /ˈbɔːrɪŋ spɔːts kɔːs/ ....

🎧 **Listen and check your answers. How many words and expressions did you get right?**

3 | Problem sounds: /b/ and /v/, /t/ and /θ/

🎧 **Look at the pictures. They show how we make these sounds. Listen and practise the sounds.**

/b/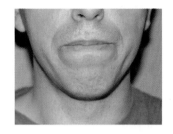

/v/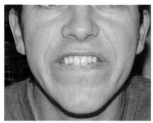

/t/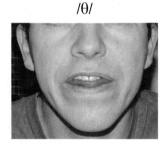

/θ/

Now say these expressions.

1. Bring that book for Barry.
2. a very violent Vietnamese video
3. She's a totally typical teenager.
4. I thought Thursday was the third.
5. They gave that thriller terrible reviews.
6. It's lively every evening.
7. The views from our bed and breakfast place were brilliant.
8. The toilets in the venue were terrible.
9. His thighs are too thin!
10. I'm thinking of trying that Thai place.

Try to write your own sentences using the sounds above. Read your sentences out to the class.

Who had the most sounds? Which was the funniest sentence?

I fell off a horse. • You should have that looked at. • It's really badly bruised. • It really hurts. • I had to have twelve stitches. • I had three fillings. • I slipped on the ice and fell over. • Maybe you should put a bandage on it. • Can you bend it at all? • I've still got the scar today. • There was blood everywhere. • They gave me two injections. • I was running for the bus and I tripped. • I can be so clumsy sometimes. • Let me call you a taxi. • What seems to be the problem? • It looks quite nasty. • It was all my fault. • Don't be silly! It's fine.

Conversation

1 | Talking about what's wrong with you

Have you ever seen anybody have an accident? Where? What happened? Did you help?

Look at the picture. What do you think has happened? With a partner, have the conversation these two people would have.

♫ **Listen to this conversation between the two people in the picture – David and Ruth. Complete the conversation.**

D: Aaagh!

R: Oh, (1) .... ?

D: Yes, I think so.

R:: (2) .... ? That was quite a nasty fall.

D:: Yes, I don't know what happened. I think I just tripped.

R: Yes, you need to be careful. Can you (3) .... ?

D: Yes, I think so. Ow, ow!

R: (4) .... have that arm looked at. (5) .... broken.

D: No, it'll be all right. It's probably just bruised.

R: It doesn't look like it to me. Honestly, I really think you should (6) .... You don't want to be walking round with a broken arm.

D: Yes, maybe you're right. It IS quite painful.

R:: Shall I (7) .... to take you to the hospital?

D: Would you mind?

R: No, of course not. Just sit there for a minute and I'll see if I can get one. I'll be back in a second.

D: OK. Thanks. I really (8) ....

Practise the conversation with a partner.

2 | Grammar questions

Look at the conversation in Activity 1 again. Match two of the missing expressions with these explanations.

a. I think it's a good idea for you to ... =
....

b. It's possible it is ... = ...

In you should have it X-rayed, who does the X-ray?

3 | Using vocabulary: health problems

Match these things with the photos.

1. stitches ☐
2. a bandage ☐
3. some cream ☐
4. a rash ☐
5. a filling ☐
6. an X-ray ☐

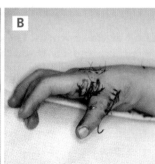

A

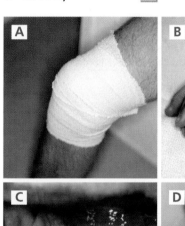

B

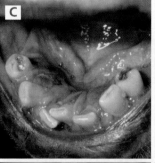

C

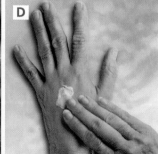

D

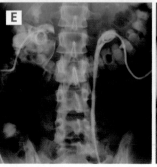

E

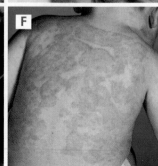

F

4 | Practice

Complete the conversations with the groups of words in the box.

> have a check-up + nothing + worrying
> have it looked at + filling + an appointment
> have it looked at + red + cream
> have it looked at + stitches + a bandage
> have it X-rayed + broken + bruised

1. A: Are you all right?
    B: Yes, I've just cut myself.
    A: Maybe you should go to the hospital and
       .... It might need
       ....
    B: No, it'll be all right. I probably just need to put
       .... on it.

2. A: Are you all right?
    B: Yes, I've just banged my arm.
    A: Maybe you should go to the hospital and
       .... It might be
       ....
    B: No, it'll be all right. It's probably just badly
       ....

3. A: Are you all right?
    B: No, not really. I woke up this morning with this
       horrible toothache.
    A: Maybe you should go to the dentist and
       .... You might need to
       have a .... or something.
    B: Yes, maybe you're right. I'll ring them and make
       .... later.

4. A: Are you all right?
    B: Yes, but I've had this rash on my hand since
       yesterday.
    A: Maybe you should go to the doctor and
       .... It looks really
       ....
    B: No, it'll be all right. I just need to put some
       .... on it or something.

5. A: Are you all right?
    B: Not really. I've been feeling really sick for the last
       two weeks. I'm worried it might be something
       serious.
    A: Maybe you should go and ....
       It might be ....
    B: Yes, maybe you're right. I don't want to be
       .... about it all the time. I'll ring the
       doctor now.

Spend two minutes trying to memorise the suggestions which begin 'Maybe you should'.

With a partner, practise the conversations. Your partner will choose a problem. You should close your book and make a suggestion. Begin like this:

A: Are you all right?'

Have you ever had an X-ray? When? Why?

5 | Vocabulary: describing accidents

Complete the collocations with the words in the box.

broke	fell off	got bitten	hit	slipped
cut	fell over	had it	put	tripped

1. It was icy and / The floor was wet and / It was muddy and I ....
2. I tripped and / I slipped and / I was running in the park and I ....
3. I .... my head / my elbow on the side of the table / my knee on the door.
4. I .... my arm / my nose / a bone in my foot / my leg in three places.
5. I .... on the stairs / over / over the cable on the floor / on the carpet.
6. I went and .... looked at / checked out / stitched / X-rayed.
7. I .... my hand on some glass / it really deeply / my head / myself shaving.
8. I .... a bandage on it / a plaster on it / some cream on it / some ice on it.
9. I .... a horse / my bike / a ladder.
10. I .... by a dog / by a snake / by about 100 mosquitoes!

6 | Vocabulary: in hospital

Put the words in order and make questions.

1. be / seems / the / What / problem / to
    .... ?
2. happen / did / How / it
    .... ?
3. all / Does / at / hurt / this
    .... ?
4. up / Can / you / stand
    .... ?
5. you / arm / your / Can / lift
    .... ?
6. all / you / Can / bend / it / at
    .... ?
7. hit / you / all / your / Did / head / at
    .... ?

With a partner, use the questions to have a conversation between the doctor and the man who fell down the steps in Activity 1.

Reading

1 | Before you read

You are going to read about accidents which happened in the places in the photos. With a partner, discuss what could happen in each place.

2 | While you read

∩ Now read the stories and find out if they mention any of the accidents you thought of.

3 | Comprehension

With a partner, check you understand what happened in each story. Which of the accidents:

1. were really stupid?
2. were just bad luck?
3. sound really nasty?
4. don't sound that bad?

It really  hurt!

Stuart I've got a horrible scar on my back. I got it at school when I was about 13 or 14. I was playing rugby and I was trying to get the ball when suddenly I felt this awful pain on my back. I screamed in pain and could feel blood running down my back. One of the players in the other team had scratched me really hard with his really long nails! I was really angry about it!

Chris When I was 18, I went out to a club in Boston with some friends to celebrate my birthday. We had a few drinks and the music was really good, so we all started dancing. I was dancing and having a really great time, but then I slipped over on a drink someone had spilled and somehow put my hand through a window. It really hurt. I had to go to hospital and have eight stitches. I've still got the scar today!

Katy I've got a horrible scar on my right knee. When I was younger, I was trying to learn to skateboard and one day I was skateboarding downhill when I suddenly realised I didn't really know how to stop. So I just put my knee down and hoped that would work! It was incredibly painful and the wound went through to the bone!

Will When I was five or six, I was playing outside with a friend from the neighbourhood and when it started getting dark, I ran inside my house to get a coat. I put it on and put my hands in my pockets to keep warm. I was running back outside and I tripped on a step. I couldn't stop myself because my hands were in my coat pockets and I hit my forehead on one of the steps. It was horrible! There was blood everywhere! My uncle took me to hospital and I had to have five stitches.

Zeynep One day when I was eleven or twelve, we went to the beach. I went out into the water and was sitting on one of those wooden things you get in the water sometimes, the ones you lie on or rest on after you've been swimming. There were lots of people around and next to me was a little girl who wasn't very good at swimming. I remember someone pushing her off the wooden thing and I remember her screaming. I managed to catch her OK, but she was so scared that she bit me really hard on the shoulder. It really hurt! I've still got a mark there today!

Barney When I was about eight or nine, I was showing off to some friends of mine in the swimming pool and decided to jump in backwards. I didn't jump back far enough and hit my chin on the side of the pool. I only got a small cut, but there was blood everywhere. I had to go to hospital and had about five stitches. The worst thing was the injection for the local anaesthetic – the doctor did it into my chin bone! Ouch!

4 | Word check

Complete the sentences with the words in the box.

blood	injection	screaming	stitches
hurt	scar	slipped	tripped

1. It was horrible! There was .... everywhere!
2. It was icy and I .... and fell over.
3. I was trying to lift this really heavy box and .... my back while I was doing it.
4. I .... over my shoelaces and hit my head as I fell.
5. I had to go to hospital and had twelve .... in my leg. I've still got the .... today. Look.
6. I can remember .... in pain. It was horrible!
7. I had to have an .... into my neck to kill the pain. It was horrible!

With a partner, discuss these questions.

a. Can you think of three things you can slip on?
b. Can you think of three things you can trip over?
c. Can you think of three ways you could hurt your back?

5 | Using grammar: past simple and past continuous

We often use the past simple and the past continuous to talk about accidents:

• I was running back outside and I tripped on a step.

Look at the above example and discuss the questions with a partner.

1. Which action started first – the running or the tripping?
2. Which action took longer – the running or the tripping?

Match the sentence beginnings with the endings.

1. I was drilling a hole in the wall
2. I was cutting some onions
3. I was changing a light bulb
4. I was running down the stairs
5. I was messing about with some matches
6. I was making coffee

a. and someone knocked me, and I poured it all over my hand and burnt myself.
b. and I dropped one of them and burnt a hole in my jeans.
c. and I slipped and fell off the chair.
d. and the knife slipped and I nearly cut the end of my finger off.
e. and the drill slipped and hit my hand. It really hurt.
f. and I tripped and fell and knocked three teeth out.

6 | Practice

Complete the sentences with the past simple or the past continuous form of the verbs.

1. The other day, I .... the road. I .... over and .... my head on the pavement. I .... a terrible bump. (cross, trip, bang, get)
2. Yesterday afternoon, I .... the tea and Alan .... my arm. The tea .... all over my hand and .... me really badly. (pour, knock, go, burn)
3. I .... home the other day and a dog .... out in front of me. I .... it and .... it. It .... awful! (drive, run, hit, kill, be)
4. My sister .... the windows sometime last week and she .... off the ladder and .... her back really badly. (clean, fall, hurt)
5. I .... my floor the other day and I .... my thumb with the hammer. It really .... and my nail .... all black and purple. (fix, bang, hurt, go)

Cover the six stories you read and look back at the photos. With a partner, discuss what you remember about the accidents.

> For more information on using the past simple and past continuous, see G30.

7 | Free practice

Have you ever had an accident? Spend two minutes thinking about how to describe what happened. Use your dictionary to help you if necessary.

Now tell some students your story.

Try and use these expressions when responding to other students' stories.

• Ouch! Nasty!
• Oh no, were you OK?
• Did you have to go to hospital?
• Do you still have a scar?

Listening

1 | Apologising

Look at these statements. Decide if they would be said by the person who caused the accident (**A**) or the other person (**B**). The first two have been done for you.

1. I don't know what I was doing.   A
2. Don't be so silly! It's fine.   B
3. I'm afraid you'll have to pay for it.
4. Don't worry about it!
5. I'll pay to get it cleaned.
6. I didn't see them there.
7. Let me help you.
8. It's OK. I need to get a new one anyway.
9. It was partly my fault.
10. I can be so clumsy sometimes.
11. It was an accident!
12. I'm really sorry.
13. Forget about it.
14. It just slipped from my hand.
15. Let me get a cloth.
16. Look where you're going!

2 | While you listen

🎧 **Listen to two conversations in which things go wrong. Which expressions in Activity 1 do you hear?**

Compare what you heard with a partner. What happened in each conversation?

3 | Comprehension

Now read what each person reported to a friend the following day. Some of the information is wrong. With a partner, correct the stories.

Report 1

I went with Jenny to this shop in Bond Street to look for a present for Chris and Anna's wedding. While we were in there, I was walking past this table and I caught a vase with my bag and it fell onto the floor and broke. It was awful because the vase cost £150. I offered to pay for it, but luckily, the shop assistant said they had insurance to cover things like that. They were really nice about it, which was lucky, because there's no way I can afford to give away £150 at the moment.

Report 2

It was really awful, because I spilt water all over her dress. It was this brand new white dress – really nice, really expensive, and there was this huge stain on it. It was so awful. I don't know how it happened. I guess I just caught the table when I was getting up and knocked her glass over. Anyway, as you can imagine, she was really annoyed. She just went home and I felt I had to offer to pay for a new dress. It cost me 200 euros!

Listen to the conversations again and check your corrections.

4 | Speaking

What would you do in these situations? Discuss the choices with a partner. Do you agree with your partner's decisions?

1. If I broke something in a shop:
   a. I'd pay for it.
   b. I'd refuse to pay for it.
   c. I'd leave the shop before an assistant saw me.
   d. I'd do something else. (say what)

2. If someone spilt wine on my new jumper:
   a. I'd get really angry.
   b. I'd ask them to pay to get it cleaned.
   c. I would lie and tell them not to worry because the jumper is quite old anyway.
   d. I'd do something else. (say what)

Have you ever done anything similar to the people you heard about? What happened?

Which of these statements describes you?

a. I'm a really clumsy person. I'm always breaking things and bumping into people.
b. I'm quite clumsy. I often knock things over.
c. I'm not very clumsy. I can't remember the last time I broke something.
d. I could never live with anyone who was really clumsy.

Do you know any good ways to get rid of different kinds of stains?

5 | Role play

With a partner, look at the expressions in Activity 1 again. Which expressions could you use in the situations below? Can you think of any other expressions you would use?

1. You break a large, expensive bowl in a shop.
2. You're having a cup of tea at a friend's house and you knock your cup over and spill tea all over their carpet.
3. You bump into someone and they drop their papers all over the wet floor.
4. You accidentally sit on someone's glasses.
5. You've borrowed a friend's electronic dictionary and you drop it and break it.
6. You bump into someone at a party and they spill red wine all over their shirt.

Role play the conversations with a different partner.

6 | Using grammar: *will*

We often use I'll + verb when we offer to do things.

Complete the offers with the verbs in the box.

call	carry	have	help	show

1. I'll .... you a taxi, if you like.
2. I'll .... you where to go.
3. I'll .... you move it, if you like.
4. I'll .... a look.
5. I'll .... that upstairs for you, if you like.

Now complete these offers with the verbs in the box.

ask	clean	pay	save	show

6. I'll .... you how to do it, if you like.
7. I'll .... that up for you.
8. I'll .... you a seat.
9. I'll .... for everything with my card.
10. I'll .... him when I see him, if you like.

🎧 **Listen and check your answers. Then listen again and practise saying the sentences. Remember that in normal spoken English, we pronounce I will as /aɪl/.**

Some languages use a present tense to make offers like those above. What tense does your language use?

▶ For more information on using *will*, see G31.

7 | Speaking

Discuss these questions with a partner.

1. When would you offer to do the things above and who to?
2. Which offers could you use in class?
3. Are any of these things something you would never offer to do? Why?

8 | Practice

Write three more offers you commonly make.

- I'll ....
- I'll ....
- I'll ....

Real English: Let me

We often use Let me instead of I'll to offer to do something.

Let me get a cloth.
Let me call you a taxi.
Let me help you.
Let me take your coat.
Let me pay.
Let me.

When would you say simply Let me?

9 | Further practice

Look at these sentences. When can you use Let me instead of I'll?

1. I'll be all right.
2. I'll answer it.
3. I'll show you round.
4. I'll be back in a minute.
5. I'll go and get your coat.
6. I'll take you to the airport.
7. I'll help you with that.
8. I'll probably go later.
9. I'll get these drinks. You paid last time.
10. I'll see you later then.
11. I'll go and get a seat.
12. I'll meet you outside the train station.

With a partner, practise the offers. For example:

A: Let me answer it.
B: OK. Thanks.

A: Let me take your bag.
B: It's OK, I can carry it.

A: Let me help you with that.
B: It's OK. I can manage, but thanks anyway.

I've got a problem with my landlord. • It'll sort itself out. • It's making a funny noise. • The batteries are dead. • Have you cancelled your cards? • It's such a pain! • I need to sort out what I'm going to take on holiday. • He jumped the queue! • They've just introduced a new law. • Can you save my place in the queue? • Is there a cashpoint near here? • Oh well, never mind. • I've just bought myself a food processor. • It's leaking. • I need to get it fixed. • It hasn't had any effect. • There's nothing wrong with it. • It's covered by the guarantee.

18 Problems

Conversation

1 | Speaking

Discuss with a partner what problems you could have with these things.

a bag	a mini-disc player
a cash card	a passport

Have you ever had any problems with any of these things? What happened? What did you do about it?

2 | Using vocabulary: sorting out problems

Match the sentence beginnings with the endings.

1. I've had my bag stolen,

2. I've lost my passport,

3. A cash machine has just eaten my credit card,

4. I bought this mini-disc player the other day, but it's not working properly,

5. I'm doing an English course at the moment, but they say I haven't paid,

6. I'm having some problems with this guy at work,

a. so I need to go to the Embassy and see if I can get a replacement.

b. so I need to go to my bank and see what the problem is and if I can get any money out.

c. so I need to go to the finance office and find out what's happened.

d. so I need to go and talk to my boss about it.

e. so I need to report it to the police and cancel all my credit cards.

f. so I need to take it back to the shop and see if I can get a new one.

3 | Problems on holiday

🎧 **Listen to this conversation between two people – Tony and Adriana. They are both on holiday. The first time you listen, find out what problem Tony's got and what he's going to do about it.**

Listen again and complete the conversation.

T: Hello. How are you?

A: Great. I've seen lots of interesting things. I'm really enjoying it.

T: Yes, it's a nice place, isn't it?

A: Yes, lovely. So what are you doing today?

T: Oh, (1) .... , so I need to go to the Embassy and see if I can get a temporary one.

A: Oh no! Where did you lose it?

T: I'm not sure. The last time I remember (2) .... was in the bank the other day.

A: Have you been back there to see if anyone's (3) .... ?

T: Yes, I went there yesterday, but they didn't have it.

A: (4) .... !

T: Yes, it's a real pain. Anyway, listen, (5) .... The Embassy opens at ten and I want to get there early.

A: Yes, sure. Well, good luck. I hope you (6) ....

T: Yes, thanks.

With a partner, have similar conversations about some of the problems you discussed in Activity 1. Begin by asking So what are you doing today?

Real English: It's a real pain

If something is **a pain**, it is annoying and it usually takes a long time to do.

I hate queuing! It's such a pain.
I've missed the last bus. What a pain! I'll have to walk now!

Can you think of anything else that is **a real pain**? Have you heard the expression which means the same – *It's a pain in the neck*?

---

4 | Using grammar: present perfect questions

You heard this extract in the conversation.

T: The last time I remember having it was in the bank the other day.

A: Have you been back there to see if anyone's handed it in?

We often ask a question in the present perfect when someone has a problem. It's often a way of making a suggestion.

Complete the questions with the present perfect form of the verbs.

1. A: I've got a bit of an upset stomach. I've had it for a couple of days now.
   B: .... to the doctor's about it? (be)

2. A: There's something wrong with this Walkman.
   B: .... changing the batteries? (try)

3. A: I had my bag stolen this morning when I was sitting in a café.
   B: Oh no! .... it to the police? (report)

4. A: I've got a terrible headache. I've had it all morning.
   B: Oh no! .... anything for it? (take)

5. A: I've lost my keys. You haven't seen them, have you?
   B: .... in the living room? I remember seeing them on the table last night. (look)

6. A: I lost my wallet last night. It had all my cards in and everything.
   B: .... them all? (ring up and cancel)

7. A: There's a guy in my class who is really annoying me. He keeps saying stupid things to me.
   B: .... to the teacher about it? (talk)

8. A: All the hotels I've rung are fully booked. Where are we going to stay?
   B: .... ringing the tourist office? They can often help. (try)

Now match the answers with the questions above.

a. Yes, I picked them up from there this morning, but now I've put them down again. ▢

b. Yes, I bought some new ones yesterday, but it's already playing slowly. ▢

c. Not yet, but I've made an appointment for this evening. ▢

d. Not yet, I'm going to go to the station this afternoon. ▢

e. That's a good idea. I'll do it now. Do you know where I can get their phone number? ▢

f. Yes, I had an aspirin earlier, but it hasn't had any effect. ▢

g. Yes, I did it this morning, as soon as I realised I didn't have them. ▢

h. No, but it's a good idea. Maybe I'll do it after the next class. ▢

5 | Grammar questions

Read the answers in Activity 4 and find examples of:

a. the past simple ....

b. going to + verb ....

c. will + verb ....

Discuss these questions with a partner.

1. Which tense is used in the 'Yes' answers?

2. Which form shows a decision you are making now? How do the answers start?

3. Which form shows a decision you made earlier? How do the answers start?

> For more information on using present perfect questions, see G32.

6 | Role play

Look at these first lines of conversations. With a partner, continue the conversations.

1. I left my bag in the classroom, but it's not there now.

2. I've had this cold for about two weeks!

3. There's some money missing from my account.

4. I'm finding the English course really difficult.

7 | Key word: *sort out*

When we find an answer to a problem, we sort the problem out. We also use sort out to mean organise or tidy things.

Find ten expressions with sort out. Mark the end of each expressions using /.

```
d i d y o u s o r t o u t y o u r p r o b l e m w i t h
t h e p a s s p o r t I n e e d t o s o r t o u t s o m e
p a p e r s I n e e d t o s o r t o u t m y t h i n g s t o
t a k e i t ' l l s o r t i t s e l f o u t I n e e d t o
s o r t o u t t h i s d i r t y w a s h i n g I ' m t r y i n g
t o s o r t o u t m y h o l i d a y h a v e y o u
s o r t e d o u t a v i s a h e n e e d s t o s o r t h i s
l i f e o u t I ' m j u s t g o i n g t o s o r t o u t t h e
h o u s e I s t i l l h a v e n ' t s o r t e d o u t t h a t
p r o b l e m w i t h m y c o m p u t e r
```

🎧 **Listen and practise the expressions.**

Now discuss these questions with a partner.

1. Have you got any problems that you need to sort out?

2. Do you need to sort out anything in your house?

3. Do you know anyone who needs to sort their life out? Why? What's wrong?

4. Are you good at sorting out computer problems?

Reading

1 Speaking

Discuss these questions.

1. Have you ever had to queue:
   a. to buy tickets?
   b. to buy food?
   c. to get into a movie?
   d. to get into a club?

2. What's the longest you've ever had to queue?

3. Have you ever pushed into a queue?

4. If you 'jump a queue', you go right to the front of it. Have you ever done that? How?

2 Before you read

You are going to read an article about queuing. These collocations are all in the article. Think about each one and its connection to queuing. Compare your ideas with a partner.

> catch my bus into town
>
> get some money out of the cashpoint
>
> introduce a new law
>
> join a queue
>
> key in your personal identity number
>
> make the right decision
>
> pay some cheques into your account
>
> save my place in the queue

3 While you read

∩ **Now read the article and see if your ideas were right.**

The queue The queue **The queue**

The queue The queue

Yesterday I went to the bank to get some money out of the cashpoint. There are two machines next to the bus stop where I catch my bus into town. I got to the bank and there were two people waiting at each machine, so I had to decide which queue to join. I was worried because I knew the bus could come at any moment, so I wanted to join the faster queue. I joined one with an old lady and a young man in front of me.

The young guy finished quickly and we moved forward. I started thinking I'd made the right decision. The old lady then started looking in her bag for her purse. As the queue next to me moved forward, I thought about changing, but I couldn't see a bus coming and anyway, just at that moment, a couple arrived and started queuing up for the other machine. 'Never mind,' I thought. 'I only have to wait for one person and the old lady has found her purse.' Unfortunately, though, she had also found several cheques, which she wanted to pay into her account. She put her card in and keyed in her PIN number. The machine seemed very slow and I suddenly noticed a bus at the end of the road. The old lady took the envelope and put her cheques in, but then she dropped one. I picked it up for her and put it in the machine.

I could see the bus coming to the stop before mine. The old lady finally finished! 'I'm going to make it,' I said to myself. I keyed in my number and asked for fifty pounds. I waited and a message came up: 'Sorry. This machine is temporarily unable to dispense money.' I wanted to scream! The bus was already leaving the stop before mine. I looked over at the three people waiting in the other queue and asked if I could jump in ahead of them. 'My bus is coming,' I tried to explain. 'I need the money to get the bus.' They just looked at me as if I was an alien. 'No, you'll have to wait like everyone else,' one of them replied. I joined the end of the queue. My bus left without me!

In this kind of situation, there should be a law that makes everyone form just one queue. This is what happens in the post office and it works well. Everyone is treated fairly. Until that law is introduced, though, the world will continue to be divided into two groups: the people like me, who always choose the wrong queue, wait for ages and never get what they want, and the people who never have any problems in life. They just jump queues, because they know someone on the door of a club or they have a friend who is standing near the front or because they're just beautiful and some stupid man lets them push in, because he thinks they like him (but they don't!).

Queuing, however, isn't always a problem. I met one of my best friends in a queue. I was 14 and my favourite band Take That were doing a tour. I started queuing for tickets the night before they came on sale. There were lots of us there and the girl sitting next to me was called Rachel. She was really nice. She shared her food and drink with me. She saved my place in the queue when I had to go to the toilet and she was just good fun. We've been friends ever since.

4 | After you read

Work with a new partner. Tell each other how much of the article you guessed correctly.

Look back at the expressions in Activity 2. Can you remember the order in which they were mentioned in the article?

5 | Word check

Complete the sentences with words from the text. Try not to look back at the text.

1. I was waiting for ages and I'd decided to go without him, but just at .... moment, he arrived.
2. Oh well, never .... There's nothing you can do about it.
3. I dropped my bag, but this nice man behind me .... it up for me.
4. They looked at me as if I was an .... I felt awful!
5. It's nice, because everyone is treated .... No-one gets treated better than anyone else.
6. You have to start queuing for tickets the night before they come on .... if you want to make sure you get one.

Now look back at the text and check your answers.

6 | Speaking

The writer said that the world is 'divided into two groups'. Can you remember what these two groups were? Which of these two groups do you think YOU are part of? Why?

Look at these ways in which the world can be divided into two groups. Do you agree with these divisions? Which groups is it better to be in? Why? Which groups are you in?

1. Those who are rich and those who are poor.
2. People who like cats and people who like dogs.
3. People who are in love and people who aren't.
4. Car owners and cyclists.
5. People who complain and people who don't.
6. People who give and people who take.
7. People who work for the state and people who don't.
8. People who like spending money and people who don't.

Write down two more divisions. Share your ideas with other people in the class.

7 | Using grammar: *must*

When we are late for something and we need to explain to the person we are talking to that we have to leave, we often say Listen, I must go and then explain why. For example:

• Listen, I must go. The Embassy opens at ten and I want to get there early.

Match the sentence beginnings with the endings to make excuses.

1. Listen, I must go or I'll be
2. Listen, I must go or I'll miss
3. Listen, I must go or my boyfriend will start
4. Listen, I must go. My girlfriend is cooking
5. Listen, I must go. I'm meeting
6. Listen, I must go. There's a film
7. Listen, I must go. I've got a dentist's
8. Listen, I must go. I've got lots of work

a. dinner for me tonight.
b. to worry.
c. to do tonight.
d. on TV I'd like to watch.
e. late.
f. my train.
g. a friend of mine at six.
h. appointment in half an hour.

Which of the above excuses do you use most often?

> For more information on using *must*, see G33.

8 | Pronunciation: *must*

🎧 **Practise saying the sentences in Activity 7. Notice that we don't pronounce the 't' of must.**

9 | Practice

Have conversations with some other students. Begin like this:

• Hi, how are you? I haven't seen you for ages.

You should both be friendly, but your partner should try to end the conversation as quickly as they can, using one of the sentences in Activity 7 – or a different excuse!

A

B

C

D

E

F

Listening

1 Using vocabulary: machines and technology

Match the words with the photos.

1. laptop ☐
2. microwave ☐
3. DVD player ☐
4. camcorder ☐
5. washing machine ☐
6. palmtop ☐
7. dishwasher ☐
8. Walkman ☐

Complete the sentences with the words above.

1. A: Thanks. That was delicious. Let me wash up these plates for you.
   B: No, it's OK. We've got a ....
   Just put everything in there.

2. These clothes still look dirty. I think we need to get a new .... !

3. Are you hungry? There's some food from yesterday in the fridge and I could just put it in the .... and heat it up for you, if you want.

4. My bag got stolen on the train yesterday. I'm really annoyed because it had my .... and my favourite CD in it. It's going to cost me about £100 to replace!

5. A: So did you get anything nice for your birthday?
   B: Ah, yes. My parents gave me this really nice .... It was really small and light. It wasn't much bigger than my mobile. It sent e-mails and everything, but I left it at work on Monday and I lost it!

6. Now I'm doing all this travelling I really need to get a .... , so I can do some work on the train and plane.

7. My dad gave me a .... for my birthday. It was kind of him, but now it means I'll have to buy all the films I have on video again!

8. A: Are you going to Jack and Diane's wedding?
   B: Yes, of course. They've asked me to bring my .... and film everything. I'm really looking forward to it.

G

H

2 | Speaking

Discuss these questions with a partner.

1. How many of the things in the photos do you have?
2. How long have you had them?
3. Which make have you got?
4. Have you ever had any problems with any of them? What happened?

3 | While you listen

🎧 **Listen to three conversations about problems with different machines. As you listen, decide which of the things in the photos are being discussed.**

Compare your ideas with a partner. Can you remember what the problem was in each conversation? Listen again if you need to.

4 | Using vocabulary: problems with machines

Complete the sentences with the words in the box.

a funny noise	leaking somewhere
crashing	working properly
it fixed	

1. There's something wrong with the camcorder. It's not ....
2. There's something wrong with the washing machine. It's making ....
3. There's something wrong with my computer. It keeps ....
4. There's something wrong with the engine. I think the oil is ....
5. The photocopier has broken down again. They really need to get ....

Now discuss these questions with a partner.

1. Can you think of three things you turn on and off?
2. Can you think of two things you can turn up and down?
3. Can you think of three things that can leak?
4. Can you think of three things that make a funny noise when there's something wrong with them?
5. Can you think of two things that can be out of order?
6. Can you think of three things that run on batteries?

5 | Role play

Who do you think says these things – someone who works in a shop (S) or the customer (C)?

1. Have you still got your receipt?
2. Can I leave it with you?
3. I'll leave it. It'll be cheaper to buy a new one.
4. It isn't working properly.
5. I can't promise anything.
6. How long have you had it?
7. We'll see what we can do.
8. How much do you think it'll cost?
9. Don't worry. It's still covered by the guarantee.
10. It should be ready by the weekend.

Now translate the questions and sentences into your own language. Use a dictionary if you need to – or ask your teacher. Compare your ideas with a partner who speaks the same language as you.

Work in pairs.

Student A: Choose one of the things in the photos. You have a problem with the thing you have chosen, so you have taken it to the shop to get it fixed. You will need to decide what the problem is. Ask your teacher for help if you need to.

Student B: You work in a shop which sells electrical goods.

Role play the conversation in the shop. Try to use some of the sentences and questions above. Begin like this:

A: Hi. I wonder if you can help me with this.

B: What's the problem with it?

6 | Using vocabulary: *I couldn't live without it*

How important to you are the things in the box?

calculator	CD player
hair dryer	digital camera
mobile	electronic personal organiser
printer	electric razor
scanner	food processor

Compare your ideas with some other students. Use these expressions.

*   I couldn't live without my ... . I use it all the time.
*   I could live without my ... quite easily. I don't use it very much.
*   I don't even have a ... .
*   I don't have a ... , but I'd like one.

Who likes technology the most? Who likes it the least?

19 Money

Have you got that £10 you owe me? • I'll pay you back tomorrow, I promise. • Do you want me to lend you some? • Would you mind? • It's a waste of time. • I'm going to take out a loan. • I can't remember my new PIN number. • Can I change this into dollars, please? • I'd like to pay this into my account, please. • They charge £4 commission. • I can't afford it. • Do you get any sick pay? • She's £500 in debt. • She's very well off. • Have you got that money you owe me? • It's junk mail. Just throw it in the bin. • It cost a fortune.

Conversation

1 | Speaking

Check the words in green in a dictionary or with your teacher. Then work in groups and ask each other the questions.

1. Do you know anyone who is really generous or really mean?

2. Have you ever had to borrow money from someone? Why?

3. When was the last time you lent money to someone? Why? Did they pay you back?

4. Are you good at saving money? Are you saving up to do anything at the moment?

Real English: borrow / lend

Remember that you borrow money from somebody, but lend money to people. If you borrow money, make sure you pay it back. It's horrible when you owe people money.

Could I borrow ten euros from you? I'll pay you back on Friday, I promise.

A: *Have you got that money you owe me?*
B: *Oh, sorry. I forgot.*
A: *That's the last time I ever lend you anything!*

---

2 | Borrowing money

🎧 **Listen to this conversation between two friends – Bob and Tim. The first time you listen, find out why Tim needs to borrow some money. Don't look at the conversation while you listen.**

Listen again and complete the conversation.

B: Have you got time (1) .... ?

T: Yes, OK. Where do you want to go?

B: (2) .... that place on the corner?

T: Yes, fine. Oh no!

B: What's the (3) .... ?

T: Oh, I've just realised I've left my wallet at home.

B: Don't worry. It's OK. (4) .... the coffee.

T: Yes, thanks, but it's not just that. I'm meeting someone at two and I'll have to go back home and get it. I can't spend the whole day without any money.

B: Well, do you want me to (5) .... ?

T: Would you mind?

B: No, (6) .... How much do you need? Is 30 euros (7) .... ?

T: That'd be great, if you can.

B: Yes, sure. No problem. I'll just have to go to (8) .... , though. Do you want to meet me in the café? I'll be there in a minute.

T: OK.

Five minutes later

B: There (9) ....

T: Great. That's brilliant. I'll pay you back next week, when I see you.

B: Yes, fine. There's (10) .... Have you ordered?

T: No, I was waiting for you to get here. I wasn't sure how you like your coffee.

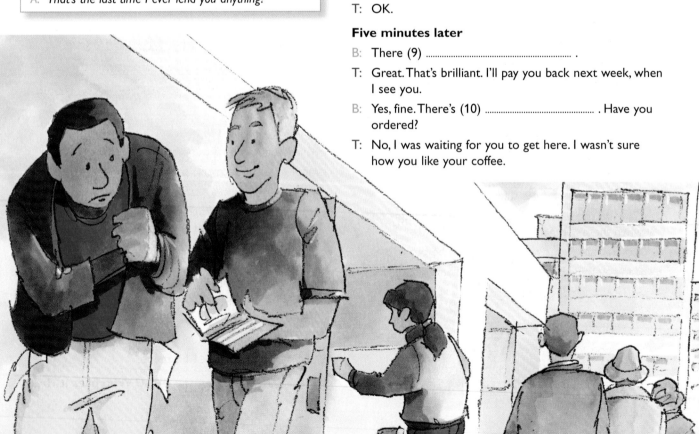

3 | Pronunciation

We usually stress the most important words in each sentence: the nouns and main verbs – the words which carry most of the meaning. We usually don't stress the other words: the pronouns, prepositions, auxiliary verbs – the grammatical words. For example:

A: Have you got TIME for a COFFEE?

B: Yes, OK. WHERE do you WANT to GO?

With a partner, decide which words in the conversation above should be stressed.

Listen to the conversation again and check your answers.

Now practise reading the conversation with a partner. Look at the tapescript if you need to. The stressed words are in CAPITAL LETTERS.

4 | Vocabulary: *time* and *money*

In the conversation, Tim said: 'I can't spend the whole day without any money.' In English, you can use the word spend to talk about using money and passing time. We use the word waste to say that we use our time or money badly.

Complete the sentences with money or time.

1. My dad's quite mean. He doesn't spend much .... on me.

2. My parents didn't spend much .... with me when I was younger. They were too busy.

3. My grandparents are quite generous. They always buy me nice presents and give me .... when they see me.

4. I don't spend much .... studying outside class.

5. I spend most of my free .... watching TV.

6. I spend a lot of .... on clothes.

7. I think buying CDs and music is a waste of ....

8. I think studying history or Latin is a waste of .... It's better to spend the .... studying computing or business, or something like that.

9. I spent all Sunday morning in bed. I got up just in .... for lunch.

10. I've spent £300 since last week! I don't know where all my .... goes.

Compare your answers with a partner. Are any of the sentences above true for you? If not, can you change the sentences so that they are true? For example:

*   My dad's quite generous.

*   I spend most of my free time playing sport.

*   I don't spend much money on clothes.

5 | Using grammar: making and responding to offers

Put the sentences in order and make conversations. The first in each has been done for you.

Conversation 1

a. No, of course not. What would you like in it? Is cheese OK?

b. Would you mind?

c. Do you want me to make you a sandwich?

d. That's OK.

e. I'm really hungry.

f. That'd be great, thanks.

1. [e] 2. [ ] 3. [ ] 4. [ ] 5. [ ] 6. [ ]

Conversation 2

a. Well, that'd be great. Thanks.

b. Would you mind?

c. I've got to go, or I'll miss my train.

d. That's OK. I'll just go and get my keys.

e. Do you want me to drive you?

f. No, of course not. I've got to go near there anyway.

1. [c] 2. [ ] 3. [ ] 4. [ ] 5. [ ] 6. [ ]

6 | Practice

Complete the conversations with the offers you would make.

1. A: It's a bit cold in here.
    B: Do you want me to .... ?

2. A: This bag's really heavy.
    B: Do you want me to .... ?

3. A: The cash machine's not working.
    B: Do you want me to .... ?

4. A: I want to go shopping, but I have to stay with the baby.
    B: Do you want me to .... ?

5. A: I don't know where to go.
    B: Do you want me to .... ?

6. A: I hate walking home in the dark.
    B: Do you want me to .... ?

With a partner, have conversations similar to that in Activity 2. Continue the conversation for as long as you can.

> ▶ For more information on how to make and respond to offers, see G34.

Reading

1 | Vocabulary: banks

Complete the sentences with the words in the box.

account	a new account	my credit card
a loan	banks	

1. I'd like to open ....
2. I don't have a bank ....
3. I'm thinking of changing ....
4. I'd like to take out ....
5. I need to cancel ....

Now complete these sentences with the words in the box.

apply for	change	make	pay	transfer

6. I'd like to .... a complaint.
7. I'd like to .... my PIN number.
8. I'd like to .... some money from my account in Japan to my account here.
9. I'd like to .... some money into my account.
10. I'd like to .... a credit card.

With a partner, discuss why the person wants to do these things. For example:

A: I'd like to take out a loan.

B: Maybe he wants to buy a car or perhaps he wants to go and study abroad for a year.

2 | While you read

You are going to read an article called 'Eight things I hate about banks'. Before you read, check you understand the expressions in the box.

be served	fill in a form
charge commission	get a cheque cashed
charge interest	owe someone five dollars

∩ **As you read, mark the text with:**

✓ where you agree with it.

✗ where you disagree.

? where you don't exactly understand.

Eight things I hate about

1 They're rich

Maybe I'm just jealous, but I think banks are too rich. The big banks in Britain made over £15 billion last year. If you ask me, they shouldn't be allowed to make so much money.

2 They're mean

One reason they make so much money is that, like all rich people, they are mean! That's why they give us about 0.2% interest when WE have money in the bank, but when we borrow money from THEM, they charge us anything from 8% to 25% interest. It's terrible!

3 Bank charges

Imagine you borrowed my car and I said, 'Listen, can you bring it back by six o'clock, because I need to go out somewhere?' You bring the car back at 6.01 and I ask for £40, because you brought it back late. The following day, I write you a letter telling you that you gave me £40. I then also charge you another £15 because I had to send you a letter. On top of that, I ask for another £5, because my car is less valuable now, because you drove it for two hours. I then phone you to say you can borrow my car whenever you like. It doesn't sound fair, does it? But that's the kind of thing banks do if you spend £1 more than you should. The only difference is, they don't ask you for the money, they just take it from your account!

4 Changing banks

It's very difficult to change banks. In fact, it's more difficult than getting divorced! You have to write to so many people to tell them you've changed banks, you get bored and you stop. And anyway, you know it's a waste of time, because (unlike a new wife or husband!) your new bank will be exactly the same as your old one!

banks

5 Junk mail

Every day I receive letters from different banks asking me if I'd like to take out a loan or get a new credit card. I always throw these letters in the bin. I wish the banks would stop sending me them. It's such a waste of paper.

6 They're bad for poor countries

One way banks make their money is by charging a lot of interest to poor countries for loans they have made to their governments. A lot of these countries now spend so much on the interest to the banks, they can't afford to spend money on education, health and other basic services.

7 Banks abroad

I often hope that when I go abroad, banks will be better than they are here. When I go to change money, there are almost no customers in the bank. However, I still have to wait for hours to be served. Then you have to fill in a form, have proof of ID and sign your name about six times – just to change £50. Then they charge you 3% commission for the service!

8 I need them!

Perhaps the thing I hate most about banks is the fact that I need one! They're like men – you can't live with them, but you can't live without them! For a while, I tried to live without having a bank account, but it was impossible. Everything just took a very long time. It was difficult to get paid, it took a long time to pay bills, and if people gave me cheques, I had to pay the bank to get them cashed. And I worried about having lots of cash in the house and carrying it around in the street. I couldn't do it, and in the end, I opened a new account. I was lucky, because millions of people can't open an account. The bank won't let them, because they don't have enough money – which is another reason why I hate banks!

3 | Comprehension

With a partner, compare which parts of the text you have marked ✓, ✗ and ? Explain your reasons. For example:

- I don't agree that banks are too rich. In my country, they don't make much money.
- I agree they are mean. I only get one per cent interest in my bank.
- I don't understand this bit about the car and bank charges.

Did you agree with each other?

4 | Role play

Complete the conversation with the words in the box.

cash	change	fill in	ID	sign

A: Yes. How can I help you?

B: I'd like to .... some money.

A: Certainly. How much?

B: 700 euros in ....

A: OK. Have you got any proof of .... , like a passport or driver's licence?

B: No, sorry.

A: Well, in that case, I need you to .... this form.

B: OK. Have you got a pen?

A: Can you just .... here at the bottom?

B: Oh right.

A: That's fine. Here's your money, and your receipt.

Practise the conversation with a partner. Then have other conversations between a bank employee and customer. Answer the question How can I help you? with the sentences in Activity 1.

Listening

1 While you listen

Look at the people in the photos and decide what money problems they could have.

1 a 16-year-old student

2 an office worker

3 a shopaholic

4 a foreigner in another country

⋒ Now listen to four conversations and see how many of your ideas the speakers mention.

Make sentences about the people in the photos.

1. He can't afford to ... because ... .
2. He can't afford to ... because ... .
3. Jenny can't afford to ... because ... .
4. He can't afford to ... because ... .

2 Word check

Who said these words? Complete the expressions.

1. .... unfair.
2. .... a supermarket
3. I cycle ....
4. take time off work .... interviews
5. some .... designer ....
6. She's .... debt.
7. A snack like this would only .... or seven.
8. It's .... similar ....

Listen again and check your answers – or read the tapescript.

3 Speaking

Discuss these questions with a partner.

1. Which of the speakers do you feel sorry for? Why? Have you ever had any similar problems?
2. Did you use to get pocket money when you were younger? How much? Was it enough?
3. Did you ever have to work part-time when you were growing up?

4 Using grammar: comparing prices

In the fourth conversation, one speaker said: 'everything's cheaper in my country than it is here'. Match the comparisons with the prices.

1. Beer is much cheaper in the north than it is here. ☐
2. Cigarettes are much cheaper in Indonesia than they are here. ☐
3. Jeans are much cheaper in America than they are here. ☐
4. Taxis are much cheaper in Bangkok than they are here. ☐
5. Watching football is much cheaper in Russia than it is here. ☐
6. Bread is much cheaper in Scotland than it is here. ☐
7. Getting your hair cut is much cheaper in Korea than it is here. ☐
8. Eating out is much cheaper in Iran than it is here. ☐

a. I mean, a pint only costs about £2 or so in Manchester.
b. I mean, tickets for a match there only cost about 60p.
c. I mean, a pair of Levis there only costs about £30.
d. I mean, a half-hour ride there only costs about £2.
e. I mean, a loaf there only costs 60p or so.
f. I mean, an average meal there only costs £4 per person!
g. I mean, a wash and cut there only costs around £10!
h. I mean, a packet there only costs about 30 or 40p.

5 | Practice

Have you ever been anywhere that was much cheaper than your home town? Tell a partner about this place and give examples of what was cheaper. Use these expressions.

1. ... is much cheaper in ... than it is here.
   I mean, ... there only costs about ... .

2. ... are much cheaper in ... than they are here.
   I mean, ... there only cost about ... .

Which of the words in the box can you use in sentence 1 above? Which can you use in sentence 2?

chocolate	DVDs	paper	shoes
clothes	hotels	rice	toothpaste

Now tell your partner about a place that was much more expensive than your home town.

6 | Key word: *pay*

Translate these expressions into your language. DON'T use a dictionary. Ask your teacher if you need help. Compare your ideas with a partner who speaks the same language as you.

1. How shall we pay the bill?
2. Do I get a discount if I pay cash?
3. I paid 300 to get my car repaired.
4. I'll pay you back tomorrow.
5. Can I pay in dollars?
6. I've got to pay my bill this week.
7. I'd like to pay this into my account, please.
8. How much did you pay for it?
9. How are you paying?
10. Do you get any sick pay where you work?
11. I don't get paid until the end of the month.
12. What are we doing now? I wasn't paying attention.

Now close your book. Your partner will say the translations. Can you remember the expressions in English?

7 | Practice

Complete the conversations with ONE word in each space. Can you do this without looking at the sentences in Activity 6?

1. A: Can I borrow £10? I'll pay you .... tomorrow, I promise.
   B: Yes, of course. There you are. What happened to all the money you're getting with your new job?
   A: Oh, I had to pay £300 to get my car .... the other day and I don't .... paid until the 28th.

2. A: How .... we pay the bill?
   B: Do you want to just split it?
   A: Yes, OK. That sounds good.

3. A: Wow! I like that jacket. Is it new?
   B: Yes, I got it last week.
   A: How .... did you pay for it? Was it expensive?
   B: No, it was OK, actually. I only paid £75.

4. A: Hi, I'd like to pay this cheque .... my .... , please.
   B: Certainly, sir. Is that all?
   A: Yes, that's it, thanks.

5. A: How much is that?
   B: £99.99, please. .... are you paying?
   A: Do I get a .... if I pay .... ?
   B: No, I'm afraid not.
   A: Oh right. Well, in that case, I'll pay by credit card, if that's all right.

8 | Speaking

Discuss these questions with a partner.

1. What's the best thing you've bought this year? How much did you pay for it?
2. How do you usually pay bills?
3. What day do you get paid?
4. What was the last thing you had to pay to get repaired? How much did you pay?
5. Have any teachers ever told you to pay attention? In which classes? What were you doing?

The economy is in a mess. • Unemployment is very low. • The cost of living's really high there. • The average wage is about £300 a week. • The quality of life is great. • Inflation's gone down this year. • Racism is getting worse. • She gives a lot of money to charity. • They buy a lot of designer clothes. • My brother's a vegetarian. • Do you belong to a trade union? • The factory closed down last year. • Three hundred workers lost their jobs. • She looks great for her age. • He's going deaf. • Young people today! • I never used to!

Conversation

1 | Using grammar: questions with *how long*

Complete the answers with for, since and till.

1. A: How long have you been here?
   B: .... Sunday.

2. A: How long are you going to stay?
   B: .... July.

3. A: How long are you going to stay?
   B: .... another three days.

4. A: How long have you been studying English?
   B: .... about three years now.

5. A: How long are you going to study English?
   B: .... I'm fluent.

6. A: How long have you been living here?
   B: .... I was a child.

Spend two minutes trying to memorise the questions.

Close your book. Your partner will read out the answers. Can you remember the questions?

> For more information on using questions with *how long*, see G35.

Real English: till

In spoken English, it is more normal to say till. In written English, people usually use until. The two words mean exactly the same thing.

2 | Talking about life in your country

🎧 **Listen to this conversation between two people – Martin and Alex. They meet while they are abroad. The first time you listen, find out why they're abroad and how long they're going to stay. Don't look at the conversation while you listen.**

Listen again and complete the conversation.

M: What do you do back home?

A: Well, I was working in a car factory, but it (1) .... That's why I'm here, really. I got some money when I lost my job and I decided to go travelling (2) .... to think about what to do next.

M: And what are you going to do?

A: I still haven't decided. The economy's in (3) .... at the moment. There's a lot of unemployment and people aren't spending much money, so it's going to be difficult to find a new job. I might try to retrain and do (4) ....

M: Have you got any idea what you want to do?

A: Not really. Maybe something with computers. I might try to find a job abroad for a while before I do that. What about your country? Is it easy to find work there?

M: Yes. A few years ago it was quite bad, but the economy's (5) .... at the moment. I think unemployment is about four per cent, so finding a job isn't really a problem. The problem is (6) .... Prices have gone up a lot over the last few years. Everything is more expensive, so the money you earn goes really quickly.

A: Right.

M: Sometimes I think I should move to somewhere like here. I'm sure people don't get paid very much, but the cost of living is so low and there's a better (7) .... People don't work as hard; life is more relaxed; the food's great; the weather's great; it's just very nice.

A: Yes, maybe, but don't forget that you are on holiday. Maybe it's (8) .... for the people who live here.

M: No, maybe not.

A: So anyway, how long are you going to stay here?

M: Just till Friday. I have to get back to work. What about you? How long are you staying?

A: Till I get bored or I (9) .... money. I don't have any plans.

3 | Using vocabulary: the economy

Match the sentences with the summary statements.

1. Almost everyone has a job.
2. Prices are going up very slowly at the moment.
3. The average wage is around £500 a week. Some people earn a lot more and some earn a lot less.
4. I have to give a lot of the money I earn to the government.
5. Everything is very expensive – even basic things like food and rent.
6. When I go abroad, I can buy lots of things with the money from my country.
7. The weather is nice, the people are nice. There's not much crime. It's near the beach. You don't have to work long hours.
8. Unemployment is going up, inflation's going up, factories are closing down and companies are going out of business.

a. Inflation is very low.
b. The cost of living is very high.
c. Unemployment is very low.
d. The quality of life is very good.
e. The economy is in a mess.
f. Tax is very high.
g. Most people's salaries are very good.
h. Our currency is very strong.

4 | Pronunciation: *of*

We often use the weak form /ə/ or /əv/. It is usually linked to the word before it. For example:

lots ‿ of things

⌂ **Listen and practise these expressions.**

the quality of life	lots of problems
out of business	the cost of living
a lot of money	a bit of a mess

5 | Practice

With a partner, rewrite the sentences and summary statements in Activity 3 so that they have the opposite meaning. For example:

1. A lot of people don't have a job. Unemployment is very high.

Check your answers with another pair.

Spend two minutes trying to memorise the summary statements – both those in Activity 3 and the opposites above.

Close your book. Your partner will read out the sentences. Can you remember the summary statements?

6 | Further practice

Use the words from Activity 3 to talk about your country and the countries next to yours. For example:

- The average wage in my country is about £300 a week.
- The economy in Italy is doing quite well.

Now discuss these questions with a partner.

1. Are there areas or cities in your country where the economy is doing better or worse? In what way?
2. Is the quality of life better in some areas?

7 | Using grammar: describing changes

We can use the present continuous and the present perfect to describe changes. The present continuous (be + -ing) shows the change is not finished. The present perfect (have + past participle) shows the change happened before now:

- The economy's doing quite well at the moment.
- Prices have gone up a lot over the last few years.
- The cost of living has gone down since the election.

We often use at the moment with the present continuous and over the last / past few years and since with the present perfect.

Complete the sentences with the present continuous or the present perfect form of the verbs.

1. Unemployment .... at the moment. (fall)
2. Inflation .... at the moment. (go up)
3. Children's behaviour .... worse and worse since my parents were children. (get)
4. Crime .... worse and worse at the moment. (get)
5. The world .... a more dangerous place since September 11th. (become)
6. Racism .... worse over the past few years. (get)
7. My English .... since I started this course. (improve)
8. I .... a lot at the moment. (work)
9. I .... a lot over the last ten years. (change)
10. I .... very busy over the last few weeks. (be)

Which of the sentences are true for you and your country? Can you change the other sentences to make them true?

> For more information on how to describe changes, see G36.

Reading

1 | Speaking

Look at the photos. Decide which of them was taken in:

1. the 1970s
2. the 1980s
3. the 1990s

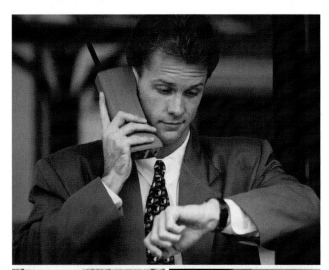

What do you think life was like for the men in the photos? Think about: work, free time, food, holidays, attitudes to women, etc.

2 | Before you read

You are going to read an article about what life was like for British men during the last thirty years of the 20th century. Before you read, check you understand the words in the box. Ask your teacher for help if you need to.

charity	hi-tech toys	the environment
designer clothes	miner	trade unions
going on strike	sushi	vegetarian

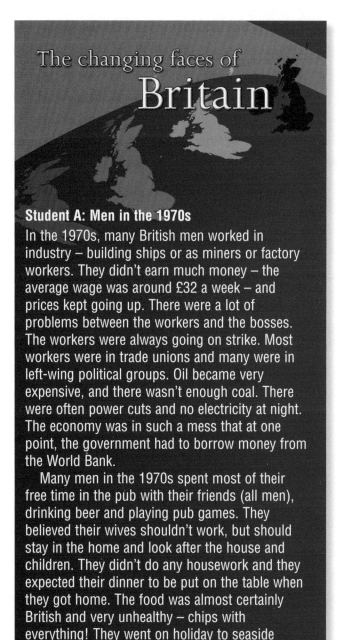

The changing faces of Britain

Student A: Men in the 1970s

In the 1970s, many British men worked in industry – building ships or as miners or factory workers. They didn't earn much money – the average wage was around £32 a week – and prices kept going up. There were a lot of problems between the workers and the bosses. The workers were always going on strike. Most workers were in trade unions and many were in left-wing political groups. Oil became very expensive, and there wasn't enough coal. There were often power cuts and no electricity at night. The economy was in such a mess that at one point, the government had to borrow money from the World Bank.

Many men in the 1970s spent most of their free time in the pub with their friends (all men), drinking beer and playing pub games. They believed their wives shouldn't work, but should stay in the home and look after the house and children. They didn't do any housework and they expected their dinner to be put on the table when they got home. The food was almost certainly British and very unhealthy – chips with everything! They went on holiday to seaside towns in Britain and spent their Saturdays watching football. They didn't understand their children, who had long hair and listened to rock music.

3 | While you read

Work in groups of three. You are each going to read about a different decade. One of you should read Text A; one of you should read Text B; one of you should read Text C.

Answer these questions.

1. What kind of job did men do?
2. How did they spend their free time?
3. What kind of food did they eat?
4. What kind of music did they listen to?
5. How did they feel about women?
6. Where did they go on holiday?
7. Were they interested in politics at all?

Student B: Men in the 1980s

In the 1980s, lots of people who worked in industry lost their jobs. Almost half the mines in Britain were closed down. Unemployment was very high. Because of this, many British men now wanted to work in business or in the stock market. Their main interest was making as much money as they could, as quickly as possible so that they could retire before they were 40. These men didn't want to belong to a trade union and they didn't like workers who went on strike. These 1980s men voted for Mrs. Thatcher and her Conservative government, and they believed that the individual was more important than society.

These men also wanted to show everyone how successful they were. They wore suits to work and in their free time they liked to wear expensive designer clothes made by Armani or Gucci. They loved new technology and spent a lot on new hi-tech toys like Walkmans, CD players and mobile phones.

Many men in the 1980s worked hard and played hard. They went on holiday to Spain, Greece and the Caribbean. They waited until much later before getting married. They had plenty of girlfriends and liked to meet them in expensive wine bars or Japanese sushi restaurants. In the little spare time they had, they played squash or golf, and then they went home and listened to pop music by Phil Collins and Dire Straits.

Student C: Men in the 1990s

At the beginning of the 1990s, men were often described as 'New Men'. Some of them were vegetarian, and they worried about the environment and people who were dying in other countries. They worked with people or for a charity. They wanted to be comfortable, but money wasn't the most important thing and they believed that Big Business didn't care for people. They had lots of female friends as well as male friends, but their best friends were their 'partners'. New Men preferred the word 'partner' to 'wife' because they didn't want to get married. The partners were more than 'girlfriends' because they lived together and were in serious relationships. Many men in the 1990s cooked foreign food for dinner (no meat, of course!) and helped with the ironing. When their babies woke up in the night, they got up and gave them bottles of milk.

In their free time New Men went out to Indian or Thai restaurants or the cinema. They listened to World music with their friends. They talked about their feelings, politics and their travel plans. They went travelling to a lot to places in Asia and South America, where there weren't too many tourists and there were interesting new cultures for them to explore.

4 After you read

Check your answers with someone who read the same text as you.

Now ask the other two people in your group the questions about the texts they read. Then discuss these questions.

1. Is there anything in the texts you found surprising or hard to believe? Why?
2. Have any of the things you talked about happened in your country? When?
3. What do you think life was like for women in the 1970s / 1980s / 1990s?

5 Word check

Complete the sentences with the words in the box. The words are all in the texts.

environment	industry	politics	retire	strike
factories	job	relationship	sacked	voted

1. He lost his .... five years ago and he has been unemployed since then.
2. My mum is 59, so she's going to .... next year.
3. You'll have to get a taxi to the airport because the bus drivers are on .... at the moment. They want more money.
4. She's done very well. She's now a very .... businesswoman.
5. I'm divorced now, but I'm lucky because I still have a good .... with my ex-wife.
6. It's a very industrial area. There are lots of .... round there making clothes and shoes.
7. I .... for the Labour Party in the last election, but I don't think I will next time.
8. I'm not interested in .... because politicians aren't interested in people like me!
9. They're building houses and hotels all along the coast. It's destroying the ....
10. The economy is doing quite well, but the car .... is still in a bit of a mess. A lot of workers have lost their jobs over the past few months.

6 Speaking

Discuss these questions with a partner.

1. Do workers in your country go on strike very often? When was the last big strike?
2. Do you know anyone who has ever lost their job? What happened?
3. Did you vote in the last election?
4. Are there any parts of your country where they are destroying the environment?

Listening

1 | Using vocabulary: talking about old and young people

Who are the oldest / youngest members of your family? What are they like?

Decide which six sentences are about teenagers (T) and which are about elderly people (E). The first one has been done for you.

1. Her eyes are very bad now. She's almost blind. `E`
2. She's going a bit deaf. You really have to shout when you talk to her.
3. She's doing very well at school.
4. She never does what she's told.
5. She goes out all the time.
6. She uses a stick.
7. He looks great for his age.
8. She's very mature for her age.
9. He's very tall for his age.
10. She's still very independent. She still does everything for herself.
11. She's very sensible.
12. He's losing his memory.

Do any of the sentences describe anyone you know? Tell a partner as much about the people as you can.

2 | Before you listen

You are going to listen to a conversation between two elderly ladies – Doris and Marge. They are chatting to each other as they take a bus. Before you listen, work with a partner and think of six things elderly people often say about young people.

Do you think any of the things elderly people say are true?

3 | While you listen

🎧 Listen to the conversation and decide if Doris and Marge talk about any of the things you thought of. Note down any other things they say about young people.

4 | Comprehension check

Decide if these sentences are true (T) or false (F).

1. There were two young people kissing at the bus stop. T / F
2. The young people at the bus stop swore at Doris and Marge. T / F
3. Marge can't walk very well. T / F
4. Marge has a pet. T / F
5. The young man in the supermarket queue let Marge go first. T / F
6. Doris sees two young girls with very short hair on the bus. T / F

Now listen to the conversation again and check your answers.

5 | Speaking

Discuss these questions with a partner.

1. Which of the sentences below best describes how you feel about Doris and Marge?
   a. I feel really sorry for them. It must be horrible for them.
   b. I can understand how they feel, but they shouldn't complain so much about things.
   c. I don't know what they're complaining about! They should just keep quiet and mind their own business!

2. Have you ever seen any young people being rude to older people? What happened?

3. Do you know any elderly people who:
   a. are good with technology?
   b. listen to modern music?
   c. still do lots of exercise?
   d. travel a lot?
   e. have a much younger partner?

6 | Using grammar: *used to*

In the conversation, Doris said: 'When we were young, we always **used to** let old people go first.'

We use **used to** to talk about things which were true for some time in the past, but which aren't true now. We use **didn't use to** / **never used to** to talk about things which weren't true in the past, but which are now. For example:

• I used to live in the North. (*I now live in the South.*)

• I didn't use to be thin. (*I was really fat when I was a boy.*)

• I never used to eat chocolate. (*Now I eat too much!*)

Match the sentence beginnings and endings.

1. People used to smoke a lot when I was young,

2. My parents always used to have a traditional English Sunday lunch,

3. The big trade unions always used to go on strike,

4. People always used to hold doors open for women,

a. but I prefer to go out and eat Italian or Japanese food at the weekend.

b. but they don't really any more. Everybody now knows about passive smoking.

c. but nowadays men don't do that kind of thing! I think it's quite sad.

d. but nowadays they don't have much power and fewer people belong to them.

Now match these sentence beginnings and endings.

5. My parents never used to travel when they were young,

6. My mother never used to lose things,

7. I never used to worry about getting older,

8. I never used to like children,

e. but since my 40th birthday, I've really started feeling my age.

f. but my brother and his wife have two now and I really love them.

g. but I go abroad on business all the time.

h. but since she retired, she's always forgetting where she's put things.

7 | Practice

Read these sentences and think about the kind of people who said them.

1. I used to go out a lot more than I do now.

2. I used to drive really fast.

3. I used to play basketball for a local team.

4. I used to live in a lovely big house in the centre of town.

5. I used to have really long hair and wear a nose ring.

6. I used to sleep until midday on Saturday mornings.

7. I never used to smoke, but I started a few years ago.

8. I never used to be interested in foreign languages, but I am now.

Now discuss with a partner why you think the changes in each speaker's life happened. For example:

1. This could be a woman who got married or maybe got a job, so she has to get up really early for it.

8 | Further practice

Complete the sentences with your own ideas.

1. People always used to .... , but they don't any more.

2. When I was younger, I used to .... , but I don't any more.

3. When I was younger, I never used to .... , but I do now.

4. My parents never used to .... when they were younger, but I do.

5. People never used to .... , but they do now.

Tell a partner about what you have written.

> For more information on using *used to*, see G37.

1 | Act or draw

Work in pairs. Take turns to choose five of the words or expressions in the box. Don't tell your partner which ones you have chosen! Without speaking, draw or act out the words for your partner to guess. Your partner has one minute to guess the words you have chosen.

a bandage	hold the door open
a bruise	industry
a camcorder	key in your PIN number
a drill	leak
a hairdrier	plug it in
a loaf of bread	push in a queue
a walking stick	rub in cream
be in a rush	sign something
burn myself	slip
cash a cheque	trip
drop something	

Were there any words you didn't know?

2 | Tenses

Choose the correct alternative.

1. We're staying / We've stayed here until next Tuesday.

2. Over the last two or three years, unemployment is going up / has gone up a lot.

3. I tripped / I was tripping when I was running.

4. I cut / I was cutting some carrots and the knife slipped / was slipping and I cut / was cutting my hand.

5. A: I'm finding my English course really difficult.
   B: Are you speaking / Have you spoken to your teacher about it?
   A: No, but I guess I should. Maybe I'm going to talk / I'll talk to her after the class today.

6. A: Excuse me, is this the way to the station?
   B: No, you need to go this way. I show you / I'll show you where it is. I'm going past there myself.

7. A: Look where you go / you're going!
   B: Oh no! I'm really sorry. Let me help you / I help you pick up the glass.
   A: No, it's OK. I do it / I'll do it.
   A: I didn't know you smoked!
   B: I'm not usually / I don't usually these days, but I used to smoke / I use smoking a lot in the past.

3 | Grammar

Complete the sentences. Write ONE word in each space.

1. A: I'm quite hungry.
   B: Do you want me to .... you a sandwich?
   A: Would you .... ?
   B: No, of course not. .... you like cheese, ham or both?
   A: Just cheese, thanks. I .... vegetarian.

2. A: Are you all right?
   B: Yes, I've just banged .... arm.
   A: Maybe you .... go to the hospital and have .... looked at. It might .... broken.
   B: No, it'll be all right. It's probably just badly bruised.

3. I know Kiev very well, because I .... to live there in .... nineties.

4. Listen, I .... go or I .... miss the start of the match.

5. Eating out is .... more expensive here .... it is in Colombia. I mean, the average meal there only .... five or .... pounds.

Compare your answers with a partner and explain your choices.

4 | Questions and answers

Match the questions with the answers.

1. What seems to be the problem? ☐
2. How did it happen? ☐
3. Can you stand up? ☐
4. How are you paying? ☐
5. How shall we pay the bill? ☐

a. I was playing football and someone kicked me.

b. Cash, if that's OK.

c. No, it's OK. I'll get it. It's my treat.

d. I've hurt my ankle.

e. Just about, but it's really painful.

Now match these questions with the answers.

6. How can I help you?

7. What's wrong with it?

8. Did you ever use to go to the bars in St Andrew's Square?

9. Can you lend me some money – just till I go to the bank?

10. How long have you been here?

e. Since Monday.

f. Not really. I went there once or twice, but I used to prefer France Street and that area round there.

g. No problem. How much do you need?

h. The mouse isn't working properly and the screen sometimes freezes.

i. Well, I'm having some problems with my computer.

In pairs, ask each other the questions above. This time give different answers.

5 | What can you remember?

With a partner, write down as much as you can remember about the texts you read about in the texts in Unit 17 and Unit 19.

Unit 17: It really hurt!

a. Stuart playing rugby

b. Chris at the club

c. Katy skateboarding

d. And the other three accidents

Unit 19: Eight things I hate about banks

a. Rich

b. Mean

c. Bank charges

d. Changing banks

e. Junk mail

f. And the other three things

Now work with another pair of students and compare what you can remember. Who remembered more?

Which text did you enjoy more? Why?

6 | Verb collocations

Complete the collocations with the verbs in the box.

| be covered   hit   lend   offer   spend |

1. .... to pay / someone a job

2. .... your head on the table / your finger with a hammer

3. .... you a book / me £5

4. .... by insurance / in blood

5. .... money like water / the weekend in bed

Now complete these collocations with the verbs in the box.

| belong   make   run out   take out   vote |

6. .... in the election / for the president

7. .... of money / of toilet paper

8. .... a funny noise / a mess

9. .... some money from the bank / a loan

10. .... to a trade union / to a political party

Work in pairs. Spend one minute memorising the words above that collocate with the verbs. Then take turns to close your book. Your partner will read out the verbs. Can you remember both collocations?

With your partner, try to think of one more collocation for each verb.

7 | Look back and check

Work in pairs. Choose one of these activities.

a. **Look back at Activities 4–6 in Unit 18 on page 127. With a partner, do the role play in Activity 6 again.**

b. **Look at the expressions in Unit 20 for talking about the economy. How many of the expressions can you remember? Do the further practice in Activity 6 on page 139 again.**

8 | Expressions

Complete the sentences with the words in the box.

do	forget	manage	plays	surprised
fault	goes	paying	promise	tell

1. I'm not ....
2. It's not too heavy. I can ....
3. He works hard and .... hard.
4. I don't know where all my money ....
5. I'll see what I can .... , but I can't .... anything.
6. You can't .... the difference.
7. It was partly my ....
8. .... about it.
9. How are you .... ?

Now discuss these questions with a partner.

1. Do you know where your money goes?
2. Can you think of a mistake or an accident which was partly your fault?
3. Do you know anyone who works hard and plays hard?

9 | Vocabulary quiz

Discuss these questions in groups of three.

1. Can you clean plates in a washing machine?
2. If you can't hear, are you deaf or blind?
3. Why would someone retrain?
4. What's the difference between I need to fix it and I need to get it fixed?
5. What do you put in a vase?
6. What happens if you don't pay attention in class? And while you're driving?
7. Can you think of two things you could show as proof of ID?
8. Can you think of three things you can turn up?
9. Complete these expressions: a loaf of ... / a pint of ... / a pair of ... .
10. What can eat your credit card?
11. When do you pay interest?
12. When you're in a rush, have you got lots of time?
13. When you're in debt, what's the problem?
14. What's the opposite of mean?
15. Do you say something nice or nasty when you swear at someone?
16. Can you think of two things that can leave a stain on your clothes? How do you get the stain out?

Pronunciation

1 | Contrastive stress: weak and strong forms

🎧 **Listen to these conversations.**

A: I'm <u>18</u>.
B: Really? I don't believe you.
A: I AM (18).

A: <u>I</u> can <u>do</u> it.
B: No you can't.
A: I CAN (do it)

A: I <u>like</u> it.
B: Really?
A: I DO (like it).

We often use auxiliary verbs (be / have / can / will, etc.) to repeat information. You don't need to say the whole sentence again. When we say the sentence the second time, we strongly stress the auxiliary verb.

Complete the conversations with the words in the box.

can	did	do	does	has	hasn't	is	will

1. A: He's married to a millionaire.
   B: Him! I don't believe you.
   A: He .... I've met her. She runs a company.
   B: No way!
   A: She .... Honestly! She's really nice.
   B: So what's she doing with him?

2. A: He's been learning English for ten years.
   B: Really? I don't believe you.
   A: He .... He told me he went to a bilingual school.
   B: No way!
   A: He ....
   B: So why is his English so bad?

3. A: She's never been on a plane.
   B: Never? I don't believe you.
   A: She .... She told me she's scared of flying.

4. A: I'll pay you tomorrow.
   B: I'll believe it when I see it.
   A: I .... , I promise. I get paid tomorrow.

5. A: I love running.
   B: You! I don't believe you.
   A: I .... I can run a mile in under six minutes.
   B: No way!
   A: I .... I'll race you, if you like.

🎧 **Listen to these pairs of weak and strong stressed auxiliaries.**

He's married. He IS.

She runs a company. She DOES.

He's been learning English. He HAS.

He went to a bilingual school. He DID.

She's never been on a plane. She HASN'T.

I'll pay you tomorrow. I WILL.

I love running. I DO.

I can run a mile. I CAN.

Now practise reading the five conversations above.

2 | Vowel sounds: diphthongs

🎧 **Diphthongs are sounds which move from one vowel sound to another. The first part is always longer and stronger than the second.**

Try and say the words in phonetic script, then write them down.

1. /jɪəz/ ....
2. /ʃeɪd/ ....
3. /kəʊst/ ....
4. /skweə/ ....
5. /weə/ ....
6. /bɪˈləʊ/ ....
7. /wɪəd/ ....
8. /heə/ ....

Now try and say these expressions and then write them down.

9. /bləʊ jɔː nəʊz/ ....
10. /ðɪs teɪsts greɪt/ ....
11. /ɪts ˈrɪəlɪ ˈsɪərɪəs/ ....
12. /ðiː eə feə/ ....

🎧 **Listen and check your answers. How many words and expressions did you get right?**

3 | Problem sounds: /w/ and /j/

🎧 **Look at the pictures. They show how we make these sounds. Listen and practise the sounds.**

/w/ 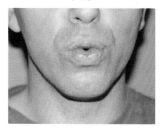   /j/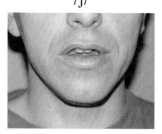

Now say these expressions.

1. I'm going away to Yemen for a year.
2. Yes, you would.
3. Yellow and white.
4. We had a week of wonderful weather.
5. Yes, it's very wet in winter.
6. Have you applied to university yet?
7. We had to queue for a while.
8. Do you want to go for a walk?
9. I worry when you want wine!
10. Do you know what? Your music is weird!

Try to write your own sentences using the sounds above. Read your sentences out to the class.

Who has the most sounds? Which was the funniest sentence?

Tapescript

Unit 1

Making friends (page 8)

C: Do you smoke?
D: No, thanks. I'm trying to stop.
C: Yes, I should too. I'm sorry, what's your name again?
D: Danko. And yours?
C: Caroline. Hi, so where are you from, Danko?
D: Croatia.
C: Oh yes? Whereabouts exactly? Zagreb?
D: No, Split. It's on the coast. Do you know it?
C: I've heard of it, but I've never been there. There was a tennis player from there, wasn't there? What's his name?
D: Goran Ivanisevic.
C: Yes, that's the one. He was lovely.
D: Yes, well, you should come to Split. There are lots of lovely people there. It's a beautiful city.
C: I'd love to go one day. So how long have you been here in Britain?
D: Almost six months now. I came here in September.
C: Right. When are you going back to Croatia?
D: In May. I've got to go back then.
C: Why? What do you do back home?
D: Oh, I'm a student. I'm at university. I have to take some exams in June.
C: Oh right. What are you studying?
D: English language and culture. That's the main reason I'm here.
C: Right, right. Well, you speak English very well.
D: Thanks. I hope so.
C: No, really.

While you listen (page 12)

(T = Tourist, L = Local)
T: Excuse me, is this the right bus stop for Burlington?
L: Yes, it is, but I'm afraid you're too late. You've missed the last bus. It went an hour ago.
T: Oh no! I'll have to walk. It's just down this road, isn't it?
L: Yes, but it's a long way to go with that heavy bag. I'll drive you there, if you like. My car's just round the corner.
T: Really? Could you?
L: Yes, of course. I'm going that way, anyway. I have a bed and breakfast place just outside the village.
T: Really? Wow! That's great. What a great place to live. You must love it here. It's so quiet and peaceful.
L: It's OK. It's not so quiet in the summer. There are a lot of tourists.
T: Sure, well, that's why I'm here. It's so beautiful. I've been in London for the last two weeks, so I'm glad to be out in the country. I mean, I liked London – there's so much to see and do – but it's a bit crowded, you know. It's nice to be away from the crowds.
L: Oh, I know. And whereabouts are you from in America? I take it you ARE from the States?
T: Yes, I'm from Washington DC.
L: Oh, really? And what's it like there?

T: It's very different to here, I can tell you. There's so much crime and violence. It's not safe to go out at night.
L: We have crime here too, you know. Oh yes. Several tourists have disappeared recently. The police think they've been murdered. They found one girl dead near here.
T: Oh, yes? Well, I'm sure I'll be all right. I don't think it can be that dangerous.
L: Maybe not. Do you have anywhere to stay, by the way?
T: No, I'm just going to try to find a place when I get there.
L: Well, why don't you stay at my guest house?
T: Sure, why not? I guess it's not too expensive.
L: Not at all. We're the cheapest place around.
T: So do you run the place on your own?
L: More or less. My mother owns the place, but she's old now and she can't do very much. Ah, here's my car.
T: Shall I put my bag in the back of the car?
L: Er… no, there's something in there already. Just put it on the back seat. You can move those clothes and the big knife, just put them on the floor. They're dirty anyway.
T: Oh, OK.
L: By the way, what's your name.
T: George.
L: Hi, George. I'm Norman. Norman Bates.

Unit 2

Likes and dislikes (page 14)

K: Do you like OPera?
J: No, I HATE it. I find it REAlly BORing. WHY do you ASK?
K: Oh, I'm THINking of GOing to SEE SOMEthing at the Opera House and I'm TRYing to FIND SOMEone to GO with.
J: NO, SORry. I just THINK OPeras go ON TOO LONG. I CAN'T sit still for FOUR hours.
K: Never MIND. I'll TRY someone else.
J: Have you asked MIRiam? I think SHE likes THAT kind of MUSic.
K: Oh, RIGHT. OK. MAYbe I'll ask HER. So what kind of music DO you like?
J: LOTS of things, really. JAZZ, POP, LAtin music. I LOVE TIto LOpez.
K: REAlly? I HATE him. ALL his songs SOUND the SAME. I like JAZZ, though. Do you like LOUis ARMstrong?
J: YES, he's OK. I QUITE like SOME of his TUNES, but I preFER GAto BarblEri.
K: Oh, RIGHT. I've never HEARD of her. Who IS she?
J: He's a MAN. He's an ArgenTINian musician. He's REAlly good. I'll LEND you a CD if you LIKE.
K: YES, OK. THANKS.

Listening (page 18)

M: Hello, Tina, how's it going?
T: All right, not too bad. How are you?
M: Oh, OK. I've just had my speaking test.
T: Oh right, yes. I forgot about that. How did it go?

M: Don't ask! I think it went really badly. I didn't know what to say. What is it you say? My mind went blind.

T: Ah, yes, you mean your mind went BLANK.

M: You see! I know nothing. I'm going to fail!

T: I'm sure it wasn't that bad.

M: No, it was terrible. I'm sure I failed. Could I have a look at your paper and see what's on? I think I'll go out and try to forget it.

T: Sure, go ahead. It's probably a good idea.

M: I like going out too much.

T: You mean you like going out a lot. I've TOLD you this before, Mario. You only use 'too' when you think it's a bad idea. You mean I REALLY like it.

M: Yes, I know, but I think I go out too much. I went clubbing last night. I got home at four o'clock in the morning.

T: Yes, that wasn't a very good idea. I'm not surprised you couldn't think this morning! Who did you go with?

M: Oh, I went on my own, but I went to a club and I know lots of people there. I was nervous because of the exam. I couldn't sleep. I thought I'd go dancing to relax, but, as I said, I like it too much. Anyway, what are you doing here?

T: Oh, I'm going shopping with my boyfriend, Hugh. He's just gone to the toilet. He'll be back in a minute.

M: Right. Let me see. What clubs are there tonight?

T: Why don't you go to see a film or something? Take it easy. Go to bed early for a change.

M: I don't really like movies.

T: You don't like going to the cinema! Why is that? Everybody likes it.

M: No, I prefer music, dancing. I just love it.

T: Oh well. Look, here's Hugh. Hugh, this is Mario, one of my old students. Mario, Hugh.

M: But you're Dale, no?

H: Dale? I'm sorry, I think you've mistaken me for someone else.

M: No, it's Dale. We met before. In the club.

H: Sorry. Tina, are you ready to go?

T: Yes, but …

H: Let's go then or the shops will close. Nice to meet you, Mario. Sorry, I'm not who you think I am.

T: OK. Bye Mario.

M: Bye. I probably won't see you again. I'm going back home on Tuesday. Bye! … But I'm sure he told me his name was Dale!

Unit 3

Explaining where things are (page 20)

P: Ouch!

S: What's up?

P: I've just cut my finger on this nail.

S: Let's have a look. Oh, yes. That's quite nasty.

P: I'd better run it under the tap.

S: Have you got any plasters? I'll go and get you one.

P: Yes, I think there are some on the shelf in the bathroom.

S: I can't see any. Are you sure they're here?

P: Do you see the cupboard by the bath? Have a look in there. I think there are some in the top drawer.

S: I've found them.

P: Thanks.

S: I also found these.

P: Oh … er … right … er … Where did you find those?

S: They were on the floor.

P: Whose are they?

S: Well, they're not mine!

Using grammar: questions with *have you got … ?* (page 21)

1. A: Oh NO! Have you got a CLOTH? I've just SPILT WINE all over your CARpet.
   B: YES, there's ONE in the KITchen by the SINK.

2. A: OUCH! Have you got a PLASter? I've just CUT myself.
   B: YES, there are SOME in the DRAWER in the KITchen.

3. A: Have you got a PEN? I've just MET an OLD FRIEND and WANT to make a NOTE of his PHONE number!
   B: YES, just a MInute. There's ONE in my BAG SOMEwhere.

4. A: Have you got any SCISsors? I just NEED to CUT this BIT of STRING.
   B: YES, there's a PAIR on the TAble in the FRONT ROOM.

5. A: Have you got a SCREWdriver? I just NEED to Open this PLUG up to SEE if the FUSE is OK.
   B: YES, there's ONE in a BOX in the GArage, I THINK.

6. A: Have you got any corRECtion FLUid? I just NEED to CHANGE this WORD here.
   B: YES, ONE minute. There's SOME on my DESK.

While you listen (page 24)

Conversation 1

A: No, I'm an only child, actually.

B: Oh really? I didn't know that. What was it like, growing up on your own? Didn't it get a bit lonely sometimes?

A: Yes, kind of. I sometimes got a bit upset because I didn't have anyone to play with, and my parents were too busy to spend much time with me, but most of the time it was OK. You just get used to it and anyway, I often used to go round to friends' houses and play there.

Conversation 2

A: Yes, why? Do you want to borrow it?

B: If you don't mind. I won't be on it long, I promise. I just need to ring work quickly and tell them I won't be in tomorrow.

A: OK. There you are. You have to press that button there first, then dial the number and then press that green button there.

B: OK. I've got it. Thanks.

Conversation 3

A: You're joking, aren't you? I haven't even got a driving licence!

B: Really? Why not?

A: I don't really know. I've just never learnt. I've lived in big cities most of my life and I've never really needed one. Public transport is usually fine for me.

A: I can't believe it! You're 54 and you've never learnt!

B: Yes, well … who knows? Maybe next year, eh?

Conversation 4

A: Yes, I have. I graduated in mechanical engineering in 1995.

B: OK, good. And have you got a Master's?

A: No, I haven't yet, I'm afraid, but I'm thinking of applying to do a part-time one sometime in the next few years.

B: Right. Well, we might be able to help you with that if we did decide to offer you the job. We could give you some free time to study in.

Conversation 5

A: Yes, but it's a really old one. It's very slow and it crashes all the time.

B: Yes? Well, why don't you get rid of it and get a new one?

A: I don't know. I don't really need a new one. The old one does everything I need it to. I mean, I can send e-mail on it, type things up on it, that kind of thing. It's not really that bad.

B: Just slow.

A: Yes.

Conversation 6

A: Yes, kind of! My son's got a little snake he keeps in his bedroom. I don't really like the thing myself, but he's very keen on it, so I let him keep it.

B: Oh, right.

A: Yes, but I'm sure that one day I'll wake up and find it dead because he's forgotten to feed it.

B: Yes, well, kids need to learn about death sooner or later, don't they? And that's as good a way as any.

Conversation 7

A: Yes, two. A boy and a girl.

B: Oh wow! That's nice. How old are they?

A: The boy's two and the girl's about seven and a half now.

B: And are you thinking of having any more?

A: No, two is enough, believe me! They're quite hard work.

B: I can imagine.

Unit 4

Making plans (page 26)

S: Are you GOing to the PARty for new STUdents toNIGHT?

E: I THINK so. And YOU?

S: YES, it MIGHT be NICE to MEET a FEW new PEOple.

E: YES AND it's FREE!

S: ExACtly. I NEver say NO to ANything that's FREE.

E: What TIME does it START?

S: SEven, but I'm GOing a bit LAter. I DON'T want to be the FIRST one there.

E: NEIther do I. I HATE going to PLAces on my OWN.

S: Do you WANT to MEET up beFORE, and THEN we could GO toGEther?

E: YES, GREAT. WHERE shall we MEET?

S: How about the CAfé NEXT to the SCHOOL? We could HAVE a DRINK FIRST.

E: YES, OK. What TIME?

S: How about a QUARter past SEven? We DON'T want to miss all the FOOD and DRINK.

E: OK. That sounds FINE.

S: What're you DOing NOW? Have you got TIME for a COFfee?

E: I don't KNOW. What time IS it?

S: JUST gone HALF past nine.

E: Half past NINE? Oh, I've GOT to GO. I'm LATE for my CLASS.

S: OK. Well, I'll SEE you in the CAfé at QUARter past SEven, then.

E: OK. BYE.

Listening (page 30)

Conversation 1

A: I think it was about three or four months ago, but it grows really quickly.

B: I can see that – and it's really thick as well, isn't it? I'll need to give it a wash.

A: OK. Fine.

B: So what do you want done to it?

A: I'd basically just like it cut a little bit, really. Just take a little bit off all round, please, and tidy it up.

B: I'll see what I can do.

Conversation 2

A: It was so long ago, I can't remember! That's why I really need to get some new things tomorrow.

B: Yes, those jeans do look a bit old.

A: I know! And this shirt is quite old as well.

B: So where are you thinking of going, then? Any idea?

A: Well, I thought I might try the High Street. There's a sale on at the department store there at the moment, so I might be able to find some cheap trousers or a jacket or something.

Conversation 3

A: It was ages ago! That's why I'm not really looking forward to going tomorrow. I'm sure he's going to tell me I have to have a tooth taken out. I've had really bad toothache for the last two or three weeks.

B: Really? That sounds awful. Are your teeth really that bad?

A: They're terrible! I've got about ten fillings. I eat too many sweets and don't really look after my teeth very well.

Conversation 4

A: It was five years ago. Just after I graduated from university, before I started working.

B: Wow! That's ages ago. How did you go so long without one?

A: I don't know. I started working here and then suddenly five years went past without me taking a break. I've just been so busy.

B: Yes. I know the problem.

A: Anyway, that's why I'm really looking forward to going away next week. I really need some time on my own, so I can just lie around and do nothing.

B: I'm sure you'll have a great time.

Conversation 5

A: It was last Christmas. They rented a house out in the countryside and the whole family stayed there for a few days. It was lovely.

B: Wow. That sounds great. So does that mean they haven't met your new girlfriend yet, then?

A: No, they haven't. That's why I'm a bit nervous about them coming down to our flat for the holidays. I'm not sure what they'll think of her.

B: Oh, don't worry about it. I'm sure they'll like her. She's really nice and friendly.

Conversation 6

A: It was nearly 20 years ago, just before I left school. I took three when I was 17 and failed them all, so I'm not really looking forward to the one tomorrow.

B: Don't worry about it. I'm sure it'll be OK. You've done really well this term, haven't you?

A: I suppose so. I'm probably just worrying about nothing.

B: Maybe, but it's only natural to feel like that. It's perfectly normal to get a bit nervous before something like this!

Review: Units 1–4

Recording word stress (page 34)

'Asian	'British
Euro'pean	'Spanish
A'merican	'Mexican
Chi'nese	Japa'nese
Bra'zilian	Pe'ruvian

Consonant sounds (page 35)

1. think
2. shot
3. crash
4. change
5. Asia
6. refugee
7. ring me later
8. I can imagine
9. dustpan and brush
10. the other day

Unit 5

Talking about things you've bought (page 36)

C: OH, I like those SHOES.   Are they NEW?
L: YES,   I only BOUGHT them   a few DAYS ago.
C: They're REAlly NICE.   They really SUIT you.
L: THANKS.   I wasn't SURE about them   to beGIN with, but I REAlly like them now.
C: YES, I LOVE the deSIGN.   WHERE did you GET them?
L: From this great SHOP   in HOCKley.   They've got a SALE on at the MOment,   and I just COULDn't reSIST them.
C: I can iMAGine.   How much WERE they?
L: They were twenty-NINE, NINEty-NINE,   reDUCED from sixty-FIVE.
C: WOW!   That's BRILliant!   Whereabouts exACTly IS this shop?   I MIGHT try to GO there later.
L: WELL,   do you know where CAStle Street is?
C: YES, I THINK so.
L: WELL,   as you're going DOWN the hill   it's about HALFway DOWN,   on the LEFT.   I THINK it's called BARrett's.
C: Oh RIGHT.   Well, THANKS for telling me.
L: That's OK.   Let me KNOW if you BUY anything!

While you listen (page 40)

Conversation 1
(J = John, B = Belinda, A = Assistant)
J: What do you think of this?
B: It's really nice. It really suits you. Is it waterproof?
J: Yes, yes, totally, which is just what I need if we're going to go camping.
B: Yes.
J: Don't you think it's a bit too big?
B: Yes, maybe a bit. Have they got anything smaller?
J: I can't see anything here. I'll ask. Excuse me.
A: Yes sir.
J: Have you got something like this, but in a smaller size?
A: I'm afraid that's all we have. You could try Black's. It's another camping shop on Judd St. It's just off this road, about halfway down.
J: Right, OK. Thanks. I'll try there.

Conversation 2
(P = Peggy, F = Frank, A = Assistant)
P: I've got the bread. Do we need anything else?
F: Yes, I must get some shampoo. I forgot to bring some with me.
P: OK. Where is it? Have you seen any?
F: No, let me ask this guy. He looks as if he works here. Excuse me, where's the shampoo?
A: I'm afraid it's at the other end of the store. The second aisle from the end.
F: OK. Thanks. ... Look at this. Don't they sell it in bottles less than a litre?
P: They're not very expensive, though, are they?

F: It's not that. It's just that it's a bit too much. I don't want to have to carry it around with me. Oh forget it. I'll leave it. I just won't wash my hair for a few days.
P: Are you sure? That's disgusting!
F: No, it'll be OK.
P: All right. Is that it then? You don't need anything else from here?
F: No, but I mustn't forget to go to the bank later. I need to cash some travellers' cheques.

Conversation 3
(C = Customer, A = Assistant)
C: Hello. I bought these batteries from you earlier, but they're the wrong size. Can I change them?
A: Yes, I guess so. What size do you want?
C: The next size down, if you've got them. Yes, those ones.
A: They're actually ten pence more expensive.
C: Oh right, OK. Can I have a paper as well?
A: That's £1.10 please. Have you got anything smaller? I haven't got any £5 notes.
C: Sorry, I've just been to the cashpoint.
A: Never mind. You'll have to have coins. That's two, three, four, five, six, seven, eight, nine, and ten.
C: OK. Thanks. Sorry about that.

Unit 6

Talking about being ill (page 42)

Conversation 1
P: HelLO.   Is that SArah?
S: YES,   HI.   How are YOU?
P: I'm FINE.   What about YOU?   You weren't in CLASS toDAY. I'm just PHOning   to make SURE you're OK.
S: Oh, THANKS.   That's really NICE of you.   I'm NOT very well, ACtually.
P: Oh NO.   What's the PROBlem?
S: I've got a REAlly BAD COLD.   I've been in BED all DAY.
P: Oh NO!   I'm SORry.   Have you been to SEE anyone aBOUT it?
S: NO,   I'll be all right.   I JUST need to   STAY in BED   for a WHILE.   I alREAdy FEEL   a bit BETter than I DID this MORning.

Conversation 2
J: HelLO.
T: Hi, JAnet.   It's TeREsa.   How's it GOing?
J: GREAT, thanks.   How are YOU?
T: NOT very well, ACtually.   THAT'S why I'm PHOning. Can you TELL RALPH   I CAN'T come to CLASS toNIGHT?
J: YES,   of COURSE.   What's the PROBlem?
T: OH,   I've just got a REAlly UPset STOMach.   I've been IN and OUT of the BATHroom   ALL day.
J: Oh NO,   that's AWful!   I'm SORry.   Can I DO anything to HELP?
T: That's really KIND of you,   but I'm all right.   I'll be FINE toMORrow.
J: Have you TAken anything FOR it?
T: NO,   I'm just DRINking lots of WAter   and TRYing to TAKE it EAsy.
J: RIGHT   THAT sounds SENsible.
T: LISten,   I've GOT to GO.
J: YES,   of COURSE.   I'll PHONE you toMORrow   and SEE how you ARE.
T: OK.   THANKS.   BYE.

While you listen (page 46)

Conversation 3

A: All right. How's it going?
B: Yes, fine. Are you OK?
A: Yes, not too bad. Did you have a nice weekend?
B: Yes, all right. I just stayed in and took it easy. What about you?
A: I spent most of it in bed. I was feeling really ill, to be honest.
B: Why? Did you have a cold or something?
A: No, no. I went to a new fish restaurant in town and I think I ate something bad. I don't know, but I was up all Friday night, being sick.
B: Oh no! That sounds awful.
A: Yes, it wasn't very nice, but I'm feeling a lot better now.

Conversation 4

A: Good morning. Do you mind if I join you?
B: No, of course not. Have a seat.
A: Did you sleep well?
B: Yes, very. What about you?
A: No, I didn't, actually. I was up till two watching a film on TV, and then I got woken up by the people in the room next to me at about five. Did you hear them?
B: No, I didn't.
A: You must be a really heavy sleeper, then, because they were making a terrible noise. It was unbelievable! Anyway, I couldn't get back to sleep for ages. Honestly, I'm exhausted.
B: Maybe you should've stayed in bed and not come down for breakfast.
A: Yes, maybe, but I need to eat in the mornings. And anyway, I HAVE paid for it.

Conversation 5

A: Hello? Is that Barbara?
B: Yes, Angus! How are you? It's been ages. So what've you been doing recently?
A: Yes, I know. I'm sorry. I've just been really busy with exams and studying. What about you?
B: Yes, everything's great. I'm in a really good mood at the moment, actually.
A: Oh yes? Why?
B: Well, I haven't really told many people yet, but I'm pregnant.
A: Wow! That's brilliant! You must be really happy.
B: Yes, I'm really pleased. I really wanted to tell people before, but I had to have a scan and check everything was all right first.
A: And is it?
B: Yes, yes. I had the scan yesterday and it's fine.
A: Wow! So when's it due?
B: September 15th.
A: Really? So you're, what, almost three months pregnant already?
B: Yes.
A: So do you know what it is yet?
B: No, I didn't want to know. I'm just going to wait.
A: Well, anyway, that's brilliant. Congratulations!
B: Thanks.
A: Anyway, listen, sorry. I've got to go or I'll be late for my art class. I'll phone you back later. And well done!
B: Thanks. See you.

Unit 7

Talking about university (page 48)

L: So what do you do, Jane? Are you working or studying or what?
J: I'm doing business management at the London Business School, actually.
L: Oh right. That sounds good. What year are you in?
J: My third, unfortunately. I've got my finals in the spring. I'm really worried about them.
L: Yes, I can imagine. So what're you going to do when you graduate? Have you decided yet?
J: Yes, I'm going to take a year off and go travelling a bit and then I'm going to try to get onto a Master's course somewhere.
L: Oh yes? What in?
J: International finance.
L: Wow. Have you applied anywhere yet?
J: Not yet, but there's a course in Leeds I'm very interested in.
L: Leeds? I've heard it's got a very good reputation. What do you need to do to get in?
J: Well, obviously, I need to get a good grade and then I have to go for an interview.
L: Oh right. Well, good luck.
J: Thanks. I'll need it. Anyway, Lee, what about you? What do you do?
L: I'm doing a one-year art course at my local college and I'd like to do art history at university next year.
J: Oh right. Have you applied anywhere yet?
L: Yes, I have, actually. I've applied to Goldsmith's College and they've offered me a place – if I pass the course I'm doing at the moment.
J: Oh wow! That's great. Congratulations! I've heard it's got a really good reputation as well.
L: Thanks, yes, they do – especially for arts subjects. I'm worried about how I'll be able to live in London, though. I've heard it's very expensive.
J: Yes, it is, believe me!
L: I'm going to work through the summer and try to save some money, but I guess I'll have to find a part-time job next year as well.
J: Yes, probably.

While you listen (page 52)

(T = Teacher, A = Adam, S = Sherry, J = Jenny, K = Kelvin)
T: OK. Let's go through the answers to Exercise 2, then. What did you get for Number 1? Anyone?
A: Hi. Morning, Miss. Morning everyone.
T: Morning? It's nearly ten o'clock, Adam.
A: Yes, like I said ... good morning.
T: And that's it? Aren't you going to apologise or explain why you're late ... again?
A: Oh, that. Yes, OK. Sorry ... I'm late because my alarm clock didn't go off, OK?
T: Right! It's not the first time THAT'S happened, is it! If I were you, I'd buy myself another one. And make sure this one works ... Anyway, open your book. We're on Page 62.
A: Please, Miss.
T: Yes, Adam. What is it this time?
A: Could you open the window? It's really hot in here. It's making me feel sleepy.

T: OK, OK. Sherry, you're the nearest. Could you just open the window there, please?

S: Yes, OK. There. Is that all right?

T: Yes, great. Thanks. Right, OK. Page 62. Exercise 2. What did you get for Number 1?

A: Sorry, Miss. I did do my homework, but I forgot to bring my books with me. I was in such a hurry to get here after I woke up late.

T: Well, why don't you just share with the person next to you, Adam? OK? Ahmed ... could you just let Adam share your book, please? Thanks. RIGHT ... Number 1 – at last!

J: It's B.

T: Yes, good. OK. And Number 2? *(sound of mobile phone)* Whose mobile it that?

A: Hello? Oh, hi. How are you? Yes, I'm fine. I'm good. Listen, wait a minute ... sorry, Miss, but is it OK if I just answer this? It's important.

T: Adam, you know the rules. You're not allowed to use mobiles in the classroom.

A: I know. I'm sorry, I really am ... but it's really really important. Is it OK if I just answer it? I'll only be one minute. It won't happen again, I promise

T: OK, OK, answer it if you have to, but could you just go outside while you're talking. And you've only got ONE MINUTE! ... OK, where were we? I've forgotten what we were doing.

K: Number 2.

T: Oh, thanks. Yes. Number 2. Anyone?

Unit 8

Talking about what you do (page 54)

J: So what do you do, Nori? Are you working or studying or what?

N: Well, I graduated a couple of years ago and now I'm working in Osaka.

J: Oh right. So what do you do?

N: I'm a civil servant. I work for the government.

J: Oh, do you? Do you enjoy it?

N: Yes, it's OK. I have to do a lot of paperwork, which is quite boring, but it's quite well paid.

J: Oh, that sounds good.

N: Yes, it is, but sometimes I get a bit bored with it. I have to work a twelve-hour day most days, and a lot of the time, I don't really have much to do, so I just sit around and kill time.

J: Do you have to work weekends?

N: No, thank goodness! Five days a week is enough.

J: Yes, I know what you mean. Do you get much holiday?

N: It's not too bad. I get three weeks a year, so that's OK.

J: And do you have to travel very far to work?

N: Yes, quite a long way. It's about an hour on the train, so I have to spend a lot of time commuting. Anyway, what about you, Jenny? What do you do?

J: I'm an estate agent, actually. I work in an office in the centre of Leeds.

N: Oh really? That sounds interesting.

J: Yes, it is, but it's quite stressful sometimes. We don't get paid that much. It depends how many houses we sell. If I don't sell anything, I don't get any extra money.

N: Oh, I see. So how's it going at the moment?

J: It's been OK this month, actually, but it's not always like that.

N: Right. And what're the other people you work with like?

J: Oh, they're OK. We all get on OK.

N: How long've you been doing it?

J: About a year and a half now. I'm still not sure that it's what I really want to do, though. I'm going to continue doing it for another six months and see if I start enjoying it more. It might get easier to sell things.

N: And if it doesn't get easier? What then?

J: Oh, I don't know. I'll have to think about it.

Listening (page 58)

V: Hello Sue! How are you?

S: Oh hi, yes. I'm all right, I guess.

V: You don't sound very well. Have you been ill? I didn't see you in class yesterday.

S: No, I know. I've just been really busy applying for jobs. I've applied to about ten different places and all the application forms are really big. They take a really long time to fill in. It's awful. I had to finish one yesterday so I could hand it in before the deadline. That's why I missed class.

V: Wow! I really don't know what I want to do when I finish. I'm just going to go on holiday and then I'll think about looking for a job after that.

S: Well, that's probably quite a good idea. Look at me. I've sent off ten application forms and I've only had one interview and that was a disaster.

V: Oh dear. What was the job?

S: Accountant.

V: Accountant! You?

S: Yes, why are you so surprised?

V: Well, you're doing a degree in biology and you're terrible with money! You're always asking to borrow money from me!

S: Yes, OK, but I was quite good at maths when I was at school, and they said they would give people training. So, you know, I thought I might have a chance.

V: I know, but usually they want people to have some experience of working in business.

S: Ah, yes ... well, that was the problem, actually. I told them in the application form I had experience of working for an accountancy company.

V: What, you mean you lied?

S: Well, it wasn't exactly a lie. My uncle runs an accountancy company, and I sometimes worked there in the holidays to get some extra money.

V: Yes, but what were you doing there?

S: Well, OK. I was making tea and posting letters and things like that, but it WAS an accountancy company!

V: Right, yes. So what happened in the interview?

S: Oh, they asked me some really difficult questions. I didn't know what to say. It was a bit embarrassing, actually.

V: Oh well, you live and learn. So what else have you applied for?

S: Well, I've sent off a couple more for accountancy jobs, one for marketing, three for jobs in drug companies, and the last one was to work in a zoo, but the money's terrible for that one, so I don't know if I really want that.

Review: Units 5–8

Word stress (page 62)

Pattern 1

upset	/ˈʌpset/
enquire	/enˈkwaɪə/
career	/kəˈrɪə/
arrange	/əˈreɪndʒ/

Pattern 2

bracelet	/ˈbreɪslɪt/
necklace	/ˈneklɪs/
lecture	/ˈlektʃə/
details	/ˈdiːteɪlz/

Pattern 3

library	/ˈlaɪbrərɪ/
opposite	/ˈɒpəzɪt/
sensible	/ˈsensəbl/
restaurant	/ˈrestərənt/

Pattern 4

imagine	/ɪˈmædʒɪn/
directly	/dɪˈrektlɪ/
appointment	/əˈpɔːɪngmənt/
revision	/rɪˈvɪʒn/

Unit 9

Restaurants (page 64)

M: Are you HUNgry?

K: YES, a BIT.

M: Do you WANT to get SOMEthing to EAT, then?

K: YES, OK. Have you got ANYwhere in MIND?

M: WELL, there's a REAlly NICE PIzza place JUST round the CORner.

K: Well, ACtually, I WENT for a PIzza LAST night. I DON'T really FEEL like aNOther one. Do you KNOW anywhere ELSE?

M: WELL, there's a REAlly NICE THAI place in SOho.

K: RIGHT. Is it VEry SPIcy? I DON'T really LIKE VEry hot food.

M: NO, it's not TOO bad. They've got LOTS of DISHes to CHOOSE from. HONestly it's REAlly NICE FOOD. I'm SURE you'll LIKE it.

K: OK then, I'll try ANYthing once.

M: Shall we WALK or do you WANT to GET the BUS?

K: I don't MIND. It's UP to YOU.

While you listen (page 68)

W: Good evening, sir.

K: Hi. We'd like a table for two, please.

W: Have you booked?

K: No, I'm afraid we haven't. Are you very busy?

W: Could you just wait one moment and I'll see what's available? Yes sir, we've got a table but it HAS been booked from half nine.

K: I don't think we'd want to stay later than that. What's the time now?

M: It's not quite seven o'clock.

K: That'd be enough time then, wouldn't it?

M: Yes, fine.

W: Would you like to follow me? Here's the menu. Can I get you something to drink?

K: What do you want to drink? Wine? Beer?

M: Um, I'm not sure. Could you just give us a moment, please?

W: Of course.

K: Wow! What a choice! Can you recommend anything?

M: It's all nice really, but when I've been before we've usually just ordered one of the set menus here. They bring you lots of different dishes and then we can just share them.

K: That sounds all right. Which one shall we get?

M: I don't mind. It's up to you.

K: OK. Well, how about menu D? I quite like the sound of the coconut soup and the beef dish.

M: OK. Fine.

K: Do you know what lychees are?

M: Oh, they're a kind of fruit. They're really nice and sweet. Are you happy having wine?

K: Yes. Red or white?

M: I prefer red, myself.

K: OK. Shall we just get a bottle of the house red, then?

M: Yes. Can you catch the waiter's eye?

W: Yes, sir. Are you ready to order?

K: Yes, we'd like the set menu D, please.

W: I'm afraid you need a minimum of three people for that menu.

K: Oh right, right.

W: You can either have this one, or there's a vegetarian option, menu E.

K: What do you think? I don't really want the vegetarian one, myself.

M: No – me neither.

W: So Menu A, then?

K: Yes, please.

W: And to drink?

K: Could we have a bottle of the house red?

W: House red.

M: Yes, and could we have some water as well, please?

W: Still or sparkling?

M: Sparkling, if that's OK with you, Kenny.

K: Yes, fine.

M: I'm sorry about that. Whenever I've come before there's been a group of us. I didn't realise you had to have a certain number of people to order that menu.

K: That's OK. Don't worry about it.

Unit 10

Talking about your family (page 70)

M: What are you doing after the class? Have you got time for a coffee?

S: No, I've got to go. I'm going round to my sister's for dinner. She gets a bit annoyed if I'm late.

M: Oh right. Where does she live?

S: Pinedo.

M: Right, that's a nice part of town. What does she do?

S: She's a doctor. She works in the Central hospital.

M: Oh, OK. So how old is she? She must be a lot older than you.

S: Yes, she's 35 years old, so she's almost 15 years older than me.

M: Wow. That's quite a big age gap. So what's she like? Do you get on?

S: Yes, she's really nice. We're actually quite similar. She's probably a bit more organised than I am, but she's quite funny and very easy to talk to. You know, she's never treated me like a baby or her little sister.

M: That's good. So is she married?

S: Yes, she got married when she was really young. I think they've been married for around twelve years. It wasn't long after they graduated.

M: OK, so have they got any kids?

S: She's actually pregnant at the moment. It's her first baby.

M: Really? That's great. When's it due?

S: November.

M: Oh right. It's quite soon then.

S: Yes, it's quite exciting. It'll be my first time as an aunt. Anyway, what about you? Have you got any brothers or sisters?

M: Yes, I've got two older brothers and a twin sister.

S: You're a twin. Wow. Do you look very similar?

M: I don't think so. We're not identical twins, if that's what you mean. Alison's a bit taller than me and her hair is darker. But yes, people are always confusing us. People she's met sometimes come up to me and say hello and start talking to me and I've got no idea who they are.

S: Right. That must be quite annoying.

M: It's OK. I'm used to it. It can actually be quite amusing!

S: So what's she like? I mean, have you got similar personalities as well?

M: Not really. She's a lot quieter than me. It's usually me who does the talking when we go out and she's a more serious person than I am. For example, she's very hard-working. Her job's really important to her. She doesn't go out very much. I guess I'm more relaxed, but she's my twin, so we're always going to be quite close.

While you listen (page 74)

S: Hello, Beth! Are you OK?

B: Salma! Fine, how's it going? I don't seem to see you so much these days. How're you finding the exams?

S: OK, I think. Hey, I saw you the other day, actually, but I couldn't stop because I was on the bus.

B: Oh yes, where was that?

S: On the Bristol Road, outside the swimming pool. You were with Mark Davies.

B: Mark! I didn't know you knew him!

S: Yes, yes. He's an old friend of mine from the school I went to before I came here. We used to be part of a big group of people who used to go out a lot together. I haven't seen him for ages though. He dropped out when I started college here and we lost touch a bit. I used to quite fancy him, actually!

B: Well, he is quite good-looking, which is one of the reasons I'm going out with him.

S: You're going out with him! I don't believe it! How do you know each other?

B: Well, actually, that time you saw us was probably only the third or fourth time we'd been out together. I actually got to know him through this chatroom on the internet.

S: You're joking! Really?

B: Yes, what's wrong with that? I don't think it's that unusual these days, is it?

S: I suppose not. You never know what they're going to look like, though, do you?

B: I guess not. Actually, the first time we met, he was on a lunch break and he was still wearing his police uniform, which was a bit of a surprise.

S: He's a policeman! You're joking! What do your parents think about that? You told me your dad's really anti the police.

B: Yes, I haven't actually told them yet. Things haven't been very good at home recently. You know my gran died a few months ago, yes?

S: No, you didn't tell me.

B: Didn't I? I forget who I've told.

S: No. I'm really sorry to hear that. Did you get on well with her? What was she like?

B: Oh, she was really nice, really kind. She used to look after us quite a lot when we were younger and she'd always buy us sweets and things. We were really close.

S: Oh, I'm really sorry. Had she been ill?

B: No, not at all. She was still quite lively right up until the night she died. She just went to bed one night and died in her sleep. The doctor said it was probably a heart attack.

S: Well, at least she didn't suffer. That's how I'd like to go – in my sleep. How old was she?

B: Eighty-one, so, you know, she'd had a good life.

S: So what about you and Mark? When are you going to tell your parents?

B: Oh, I don't know. I'm not really sure. We've only just started going out. I'll just wait and see. I don't want to give them any more bad news if it's not going to work out between us.

Unit 11

Asking for directions (1) (page 76)

(T = Tourist, P = Passer-by, L = Local)

T: Excuse me, could you help me?

P: Sorry?

T: Do you know if this is the way to The Gagosian?

P: I'm sorry. What's that?

T: The Gagosian. It's an art gallery.

P: I've no idea.

T: Sorry?

P: I'm sorry. I'm not from round here myself. I don't really know the area. Ask this guy here. Hey, excuse me, mate.

L: Yes?

P: Do you know a place round here called ... Sorry, what was it called again?

T: The Gagosian.

P: It's a gallery.

L: Oh right. Yes, I think I know the place. It's down there somewhere. Down past the park, but I'm not sure whereabouts exactly.

T: Sorry?

L: I'm not sure where it is exactly, but it's down there somewhere. Follow the signs to Hall Green. Just keep going straight on down this road, straight on until you get to a park. It's around there somewhere. Ask someone else when you get there.

T: OK. Thank you very much.

L: No problem. I hope you find it.

Pronunciation: sentence stress (page 76)

1. Excuse me, could you help me?
2. I'm looking for a gallery called The Gagosian.
3. Do you know if this is the way to The Gagosian?
4. I'm sorry. I'm not from round here myself.
5. I don't really know the area.
6. Ask this lady here.
7. It's down there somewhere.
8. It's just past the bridge on the right.
9. Follow the signs to the city centre.
10. Just keep going straight on down this road until you get to some traffic lights. Then turn right.
11. It's along that road on your left. You can't miss it.
12. Ask someone else when you get there.

Asking for directions (2) (page 77)

(T = Tourist, L = Local)

T: Excuse me. Could you help me? I'm looking for a gallery called The Gagosian.

L: The Gagosian!

T: Yes, do you know it?

L: Yes, but it's miles away.

T: But someone told me it's near the park.

L: No, no honestly. It's near Oxford Circus. I've been there.

T: Where is it?

L: Oxford Circus.

T: Ah, Oxford Circus. Yes, yes. Is it near here? Can we walk there?

L: No, as I say, it's miles away. You're best taking a bus. Go down there, until you get to the traffic lights, and then turn right. You'll see an underpass. Go under there to cross over to the other side of the main road.

T: OK. I go under to the other side.

L: Yes. Then, when you come out, you'll see the bus stop, and then you want to get the 214 bus.

T: 214.

L: Yes, and ask the driver to let you off at Oxford Circus, OK? Just tell him what stop you want to get off at.

T: OK. Thank you, thank you.

While you listen (page 81)

Conversation 1

(T = Tourist, L = Local)

T: I'm sorry, do you speak English?

L: Of course.

T: Oh ... is this the right platform for Leeds?

L: No, you're on the wrong side. You need to go over there.

T: Oh right, I wasn't sure. Thanks.

Conversation 2

(S = Ticket seller, T = Tourist)

S: Yes madam?

T: Oh, I'd like a ticket to Manchester.

S: For today?

T: Yes.

S: And returning?

T: Yes, return.

S: I mean, what day are you returning?

T: Oh, OK. Yes. Monday.

S: OK, what time?

T: Sorry, I don't know. Do I need to?

S: OK. I can give you a cheaper ticket, but it's not valid before 9.30.

T: Sorry? I ... er ... please, can you say it again?

S: Do you need to come back before half past nine in the morning on Monday?

T: I er ... I don't know. How much?

S: This is what I'm trying to tell you. If you come back before nine, it's peak hour so it'll be £175.

T: One hundred ...

S: Yes, but if you come back after 9.30 it's £50 return.

T: Fifty! Oh, still very expensive.

S: There are cheaper tickets, but you have to book in advance.

T: Eh?

S: In advance. Listen, there are people waiting. Do you want the ticket or not?

T: Yes.

S: OK, so I guess, that's the standard saver return to Manchester. It's only valid for off-peak trains. That'll be £50 pounds. How are you paying?

T: Do you take cards?

S: Yes that's fine ... can you sign here? ... OK, thank you! Next please! Where are you travelling?

Conversation 3

(R = Rep, C = Customer)

R: Yes, sir.

C: Hi. I'd like to rent a car for a week.

R: Certainly, sir. What class of vehicle would you like?

C: Um ... probably just the cheapest one you've got, to be honest.

R: I'm afraid we don't have any available, but we do have a Renault Clio, which is Class B. That's the next cheapest.

C: So how much would that be for one week?

R: Three hundred euros. That includes unlimited mileage, so you can drive as much as you like during the week without paying any extra.

C: OK. Does that include insurance?

R: No. There's a €60 charge for that, I'm afraid.

C: OK. OK. That sounds all right. I'll take it.

R: OK. In that case, I'll need your passport and driving licence, please. And then you'll need to leave your credit card number for the deposit.

Conversation 4

(T = Tourist, D = Driver)

T: Sorry, do you speak English?

D: A little.

T: I want to go to the Museu do Chiado?

D: Museu do Chiado.

T: Could you tell me what stop I have to get off at?

D: Yes, yes. Sit down.

Unit 12

Talking about your free time (page 82)

E: So what did you do last night?

F: Oh I went to see this new play, *Hello You*, at The Playhouse in town.

E: Oh right. Was it any good?

F: Yes, it was OK. I've seen better things.

E: Oh, so do you go to the theatre a lot?

F: Yes, quite often, maybe once or twice a month.

E: Wow! That's quite a lot. I hardly ever go. I prefer to go to the cinema or just go out with friends.

F: Yes, I've always really liked the theatre. I actually go to a drama club and sing with a group of people as well.

E: Really? So what kind of things do you sing?

F: Lots of things really, but mainly musicals – *West Side Story*, *Chicago*, things like that.

E: That's great. So are you any good? I mean, do you sing solo or what?

F: No. I'm OK, but I'm not that good. I just like singing.

E: Oh, that's great.

F: What about you? What do you do in your free time? Have you got any special hobbies?

While you listen (page 86)

M: What's that you're looking at?

L: Oh, it's a magazine. It tells you the courses you can do.

M: Oh yes? But you go to English classes already, don't you?

L: Yes, yes. I'm not looking for English classes. I want to study something else. My teacher said it's good for my English. I'll meet people. I'll speak more in English.

M: Oh right. Good idea. So what are you thinking of doing?

L: Well, there's a photography course that might be good. I like photography.

M: Yes, me too. Is it just about taking photos or do they teach you how to develop pictures as well?

L: Devel...? What was that word?

M: Developing. You know, when you actually go into a dark room – no lights – and actually MAKE the photos – you know, put them in chemicals and stuff.

L: Yes, yes, OK. It doesn't say. It just has the time and price.

M: Maybe you should ring up and find out more about it. Does it have a number?

L: Sorry?

M: Is there a telephone number you can ring to get more information?

L: Yes, but speaking on the telephone is quite difficult for me. I get very nervous. I'll just go to the college.

M: Would you like me to phone for you?

L: Yes? It's not a problem?

M: No, of course not. Here, pass me the magazine and I'll ring now.

L: OK, Thanks. That's great.

M: By the way, have you done any developing before?

L: Eh? Develop? Oh yes ... yes, one time, at school, but it was a long, long time ago.

While you listen (page 87)

(R = Receptionist, M = Mark, T = Teacher)

R: Hello, St Peter's College. How can I help you?

M: Oh hello, I'm phoning to enquire about the evening photography classes you run.

R: Oh yes, and what would you like to know?

M: Well, several things. The main thing is if the course is just about taking photos or do they also teach you how to develop photos?

R: Yes, they do both. The first week is in the classroom and the following week is in the darkroom.

M: OK, and do you need to have any previous experience?

R: I'm not sure. I'll put you through to someone who knows more about it. Just wait one moment, please.

T: Hello

M: Yes hello, I'm ringing about the photography class you run in the evenings.

T: Yes, what is it you'd like to know?

M: Well, just whether you need to have any previous experience to do the course.

T: No, not at all. We take absolute beginners and then we also have some people who may have done some developing before and also some who are continuing from the last course.

M: OK, and the price of the course, does that include all the materials?

T: Yes, for what you need for the classes, everything is included.

M: And just to check – the course starts next week on Tuesday, right?

T: Actually, that's a misprint, several people have had the same problem. It's actually on Thursday.

M: Thursday. OK. but at the same time – six till eight, yes?

T: That's right, yes.

M: And the course lasts for ten weeks.

T: That's right.

M: OK, that's great.

T: We've actually only got two or three places left, so if you want to join us, you'd better be quick.

M: OK, we will. Thanks for your time.

T: No problem, hopefully see you next week.

M: Yes, it sounds good. Bye.

Unit 13

Booking a room in a hotel (page 92)

R: Hello. The Old Ship Hotel. How can I help you?

A: Oh, hello. I'd like to book a room for next month.

R: Of course. When exactly would you be arriving?

A: The 19th and we're leaving on the 24th.

R: So that's five nights. And what kind of room would you like?

A: Well, there are actually two of us. So how much would two singles be?

R: That would be £60 each per night.

A: Right. And what if we shared a twin room?

R: That would be 95 for the room per night.

A: Is that with an en-suite bathroom?

R: Yes, of course. All rooms are en-suite and have all the normal facilities.

A: OK. Well, in that case, I'd like two singles, if possible.

R: Let me just check if we have those available. ... No, I'm sorry. We only have one single room available for those days.

A: Oh right. Well, never mind. We can share.

R: So you'd like one twin room for five nights arriving the 19th and departing the 24th?

A: That's right.

R: That'll be £475. We'll need to take your credit card details to make the booking.

A: Yes, sure.

R: What kind of card are you paying with?

A: Visa.

R: OK. And the number?

A: 5362 3870 6429 8479.

R: That's fine. And what's the expiry date?

A: 06 / 09.

R: OK. And your name as it appears on the card?

A: Anton Yurick. That's Y-U-R-I-C-K.

R: Great. So that's all booked for you, Mr Yurick.

Using grammar: first conditionals (page 93)

R: So, if there's anything else you need to know, please don't hesitate to get in touch.

A: Well, actually, there is one more thing. I need confirmation of the booking for my visa application.

R: Of course, no problem sir. If you fax us with your request, we'll fax you back a letter by tomorrow.

A: Great. If you wait a second, I'll get a pen. Yes, what's the fax number?

R: 0044 31 569 4482

A: OK, that's great. You've been very helpful. Thanks.

R: No problem. We look forward to seeing you.

While you listen (page 96)

J: Hi, Kasia. Have you had a good day?

K: Yes, great thanks, I spent most of the day walking round town. It's really nice.

J: Yes, it is.

K: What about you? What kind of day have you had?

J: Oh, the usual. Work. It was OK, but I'd prefer to be on holiday.

K: I'm sure.

J: Anyway, are you hungry? I'm doing some chicken for dinner.

K: Oh right. I'm not sure I'll have time to eat. I'm meeting Tom at half seven.

J: Oh yes. I forgot. Sorry. Well, you should still have time to get there if you leave here at ten past seven. There's a bus which goes at quarter past.

K: Oh, right. OK. Well, in that case, can I do anything to help?

J: You could lay the table, if you like. The cutlery is in that drawer. Thanks.

K: OK. Is it OK if I have a quick shower after I've done this?

J: Yes, of course, as long as you're quick. Dinner should be ready fairly soon. I think I left a towel in one of the drawers in your room.

K: OK, great. And ... er ... have you got an iron I could use?

J: Yes, sure. It's on the shelf in the back room where the washing machine is. There's an ironing board in there as well. It's folded up behind the door.

K: OK. Great. Where do you keep the glasses?

J: It's OK, I'll do the rest of the table if you want to go and get ready.

K: All right. Thanks. Oh and just one last thing. I completely forgot to pack my make-up. Has Sheila got any I can use?

J: Yes, I'm sure she has. You can ask her when she gets back. She should be here quite soon.

K: Oh, OK.

J: You sound as if you're getting quite dressed up. Are you going anywhere nice?

K: No, not particularly. I think we might just go to the cinema. We haven't completely decided yet.

J: OK, and you and Tom? Are you ... ? Is there ... ?

K: No! No, not at all. Why do men always think that if a woman puts on some make-up, she's looking for a boyfriend!

J: OK, OK. Sorry. I just wondered. .... So are you seeing someone else?

K: Jeremy!

J: OK, sorry. I'm just joking. By the way, are you going to be back late?

K: I don't think so, but I've got a key, so it's not a problem, is it?

J: No, of course not. Come back whenever you like, but if we've gone to bed, can you make sure both locks on the front door are locked before you go to bed?

K: Sure. No problem. OK, I'm going to have that shower.

Unit 14

What was your holiday was like? (page 98)

M: Hello, Tom. Are you all right? I haven't seen you for a while.

T: Yes, I'm fine. I was in the States all last week visiting a friend of mine. I thought I'd told you about it.

M: No, I don't think so. So whereabouts did you go?

T: Most of the time I was in Boston where my friend lives, but I went up to New York for a couple of days.

M: Right. So what was it like?

T: It was great. New York was amazing. It's just such a lively place, there's a real mixture of people, and the food's great.

M: Yes? What about Boston? What was that like?

T: Oh, it's nice. It's quite an interesting place. I didn't do much there – mainly just spent time with my friend – but it was good. I met a lot of his friends and they were really nice and friendly.

M: Sounds great. I'm quite jealous.

T: Have you ever been to the States?

M: Yes, I went there about three years ago, but I went to the West Coast.

T: Oh right, whereabouts exactly?

M: Well, we stayed for a week in San Francisco and then a week just travelling around California. It's such a big state; there are lots of things to do.

T: Yes, I've never been to that part of America, but I'd really love to go. What's San Francisco like? It's supposed to be brilliant.

M: It's great. It's really beautiful and it's very relaxed. Not like LA, which is just mad. We had a really good time there. The only disappointing thing was that it rained almost the whole time we were there.

T: Really? I thought it was supposed to be really good weather there.

M: Yes, I think it is normally. We were just really unlucky.

T: What a shame.

While you listen (page 102)

1. A: It's OK, I suppose. It's quite poor round there and it can be a bit dangerous sometimes, if you walk home on your own late at night, but it's quite a busy area and there's lots of shops and things like that round there, so it's good for shopping.

   B: Right. And what's the rent like?

   A: It's OK, actually. It's quite a cheap area to live in. I only pay about £60 a week.

   B: Wow, that's good. That's a lot less than I pay!

2. A: It's delicious! It's one of the best places to eat in town. Every time I've been there it's been great. You should try it. I'm sure you'd like it.

   B: Really? Well, I think I might take one of my clients there tomorrow evening. I've got someone coming over from Germany on business and I want to take her somewhere nice.

   A: Honestly, it'd be ideal.

3. A: Wonderful! Really great ... the food, the wine, everything! We had a really great time. The weather was nice, the people were nice. It was brilliant!

   B: It sounds lovely! And what was your hotel like?

   A: Oh, it was wonderful! It was a really old place, family-run, and they were so friendly and helpful. It was brilliant, it really was.

4. A: Awful! It was really terrible – the acting, the story, everything! It was a waste of money, it really was! Save your money, and go and see something else instead.

   B: Was it really that bad? It stars Kevin Clint, doesn't it? What was he like in it?

   A: Don't ask! It's the worst I've ever seen him act. He was awful.

5. A: Great! He's really funny. He's always making me laugh. He's very smart as well – he works with computers, so he's really good with numbers and machines, and things like that.

   B: He sounds nice. Do you see him very often?

   A: Yes, quite often. He lives quite near where I work, so we have lunch together once or twice a month.

6. A: OK, I suppose. It wasn't the best I've ever been to. It went on a bit too long, I think. I've heard that piece played much better elsewhere.

   B: Oh, really? It doesn't sound very good. What was the venue like? I've heard the building is incredible.

   A: Oh yes. The place was amazing. It's really beautiful in there. It's just a shame the music wasn't as good.

7. A: Brilliant! I'm really enjoying it. It's very practical, so we spend a lot of time making things, and looking at things and talking about them. It's really nice to be so active for a change.

    B: And what're the other students in the class like?

    A: They're all really nice – apart from this one strange English girl who never really talks to anyone, but most of them are lovely.

    B: What about the teacher? What's she like?

    A: It's a he, actually. He's great. Really interesting, really good.

8. A: It's nice. It's quite large, so there's plenty of space for the three of us. The kitchen's very modern, so that's good and the bedrooms are OK too. The bathroom is a bit small, but it's OK. I've lived in much worse places before!

    B: Oh, it sounds lovely. What're your neighbours like?

    A: I'm not sure, actually. I've only seen them on the stairs. I haven't really talked to them yet. They looked OK, though.

Unit 15

Arranging to go to the cinema (page 104)

I: What are you DOing toNIGHT?

J: I've got NOTHing PLANNED.   What about YOU?

I: Well, I was THINKing of   GOing to the CINema.   Do you want to COME with me?

J: Yes, MAYbe.   WHAT are you THINKing of SEEing?

I: Have you SEEN   *LANDS of HOPE* yet?   It's supPOSED to be REAlly GOOD.

J: YES,   I SAW it last WEEK.   It's OK,   but it's NOT BRILliant. What ELSE is on?

I: WELL, there's a FILM   with GEORGE CLOOney.

J: Oh, YES?   I DON'T really like HIM.

I: NO, NEITHer do I.   And then there's this FILM,   *CIty of DREAMS.*

J: I HAVEn't HEARD of it.   WHAT'S it aBOUT?

I: It's a FRENCH film.   It's a DRAma   about some AlGERians GROWing up in PARis.   It's got quite a GOOD reVIEW.

J: It SOUNDS quite INteresting.   What TIME'S it on?

I: SIX THIRty,   EIGHT fifTEEN   and eLEven TWENty.

J: And WHERE'S it on?

I: The ABC.

J: OK.   WELL,   shall we GO to the EIGHT fifTEEN showing? I WANT to have SOMEthing to EAT   beFORE we GO.

I: Yes, OK.   Shall I MEET you THERE, then?   You KNOW where it is, DON'T you?

J: Yes.   So I'll SEE you THERE   around EIGHT.   If I'm there FIRST, shall I get the TICKets?

I: YES.   FINE.

While you listen (page 108)

(L = Leroy, S = Ticket seller)

L: Hi. I'd like to book two tickets for the show on Saturday, please.

S: OK. Is that for the afternoon show or the evening one?

L: Oh, I didn't realise there was a choice. Let me think … um … the evening one, please.

S: Right. Let me just check if we have tickets available … Oh, I'm sorry, but I'm afraid that show is completely sold out. We do still have tickets left for the afternoon, though. It starts at four.

L: Oh right … um … well, I suppose that should be OK.

S: OK, so it's two tickets for the four o'clock show on Saturday afternoon. Whereabouts would you like to sit?

L: As near to the front as possible, please.

S: OK, I'm just checking. Oh, I'm really sorry, but the closest to the front that we've got is Row S. Does that sound OK?

L: Well, not really. We wouldn't see much from there, would we? Have you got anything upstairs?

S: I'll just check … Yes, we have. We've got a couple of seats in Row C, if you're interested.

L: That sounds great. Are those the same price as the ones downstairs?

S: No, I'm afraid they're a little bit more expensive. These are £42 and the ones downstairs are £27.

L: Forty-two pounds! Each! You're joking, aren't you? I can't afford that. I'll have to go for the two in Row U or whatever it was.

S: Certainly, sir, so that's two seats in Row S. And how will you be paying?

L: By credit card, please, if that's OK.

S: Yes, of course. What kind?

L: It's an American Express.

S: OK. And can I take your number, please?

L: Yes. It's 4926–8631–6231–9221.

S: And the expiry date?

L: It's 04 / 07.

S: And can I have the address where the card is registered, please?

L: Yes, it's 14, Beechwood Park, E17 and it's in my name, Leroy Jones. That's L-E-R-O-Y.

S: OK, that's fine. You can just pick the tickets up from the box office, any time after four today.

L: Great. OK. Thanks for your help.

Unit 16

Answering the phone (1) (page 110)

L: Hello.

P: Hi, is Jenny there?

L: I'm afraid not. She's gone out shopping.

P: Oh right. When will she be back?

L: She'll probably be about an hour. Do you want to leave a message?

P: No, it's all right. I'll just call back later.

Talking on the phone (page 111)

J: Hello.

P: Hi, is Jenny there?

J: Speaking.

P: Oh right, hi. My name's Paola. I'm a friend of Fernanda. We go to the same school to learn English.

J: Oh, OK. She told me about you. How are you?

P: Fine, thanks.

J: And how's Fernanda?

P: Oh great. She told me to say hello. Anyway, I was wondering if you could help me.

J: I'll try.

P: I'm coming to London for a few days for a visit and Fernanda said you might be able to recommend somewhere cheap to stay.

J: Well, you could stay with me if you like. I've got a spare room.

P: Really? Are you sure?

J: Yes, it's no trouble. When are you coming?

P: In two weeks' time. I'm coming down on the Friday and then I'm going to go back on the Tuesday.

J: Fine. Do you want to give me a ring a bit nearer the time just to check what time you'll be here?

P: Yes, OK.

J: OK, well, I'll speak to you then. Can you say hi to Fernanda from me and thank her for the birthday card? I'll give her a ring next week sometime. I'm actually going away for a few days.

P: OK. Great.

J: See you.

P: Yes, bye. And thanks for the offer. It's really kind of you.

J: No problem. Bye.

Pronunciation (page 114)

1. ALAN told me to TELL you he CAN'T COME tonight. He's got a MEETing.
2. ALAN told me to TELL you he's GOing to be LATE.
3. ALAN told me to ASK you if you could CALL him.
4. ALAN told me to SAY helLO.
5. ALAN was TELLing me you're GOing to THAIland in a COUple of WEEKS. It SOUNDS really GOOD.
6. ALAN told me to SAY GOOD LUCK with the eXAM.
7. ALAN told me to ASK you if you could GET some MILK on the way HOME.
8. ALAN was TELLing me you REAlly like TENnis. Do you want to have a GAME someTIME?
9. ALAN told me to SAY THANKS for the TICKets.
10. ALAN told me to TELL you NOT to be LATE. The FILM starts at EIGHT.
11. ALAN was TELLing me he's THINKing of LEAVing his JOB. Has he SAID anything to YOU aBOUT it?
12. ALAN was TELLing me about the PARty last night. It SOUNDed as if you ALL had a REAlly GOOD TIME.

While you listen (page 115)

Conversation 1

C: What happened to you yesterday?

L: I'm really sorry. There were some roadworks and the bus was really slow. It took me over an hour to get there.

C: Why didn't you ring? I would've waited.

L: I tried, but my mobile was dead, because I'd forgotten to recharge it.

C: Oh, what a shame. We did wait for about half an hour, but we didn't want to miss the beginning of the film, so we went without you.

L: Yes, I thought that was what you must've done, so I just went home again!

Conversation 2

P: Are you OK? You look a bit fed up.

K: Yes, I've just had my mobile stolen.

P: You're joking! What happened?

K: I was stupid. I was just having a coffee in that bar over the road and I stupidly left it lying on the table. Anyway, a couple of young lads came up to me and started talking really fast, and I just said I didn't understand and then they just walked off. By the time I noticed the phone had gone, they'd disappeared.

P: That's terrible. Are you insured?

K: Yes, yes. I can replace the phone easily enough, but the problem is all the phone numbers I keep in the phone.

P: Oh, no! You don't have them written down anywhere?

K: No, I just always put them straight into my mobile. I never bother to write them anywhere else.

P: What a pain.

K: Yes, I don't really know how I can contact some of them.

Conversation 3

F: Where did you say we were meeting Tom?

E: Well, I thought it was here, in front of Tesco's.

F: Don't you remember? When did you last speak to him?

E: Last week sometime. I tried calling him yesterday, but he wasn't in.

F: Have you got his mobile number on you now?

E: Yes, one minute. I think it's here somewhere ... um ... no, it's not. Sorry.

F: What a pain! So what shall we do now?

E: Let's wait five more minutes and if he doesn't come, let's just go without him.

Conversation 4

B: Is that new?

T: Yes, haven't you seen one of these yet? They're the new Fourth Generation ones. They're great!

B: Really? So what does it do, then?

T: Well, you can do all the normal things like phone and text people and it's got internet connection and games, and things like that.

B: Yes, mine has all that.

T: Yes, OK, but this one can take photos and send them and ... look ... you can watch TV on it too and download films from the internet.

B: No!

T: Yes, look. There you go.

B: Wow! That's amazing! How much did you pay for it?

T: It was only $2,000. I got it in Hong Kong.

B: ONLY $2,000! You think that's cheap!

T: Yes, it's not expensive for something like this.

B: And how long do the batteries last?

T: Ah, well, that's the problem, you see. Only about 20 minutes, usually, but they're trying to sort that out.

Review: Units 13–16

Vowel sounds (page 119)

1. visa
2. pollution
3. worst
4. harbour
5. morning
6. passport
7. the train journey
8. she teaches Greek
9. use your computer
10. boring sports course

Unit 17

Talking about what's wrong with you (page 120)

D: Aaagh!

R: Oh, are you all right?

D: Yes, I think so.

R: Are you sure? That was quite a nasty fall.

D: Yes, I don't know what happened. I think I just tripped.

R: Yes, you need to be careful. Can you stand up all right?

D: Yes, I think so. Ow, ow!

R: Maybe you should have that arm looked at. It might be broken.

D: No, it'll be all right. It's probably just bruised.

R: It doesn't look like it to me. Honestly, I really think you should have it X-rayed. You don't want to be walking round with a broken arm.

D: Yes, maybe you're right. It IS quite painful.

R: Shall I get you a cab to take you to the hospital?

D: Would you mind?

R: No, of course not. Just sit there for a minute and I'll see if I can get one. I'll be back in a second.

D: OK. Thanks. I really appreciate it.

While you listen (page 124)

Conversation 1
(V = Vernon, J = Jenny, A = Assistant)

V: Have we got everything now? Can we go home?

J: Yes, almost. I just need to go into this shop. I want to get a present for Anna. It's her birthday on Wednesday.

V: OK, but let's make it quick ...

J: Do you think she'll like this?

V: I don't know. Maybe. What is it?

J: What do you mean, what is it? It's a vase, isn't it? Men! Honestly! You've got no idea.

V: How much is it?

J: I don't know. Let me have a look ... Oh no! It's £80.

V: Eighty pounds! For that! It probably only holds one flower.

J: It is very nice, though.

V: Don't be silly, let's just put it back ...

J: ... OK, careful ... Vernon!

V: Oh no, I'm sorry, I thought I had it ...

A: What seems to be the problem?

V: I'm really sorry. I don't know what I was doing. It just slipped from my fingers as I was putting it back on the shelf. I'm really sorry.

A: Well, I'm afraid you'll have to pay for it.

V: Pay for it? You're joking, aren't you? Aren't you covered by insurance for that kind of thing?

A: I'm sorry sir, but it does say very clearly on the sign over there, any breakages must be paid for.

V: But it's £80!

A: I'm sorry, but those are the rules and we can't afford to have things broken like that. We lose money.

V: Do you think I can afford it? It was an accident!

A: I'm sorry, sir. Would you like me to call the manager?

J: Oh, Vernon, let's just pay for it. I'll pay with my card.

V: I can't believe this.

J: I know, but these things happen. Forget about it.

V: Eighty pounds! I'll have to give you the money later.

J: Don't worry about it! I'll pay for half. It was partly my fault.

V: OK, yes, I suppose. I mean thanks. But Jenny – £80. It's such a waste of money!

J: I know, but that's life.

Conversation 2
(F = Freddie, L = Lisa)

F: Would you like another drink before we go?

L: No, I'm fine. I've still got quite a bit left here.

F: OK, do you mind if I just go and ask for another one?

L: No, of course not. Go ahead.

F: Oh no, sorry. Oh no, er ... let me get a cloth ... Excuse me, excuse me. Could you bring us a cloth? We've spilt some wine. Lisa, I'm really sorry.

L: Don't worry about it!

F: Oh no, it's gone on your dress.

L: It's all right. It's not too bad. I'll just rub some salt in it. It'll come out in the wash.

F: Are you sure? It's such a lovely dress. I'll pay to get it cleaned.

L: Don't be silly! It's fine. It's only a couple of drops. It'll be fine. It's quite an old dress anyway.

F: I just feel bad. I wanted us to have a really great evening.

L: Forget about it. These things happen. I'm having a lovely time.

F: OK, I can be so clumsy sometimes. I'm sorry. Shall we just go?

L: Yes, let's and don't worry about it.

F: OK. Here, let me get your coat. Oh no, I'm really sorry ...

Unit 18

Problems on holiday (page 126)

T: Hello. How are you?

A: Great. I've seen lots of interesting things. I'm really enjoying it.

T: Yes, it's a nice place, isn't it?

A: Yes, lovely. So what are you doing today?

T: Oh, I've lost my passport, so I need to go to the Embassy and see if I can get a temporary one.

A: Oh no! Where did you lose it?

T: I'm not sure. The last time I remember having it was in the bank the other day.

A: Have you been back there to see if anyone's handed it in?

T: Yes, I went there yesterday, but they didn't have it.

A: How annoying!

T: Yes, it's a real pain. Anyway, listen, I must go. The Embassy opens at ten and I want to get there early.

A: Yes, sure. Well, good luck. I hope you sort it all out.

T: Yes, thanks.

While you listen (page 131)

Conversation 1

A: Hi, I wonder if you can help me with this.

B: What's the problem with it?

A: I'm not really sure. It's just not working properly. When you press record, the red light doesn't come on and then, even if it works, the film usually comes out looking very strange.

B: OK. Let me have a look at it ... oh, it's very dirty. How long have you had it?

A: Quite a while now. Maybe four or five years.

B: Right. That's quite a long time. And when was the last time you cleaned it?

A: Cleaned it? I didn't know I had to! I've never really cleaned it. I don't know how to do it.

B: Ah-ha! Well, that could be part of the problem. Let's open it all up and give it a good clean, and see if that makes any difference.

A: OK. Great. Thanks. Can I leave it with you?

B: Yes, of course. It should be ready later on today, if you want to come back later to collect it.

Conversation 2

A: Hi, thanks for coming.

B: That's OK. Where is it?

A: Just through here in the kitchen. There you are.

B: Right, OK. And what's the problem with it?

A: I'm not really sure. It's making a funny noise when it goes round and I think it's leaking somewhere because water keeps coming out from underneath here.

B: I see. And how long've you had it?

A: Almost four years now and I've never had any problems with it before.

B: No, it's a very good make. They don't usually break down. Let's start with the noise. Do you always check there's no money in your pockets before you put things in?

A: Well ... um ... I try to, of course, but it's possible I miss some sometimes.

B: Well, that could be it, then. Sometimes coins get stuck just here and start making a horrible noise. Let's open this up and have a look, OK? And then we'll worry about the leak.

Conversation 3

A: So what's wrong with it?

B: I've no idea! I've tried turning it on and off, but nothing happens at all. I've tried pressing all these buttons here, but that didn't make any difference. I've even tried changing the batteries in the remote control I use with it, but that didn't help either. I really don't know what to do.

A: How long have you had it?

B: Just a couple of days. I only bought it last Saturday and the man in the shop told me it was the best brand you can buy. It makes me really angry.

A: OK. OK. Calm down and let's have a look at it. It's all connected up OK.

B: I know. I checked all that earlier.

A: It's very strange. Let's start from the beginning with it, then. OK. Oh, look – you idiot!!

B: What? What have I done?

A: You haven't plugged it in over here, have you! I'm not surprised it hasn't been working!

B: Oh no. I'm really sorry. I've completely wasted your time, then!

A: Oh well, never mind. You live and learn, I suppose.

B: Yes, maybe ... but it's a really stupid mistake, isn't it?

A: You can say that again!

Unit 19

Borrowing money (page 132)

B: Have you got TIME for a COFfee?

T: Yes, OK. WHERE do you WANT to GO?

B: How about that PLACE on the CORner?

T: Yes, FINE. Oh NO!

B: What's the MATter?

T: Oh, I've just REAlised I've LEFT my WALlet at HOME.

B: Don't WORry. It's OK. I'll PAY for the COFfee.

T: Yes, THANKS, but it's NOT just THAT I'm MEEting SOMEone at TWO and I'll HAVE to GO BACK HOME and GET it. I CAN'T spend the WHOLE day withOUT any MONey.

B: Well, do you want ME to LEND you SOME?

T: Would you MIND?

B: No, of COURSE NOT. How MUCH do you NEED? Is THIRty euros enough?

T: THAT'd be GREAT, if you CAN.

B: Yes, SURE. No PROBlem. I'll JUST have to GO to the CASH machine, though. Do you WANT to MEET me in the CAfé? I'll BE there in a MINute.

T: OK.

B: THERE you ARE.

T: GREAT That's BRILliant. I'll PAY you BACK NEXT WEEK, when I SEE you.

B: Yes, FINE. There's NO HURry. Have you ORdered?

T: NO, I was WAIting for YOU to GET HERE. I WASn't SURE how you LIKE your COFfee.

While you listen (page 136)

Conversation 1
(B1 = Boy 1, B2 = Boy 2)

B1: Can't you ask your mum and dad for some?

B2: I have, but they just said I've had my pocket money already. They only give me £15 a week. I buy one CD and it's nearly all gone. It's a pain. I can never afford to go out these days.

B1: Won't they give you any more? Fifteen pounds is nothing.

B2: No, I've asked them, but they just said I should get a job. It's so unfair. You don't have a job. Gino doesn't have a job. None of my friends have one.

B1: I know. It's awful!

B2: I don't want to spend my weekends filling shelves in a supermarket for £5 an hour.

B1: I'm glad they're not MY parents.

Conversation 2
(M = Man, W = Woman)

M: So how's work?

W: Oh, don't ask! It's just the same old thing. I'm really fed up with it. You know, I'm earning the same money as I was when I first started there five years ago.

M: That's terrible. Haven't you had any pay rise in five years?

W: No, nothing.

M: So how much do you get?

W: Seven euros an hour.

M: Seven? That's awful. How do you survive?

W: Well, I have to live at home with my parents, I cycle to work, that kind of thing. I manage, but it's terrible money. I never have any money at the end of the month.

M: So why don't you get another job?

W: I can't afford to take time off work to go to interviews. And there aren't that many jobs around at the moment, anyway.

M: That's awful.

Conversation 3
(G1 = Girl 1, G2 = Girl 2)

G1: Did you see the new jeans Jenny was wearing?

G2: Yes, they looked OK. I'm not sure I would wear them, though.

G1: No, me neither. But you know how much they cost?

G2: No. Were they expensive?

G1: Two hundred and fifty pounds.

G2: Two hundred and fifty pounds for a pair of jeans! You're joking.

G1: No, honestly, she told me herself. She got them in some fancy designer shop on Saturday.

G2: That's crazy. Is she really well off, then?

G1: I don't think so. She's a nurse. She works at the Springfield hospital. I think she just pays for everything on her credit card. I went out with her the other day and she probably spent £150 then. Honestly, she just spends money like water.

G2: Maybe she's from a rich family.

G1: I don't think so – and she was complaining she couldn't afford to go on holiday in the summer, because she's in debt!

G2: I'm not surprised.

Conversation 4
(T1 = Tourist 1, T2 = Tourist 2)

T1: Did you get the bill?

T2: Yes.

T1: How much was it?

T2: Fifteen pounds.

T1: Really? Let me have a look. ... What? Two fifty for a coffee. That's terrible!

T2: No, that's quite normal, isn't it?

T1: No way! Things like that are much cheaper in my country than they are here in London. I mean, you probably only pay about a pound for a coffee and a snack like this would only cost about six or seven.

T2: Oh, in my country it's fairly similar to here. The only thing which is cheaper there is public transport. Buses and trains are much cheaper than they are here. And they're nicer as well.

T1: Yes, well, everything's cheaper in my country than it is here. That's why I can't afford to stay here in the UK much longer. I'm running out of money – fast!

Unit 20

Talking about life in your country (page 138)

M: What do you do back home?

A: Well, I was working in a car factory, but it closed down. That's why I'm here, really. I got some money when I lost my job and I decided to go travelling for a while to think about what to do next.

M: And what are you going to do?

A: I still haven't decided. The economy's in a bit of a mess at the moment. There's a lot of unemployment and people aren't spending much money, so it's going to be difficult to find a new job. I might try to retrain and do something completely different.

M: Have you got any idea what you want to do?

A: Not really. Maybe something with computers. I might try to find a job abroad for a while before I do that. What about your country? Is it easy to find work there?

M: Yes. A few years ago it was quite bad, but the economy's doing quite well at the moment. I think unemployment is about four per cent, so finding a job isn't really a problem. The problem is the cost of living. Prices have gone up a lot over the last few years. Everything is more expensive, so the money you earn goes really quickly.

A: Right.

M: Sometimes I think I should move to somewhere like here. I'm sure people don't get paid very much, but the cost of living is so low and there's a better quality of life. People don't work as hard; life is more relaxed; the food's great; the weather's great; it's just very nice.

A: Yes, maybe, but don't forget that you are on holiday. Maybe it's not like that for the people who live here.

M: No, maybe not.

A: So anyway, how long are you going to stay here?

M: Just till Friday. I have to get back to work. What about you? How long are you staying?

A: Till I get bored or I run out of money. I don't have any plans.

While you listen (page 142)

D: Did you see those two young people at the bus stop?

M: I did. Young people nowadays have got no shame. We were never allowed to kiss in public like that, were we, Doris?

D: No. We lived in a more polite time. The language young people use today – it's awful. They swear all the time – using all those bad words. Honestly, it's shameful.

M: I know. Did I tell you what happened to me in the supermarket the other day?

D: No, what happened?

M: Well, you know I have a bad leg.

D: Oh yes. You have to use a stick sometimes, don't you?

M: Yes. Well, I did my little bit of shopping – you know, just a little bit of bread and cheese – I don't eat much these days. And then I bought some tins of cat food.

D: Just a few things, then.

M: Yes, and I came to the checkout to pay and there was a queue. Well, my leg was hurting because I'd been walking round the shop, you know.

D: Well, you've got a bad leg, haven't you?

M: Mm. But no one offered to let me go first. I just had to wait.

D: Oh, young people! When we were young, we always used to let old people go first, didn't we?

M: I know, but it just doesn't happen any more.

D: No. Young people today – they're always in such a rush.

M: Anyway, I told the boy in front of me. I said, 'My leg's hurting. They should have help for old people like me. We should get treated better.'

D: Good for you.

M: But do you know what he did then? He called me something which I'm not going to repeat and he laughed at me!

D: No! That's terrible, Marge. They've got no respect, these young people. Oh, look at those two standing by the door. Are they boys or girls? You can't tell the difference sometimes with these girls with their short hair and trousers and the boys with rings in their ears and noses and everywhere.

M: Oh, I know. It wasn't like that in our day. Girls were girls and boys were boys. (sound of a mobile phone)

D: Oh that's mine. Hello, Reg. Is that you? Yes, I'm on the bus. I said I'm on the bus!

Review: Units 17–20

Vowel sounds: dipthongs (page 147)

1. years
2. shade
3. coast
4. square
5. where
6. below
7. weird
8. hair
9. blow your nose
10. this tastes great
11. it's really serious
12. the air fare

Grammar introduction

The authors speak

We both teach General English every day. We know how worried many students are about their grammar. The first thing we usually tell our students at this level is that you WILL make mistakes when you speak English – this is normal and there's no way to avoid it! It takes a long, long time to become totally accurate in English. In fact, we are both married to non-native speakers of English. They have both lived in England for a long time, but they both sometimes make mistakes. If you worry too much about making mistakes, you'll never say anything! In the real world, away from the language classroom, people don't worry too much about grammar mistakes if they can understand what you are trying to say. We've both heard lots of conversations in Britain between non-native and native speakers, where lots of mistakes are made. This doesn't stop people buying tickets, finding out where places are, booking rooms – or making friends!

This doesn't mean we don't think it's important to become more accurate. Learning grammar is similar to learning words. Lots of the most common words in English – words like *get, have, make, do* – are used in hundreds of different ways and connect with hundreds of other words. In the same way, different grammatical structures have different meanings – some of them are very common and easy to understand; some of them are much more unusual and more difficult to understand. It's good to remember that you can't learn everything at once. You need to take things step by step. Becoming grammatically accurate takes time, but it is possible at this level to be accurate in limited ways. You can learn how to use the most common, useful structures in English in a small number of ways – and you can learn how to use them accurately within those limits.

In the grammar exercises in this book, we have deliberately tried to make life easy for you. We don't believe that grammar should be made difficult for students or that it should scare you. We think it is important that you feel that the patterns and uses of grammar are easy to understand. You need to see good examples of how grammar works in everyday conversations and you need the chance to practise using grammar in these kinds of conversations yourself. We hope this book allows you to do that.

We have also tried to make sure that this book allows you to meet the most important grammatical structures of English more than once. It's useful to meet things like the present perfect and the past simple two or three times and to do different things with them at different times. Your ability to use these structures accurately will hopefully get better each time you meet them. We have also tried to write vocabulary exercises which also have a gentle focus on grammar. For example, in Unit 5, there is this exercise:

1 | Using vocabulary: problems with clothes

Match the problems with the pictures.

1. I can't wear this. It's too big.
2. I can't wear this. It's too tight.
3. I can't wear this. It's too small.
4. I can't wear this. It's too bright.
5. I can't wear this. It's too old-fashioned.
6. I can't wear these. They're too trendy!

In which picture(s) would the speaker add It doesn't fit me and in which would they add It doesn't suit me?

Do you have any clothes that you don't wear any more? Why?

What kind of clothes suit you? What colours suit you?

This activity is looking at adjectives for describing clothes – *big, tight, old-fashioned*, and so on. It also helps you revise and remember how to use *can't* and *too + adjective*. We also want you to notice the expressions which we use with grammar in everyday conversation, so here the expressions in the first question are important. The way we have highlighted words in colour in this book will also help you notice words which go together.

In some activities, you will meet expressions which are also good examples of common grammatical structures. You can learn and reuse them as whole fixed expressions. Learning lots of these fixed expressions will help you become more accurate. For example, in Unit 2, you meet the expression *I've never heard of it*. You can understand, learn and use this expression without spending hours studying the present perfect. This book helps you to meet lots and lots of expressions like this.

Many individual words also have their own grammatical patterns and we will help you learn what kind of grammar you can use with some important everyday words like *want* and *hope*. Finally, although it is important to look at grammar and to try to be accurate, it is more important to be able to say what you want to say. Without grammar, you can't say very much, it's true. But, without words, you can't say anything at all. If you spend time studying English outside class, make sure you spend more time learning words and expressions than doing grammar exercises. Remember – the way we present vocabulary in this coursebook and in the workbook will make you more grammatically accurate anyway.

We hope you enjoy using this book, we hope you find the Grammar commentary useful, and we hope you feel your English improving as you work through INNOVATIONS.

Hugh Dellar & Andrew Walkley

Grammar commentary

Unit by unit grammar notes

G1 | Past simple (page 11)

We use the past simple to talk about things in the past that we see as completed. We often use time expressions with the past simple to make it clear we are talking about the completed past. We can use the past simple to talk about things that happened only once, things that happened over a long period of time, or things that happened a lot in the past. Look at these examples:

> I missed my bus this morning.
> I worked in a shoe shop for two years after I left university.
> I played a lot of tennis when I was younger.

Look at these common ways of answering past simple questions both positively and negatively:

> A: Did you watch that film on Channel 3 last night?
> B: Yes, I did. It was great, wasn't it?
> B: No, I didn't. I didn't have time.

G2 | There's ... / There are ... (page 12)

We use *There's* and *There are* to introduce nouns for the first time and to say that they exist somewhere. We use *There's* with singular nouns and uncountable nouns. When we introduce a singular noun, we usually say *There's a* + (noun) or *There's* + (someone / something / no-one / nothing)*, etc. Look at these examples:

> There's a bank near the station. You could try there.
> There's something wrong with this machine!
> There's nothing wrong with it.

There are lots of nouns in English that can be uncountable. There is no easy way of remembering them. You just have to try to learn them. It's also important to look at the other words we use with *There's* and *There are*. Here are some useful examples:

> There's a lot of traffic on the roads this morning.
> There's some milk in the fridge.
> There's too much sex and violence on TV.

We use *There are* with plural nouns. We usually use a quantifier with the noun – *lots of, some, plenty of,* etc. Look at these examples:

> There are lots of hotels near the station.
> There are some lovely beaches on the west coast.

Look at these common ways of answering questions using *There's* and *There are* both positively and negatively:

> A: Is there any / much rice in the cupboard?
> B: Yes, loads. / Yes, quite a lot. / Yes, a bit.
> B: No, not much. / No, none at all.
>
> A: Are there any / many shops near your house?
> B: Yes, loads. / Yes, quite a few. / Yes, a few.
> B: No, not many. / No, none at all.

G3 | Too (page 19)

We often use *too + adjective* to explain why we don't like something or cannot do it:

> It's too hot in here. Is it OK if I open a window?

We often use the pattern *too + adjective + to + verb*:

> I'm too fat to get into my trousers. I need to lose weight!

We sometimes use the structure *too + adjective + for someone / something* – especially to talk about problems with clothes:

> Those jeans are too small for you. Try the bigger ones.

We can also use *too + adverb*:

> I arrived too late and missed my flight.

You can use *too* with *much + uncountable noun* and *many + plural noun*:

> I put too much garlic in here. It tastes horrible.
> You can't go to Intermediate level yet. You make too many mistakes.

G4 | Questions with *have you got ... ?* (page 21)

When we ask *Have you got a ... ?*, we add a singular noun. When we ask *Have you got any ... ?*, we add a plural noun or an uncountable noun. Look at these useful examples and notice the possible answers:

> A: Have you got a pen I can borrow?
> B: Yes, there's one in my bag somewhere. One minute.
> B: No, sorry. Ask Jenny. I think she's got one.
>
> A: Have you got any plasters?
> B: Yes, there are some in the bathroom.
> B: No, none at all. Sorry.

G5 | I'm thinking of ... (page 23)

We often report ideas we have about the future using *I'm thinking of ...* . It means we are not 100% sure about the idea yet, but have already started thinking about it:

> I'm thinking of doing a French course next year. My boss said it's a good idea and might help me at work.

Did you notice that after *I'm thinking of ...* , we also add a verb in the *-ing* form? You may also hear people say *I was thinking of ...* to talk about future plans. This has a very similar meaning, but suggests the speaker is less certain.

G6 | One / ones (page 25)

We use *one* or *ones* to talk about something that has already been talked about. We don't usually repeat main nouns. Look at these examples:

> It's an OK book, but I prefer the last one she wrote.

> I like these glasses better than the ones we looked at earlier.

G7 | Present continuous for arrangements (page 27)

The most common way to ask someone about their arrangements in the near future is to use the present continuous:

What're you doing today after class?
What're you doing this weekend? Anything good?

When we want to talk about things in the future that we have already arranged to do – usually with other people – we use the present continuous. We usually only use a small number of verbs to report these arrangements – *come, go, have, meet, stay* and a few more. Look at these examples:

My mother is coming to London this weekend. She's staying with me for three days.
I'm going out with some friends tonight.
I'm meeting an old friend of mine this afternoon.
I'm having dinner with an important client later.

G8 | Present simple with *hope* (page 29)

We use *hope* to talk about things we want to happen in the future. After the verb *hope*, we use the present simple tense:

A: I hope you have a good time in Switzerland next week.
B: Thanks. So do I.

Note that we do NOT use *wish* to talk about the future in sentences like these. This is a common mistake.

G9 | Time expressions (page 30)

When you are learning to use different verb structures, it's important to make sure you also notice the words which often go with these structures. Keep a page in your notebook where you record new examples of time expressions which can be used with different structures. Here are some useful examples:

I went there
the other day / the week before last / years ago / when I was eight or nine.

I'm going there
in an hour or two / a week tomorrow / in a few weeks' time / in a couple of months / sometime next year.

Remember that there is no difference between the following:

in a few minutes   in a few minutes' time

G10 | Prepositional expressions (page 37)

Keep a page in your notebook where you record new expressions you meet. Here are some everyday examples:

Describing where places are in a town

It's next to the police station.
It's directly opposite the bank.
It's on the corner of Gillespie Road and Avenell Road.
It's just round the corner from the station.
It's right next door to the primary school.
She lives about three doors down from Mark's house.
It's just up the road from where I work.

G11 | Not enough (page 40)

We often use *not* + *enough* to talk about problems. *Enough* comes before nouns, but after adjectives and adverbs. Look at these examples:

I don't have enough money to buy it. I'll just leave it, thanks.
There aren't enough places for young people to meet.

I'm not old enough to vote yet. It's really annoying!

Did you notice the structures *not (adjective) enough + to do something* and *not (adjective) enough + for somebody*?

G12 | Negative questions (page 41)

We often ask negative questions after the person we are talking to has said something that surprises us or that we don't agree with. Look at these examples:

A: I really love that film.
B: Really? Don't you think it's a bit boring?
A: Oh no, not at all.
A: I really like the new girl in Class 3.
B: Do you? Don't you think she's a bit strange?
A: No, not really. Why? Do you?

Did you notice that after *Don't you think*, we just add our opinion? We don't change the word order of the second part of the sentence. It's like a normal positive sentence.

G13 | Can't / couldn't (page 45)

Look at these examples of using *can't / couldn't*:

1. **No ability**

I can't drive. I've failed my test three times.
I couldn't speak much English before I started this course.

2. **No permission**

I can't have parties in my flat. My landlord won't let me.
His parents said we couldn't see each other any more.

3. **Avoiding bad consequences**

I can't be late or my girlfriend will kill me!
I couldn't say no to him. He's one of the boss's best friends!

To talk about these ideas in the future, use *will / won't be able to*:

Hopefully, I'll be able to find a good job after I graduate.
If I drink this coffee, I won't be able to sleep tonight.

G14 | *Going to* and *might* (page 49)

Here are some more examples of decisions people have made:

My brother is going to move to Australia next month.

Don't try to stop me, because I've already made my decision. I'm going to tell him I don't love him and ask for a divorce!

We use *might + verb* to talk about things we think are possible in the future, but not probable. *I might* means there is a 50–50 chance that I will. We often show that we are not sure by using other expressions:

I'm not really sure yet. I suppose I might …
I haven't really decided yet. I think I might …

A: What're you doing this weekend?
B: I'm not really sure yet. I think I might go to the beach. It depends on the weather. What about you?
A: I haven't really decided yet. I might just stay in and have a quiet weekend at home. I'll see how I feel.

G15 | Asking for permission (page 52)

There are lots of different ways of asking for permission in English. *May I ... ?* sounds very formal and quite old-fashioned now. *Can I ... ?* sometimes sounds a bit too informal and rude if you're talking to someone you don't know very well. The most useful and common ways of asking for permission are:

Do you mind if I + verb?   Is it OK if I + verb?

It's important that you also learn the normal ways of answering these questions. Look at these examples:

A: Is it OK if I take this chair?
B: Yes, sure. Go ahead. Feel free.

A: Is it OK if I smoke in here?
B: No, sorry. You're not allowed to, actually. Look, there's a No-smoking sign there.

Remember that when we want to say OK to *Do you mind if I ... ?*, we answer *No, of course not.*

A: Do you mind if I join you?
B: No, of course not. Go ahead. Feel free.

A: Do you mind if I use your bathroom?
B: Well, actually, I'd rather you didn't. We're painting it and it's in a terrible mess at the moment.

G16 | Making requests (page 53)

There are lots of different ways of making requests in English. *Can you ... ?* sometimes sounds a bit too informal and rude if you're talking to someone you don't know very well. A very useful and common way of making requests is *Could you + verb?* We sometimes add *for me* at the end and it's polite to finish with *please*. It's also important that you learn the normal ways of answering these questions. Look at these examples:

A: Could you help me carry this, please, Tony?
B: Yes, sure. No problem.

A: Could you just move up a bit so I can sit down?
B: Sorry, but I'm saving this seat for a friend.

Did you notice that with small requests, we often make them sound 'soft' by adding *just*?

G17 | *Have to* and *don't have to* (page 55)

We often use *have to* to talk about things we don't really want to do, but have no choice about. Maybe we have no choice because of rules or laws, or because someone important tells us to do something. Here are some examples:

The doctor told me I have to take it easy for a few days, so I'm not going to go to work today.

We use *don't have to* if we have a choice about something unpleasant. If we say we don't have to do things, it usually means we're happy. For example:

I'm living with my cousin, so I don't have to pay any rent.
Thank goodness it's Saturday. I don't have to get up early.

To ask questions using *have to*, we say *Do you have to ... ?*

A: Do you have to work long hours?
B: Yes, I do. It's awful.

In British English, you might hear people say *I've got to + verb* to talk about specific things they have no choice about doing in the future. For example:

I've got to work late tomorrow.

We don't often use *have got to* in negatives or questions.

G18 | Present perfect simple (page 57)

We form the present perfect simple by using a noun or pronoun + *has / have* + past participle – the 'third form' of the verb. We use it to talk about something that happened in the past, but that has a connection to now – perhaps there is a present result or we want to talk more about this experience now.

We never use this structure with a past time expression like *when I was a kid, in 2001* or *the day before yesterday.*

Many verbs have regular past participles – they are formed by adding *-ed* to the verbs, just like past simple forms. However, lots of very common verbs have irregular past participles. The best way to deal with this is simply to learn each one by heart. Here are some examples:

I've lost my glasses. Have you seen them anywhere?

A: Have you done your Christmas shopping yet?
B: I've bought a few things, but I still need to get some more stuff later.

When we answer questions about our experiences, we use the past simple to give details about when they happened – and we add past time expressions:

A: Have you read any good books recently?
B: Yes, I have, actually. I read a great book by Anne Tyler the other week.

G19 | Some / any (page 65)

The rules for using *some* and *any* are quite complicated. It is often true that we use *some* in positive sentences and *any* in negative sentences and questions. This is not a 'rule'. It is only a piece of good advice:

A: Have you got any plasters?
B: Yes, there are some on the shelf in the bathroom.

A: Have you got any money on you?
B: Yes, a bit. Why?

However, we often use *some* in questions that are offers or requests. In the following examples you could also use *any* and the meaning would be basically the same. It's just more normal to use *some* in these situations:

A: Could you lend me some money? Just until pay day.
B: Yes, sure. How much do you need?

We also use *any* in positive sentences after the word *if*:

If there are any phone calls for me, could you say I'm out?
If you need any help, just ask me, OK?

When we talk about what we like and don't like, we can use *any* in positive sentences to mean it doesn't matter which one:

A: Which one do you want?
B: Any of them will be fine. They all look OK.

The words *someone, something, somewhere, anyone, anything* and *anywhere* work in the same way as *some* and *any*:

I just need to go and talk to someone about something. I'll be back in a minute.

A: Do you want me to put your coat and bag somewhere?
B: Oh thanks. That's great.

A: Has anyone seen Noel today?
B: No, but if I see him, I'll tell him you're looking for him.

I haven't got anything to wear to the party tonight!

A: Have you found anywhere to stay yet?
B: Not yet. We're still looking.

G20 | Comparatives (page 71)

Here are some more examples of comparatives:

Adjectives of three syllables

It's more expensive in this shop than in the other one. Let's go back there.
I find my older brother more interesting than my sister. He has more to say about things.
It's more difficult to find a job now than it was when my parents were young.

Adjectives of two syllables

Oxford Street is always more crowded at the weekend than during the week.
I'm getting more and more tired every day. I need a holiday!
I'm more nervous about tonight than I've ever been in my life.

Adjectives of two syllables that take -er

My brother is quieter than I am. He's very shy.
The streets in my hometown are a lot narrower than the ones here.
My sister is much cleverer than me. She went to university. I left school at 16!

Adjectives of two syllables that end in -y

I think Dave Gorman is much funnier than any of these people.
I'm happier now than I've ever been in my life.
This is easier than I thought it would be.

Adjectives of one syllable

My dad is about two feet taller than my mum. They look really funny together.
My sister is exactly one year and one day younger than me.
It's embarrassing, because my mum is fitter than I am – and she's thirty-five years older!

Remember that the following adjectives have irregular comparative forms:
good – better
bad – worse
far – further (or farther, but this sounds a bit old-fashioned now)

G21 | Indirect questions (page 77)

We often make indirect questions by starting *Do you know*. Indirect questions are more polite than normal questions – especially if it is a difficult question to answer and the other person might not know. Notice the word order after *Do you know*:

Does she work on Saturdays?
Do you know if she works on Saturdays?

Where's she staying?
Do you know where she's staying?

Did you notice that if the question is a Yes / No question, we add *if* after *Do you know*? Here are some examples of other ways of asking indirect questions:

A: Can you remember what number his house is?
B: Yes, I think it's Number 33.

A: Sorry to bother you, but could you show me where the finance office is, please?
B: Yes, of course. It's just up here. Follow me.

G22 | Expressions of frequency (page 83)

We use expressions of frequency to talk about how often we do things. We often use them with the present simple. We usually give a general answer and then add more details about exactly how often. Here are some examples:

A: Does he go to the pub a lot?
B: Yes, all the time. He's there almost every evening.

A: How often do you try to read in English?
B: Not that much / Not that often. It's too difficult. I only try it once or twice a year.

Here are the most common follow-up comments:

once or twice a week / month / year
two or three times a week / month / year
once a week / month / year
once every five or six weeks / three or four months / two or three years

G23 | Superlatives (page 85)

Here are some more examples of superlatives:

Adjectives of three syllables

It was the most expensive meal I've ever had in my life!
She's one of the most interesting people I've ever met. She's been all over the world.

Adjectives of two syllables

Central Tokyo is the most crowded place I've ever been to!
Sadie's one of the most relaxed people I've ever met

Adjectives of two syllables that take -er

I'm probably the quietest person in my family. My two brothers never stop talking!
Charles is one of the cleverest people I know.

Adjectives of two syllables that end in -y

He's the funniest person I've ever met.
I think that's one of the easiest exams I've ever taken.

Adjectives of one syllable

It's not much fun being the youngest person in the class.
Rachel's one of the fittest people I know. She ran the London marathon last year.

Did you notice that we often say *one of the + superlative*? When we use *one of the*, we then use a plural noun – *people, places, exams, films, books*, etc. We also often say *one of the + superlative + I've ever ... (in my life)*.

G24 | First conditionals (page 93)

We often use first conditionals when we offer or promise to do something, or to warn somebody about something. Look at these examples:

I'll help you with that, if you want.
If you can lend me £10, I'll pay you back tonight. I promise.
If you give me your credit card details, I can post the tickets to you today.

Notice that the *if*-part of the sentence can come first or second. It depends which part of the sentence we think is more important – the condition or the result.

G25 As long as (page 97)

Some people say *so long as* instead of *as long as*. It means exactly the same thing. Here are some more examples:

A: Is it OK if I put some music on?
B: Yes, of course, as long as it's not too loud.
A: Do you mind if I make myself something to eat?
B: No, of course not, as long as you make some for me as well!

You can stay at my house – as long as you're happy sleeping on the floor!

G26 Present perfect questions (page 99)

We use the present perfect to ask questions about general experience in the past. We often use the word *ever* to add the meaning of *ever in your life before*:

Have you ever been to New Zealand?
Have you ever seen the *Lord of The Rings* films?
Have you ever read anything by William Burroughs?

When we reply to questions like these, we don't usually just reply *Yes, I have* or *No, I haven't*. We usually say *Yes* or *No* and add a comment or a question. If the answer is *Yes* and we want to give more information, we usually use the past simple. Look at these typical ways of answering present perfect questions:

A: Have you ever been to Africa?
B: Yes, I went to Morocco a few years ago. I spent a week in Marrakech. It was amazing!
A: Have you heard the new Charlie Feathers album?
B: Yes, I have. I bought it the other day. It's really good.
A: Have you been to that clothes shop in Hanway Street?
B: No, not yet. Have you?
A: No, but I'm thinking of going there later on today. Do you want to come with me?

Notice that we never use the word *ever* in answers to present perfect questions. This is a common mistake.

> For more information on how to use the present perfect simple, see G18.

G27 Asking longer questions (page 103)

We often put lots of ideas into one question instead of making two or three connected sentences. For example:

You went to a restaurant. You went there last Friday. What was the restaurant like? (= What was that restaurant you went to last Friday like?)

We usually use *that* before the noun, because we make it clear which thing we are talking about. Any time expression in the question – *on Friday* – usually comes just before the word *like*.

Here are some other longer questions:

You went to see a film. You went last night. What was the film like? (= What was that film you went to see last night like?)

You worked in a shop. You worked there last summer. What is the shop like? (= What's that shop you worked in last summer like?)

G28 Passives (page 109)

Look at how we make passive sentences in different tenses:

Past simple

The temple was built in the ninth century.
He was arrested at the airport for trying to bring a gun into the country.

Present simple

English is spoken all over the world now.
Most of their clothes are made in Mexico.

Present continuous

My watch is being repaired at the moment. I've got to pick it up tomorrow.
The lift is being fixed. You'll have to take the stairs.

Present perfect

She has been promoted at work. She's the manager now.
My flight has been delayed, so I'll be late getting into Nantes.

Future

This road is going to be improved next year.
You'll be met at the airport and taken to your hotel.

G29 Reporting what people say (page 114)

This is one of the most complicated areas of English grammar. We use lots of different verbs to report what people have said to us – *tell, ask, say, persuade, explain,* etc. Some books tell you to change the tense of the things you're reporting. At this level, it's best to keep things simple. You can report almost everything anybody says to you using the verb *tell*. Look at these examples:

Kenny told me to say hi to you.
Kenny told me to tell you he's having a party next week and he wants you to come.
Kenny told me to ask you when your mum's birthday is.
Kenny told me to ask you if you're going to go shopping tomorrow afternoon.
Kenny was telling me about the problems he had at work. It sounded horrible.
Kenny was telling me about the flat he's going to move to. It sounds great.

G30 Past simple and past continuous (page 123)

When we are telling stories, we often begin with the action or actions that started first and were in progress when the main actions happened. We use the past continuous to do this. Most of the details of the story are then told in the past simple. This is used much more often than the past continuous. Look at these examples:

I was staying in the centre of the city and there was a bomb scare. They closed all the roads, so we missed our flight home.

I was putting a new wooden floor down in my flat and I was using a hammer and I tried to hit a nail, but I missed it and hit my hand. I broke my little finger in two places. It really hurt!

I was shopping in town with my mum when she met an old friend of hers. They went to have a coffee and a chat and I went with them. It was so boring. They sat in Starbucks for hours.

G31 | Will (page 125)

We often offer to do things for other people by using *I'll* + verb. In all of these situations, you can also say *Let me* + verb:

I'll help you with that.	Let me help you with that.
I'll pay for these.	Let me pay for these.
I'll talk to him about it.	Let me talk to him about it.

We also use *I'll* when we make promises to people. You can't use *Let me* in this situation:

I'll pay you back tomorrow, I promise.
I'll phone you tomorrow.
I won't be long. I'll be back in a minute.

G32 | Present perfect questions (page 127)

Look at these three common ways of answering present perfect questions:

1. We use *Yes* + *past simple* in positive answers:

    A: Have you cancelled your credit cards?
    B: Yes, that was the first thing I did after it happened.

    A: Have you tried the sales desk? They might be able to help.
    B: Yes, I spoke to them earlier, but they couldn't help me.

2. We use *Not yet, but I'm going to* + verb when we have already decided or planned to do the thing suggested in the question:

    A: Have you tried talking to your boss about the problem?
    B: Not yet, but I'm going to go and see him later on today.

    A: Have you been to the doctor's about your arm?
    B: Not yet, but I'm going to see her tomorrow morning.

3. We use *I'll* + verb to show we are making a decision about what to do now:

    A: Have you tried cleaning it? It might just be dirty.
    B: That's a good idea. I'll do that now.

    A: Have you phoned the Embassy? They might be able to help.
    B: Oh, that's a good idea. I'll call them now.

For more information on how to answer present perfect questions, see G26.

G33 | Must (page 129)

We use *I must* + verb to talk about things we think it is important for us to do. Here are some examples:

I must remember to post these letters later.
I must get my mum something for her birthday.
I must just make a quick phone call. I won't be a minute.

We don't usually say *You must* + verb to talk about things we think other people need to do. It's much more common to say *You should* + verb if we are giving advice or *You have to* + verb if we are telling them about rules. For example:

You should go and see them. They'd love to see you.
You have to be a relative before they'll let you in to see him. He's really ill.

G34 | Making and responding to offers (page 133)

Another common way of offering to do things for people is to ask *Do you want me to* + verb? A common way to reply is *Would you mind?* Look at these examples:

A: Do you want me to take your coat?
B: Would you mind?
A: No, of course not.

We can also ask people to do things using *Would you mind* + *-ing?*

A: Would you mind holding this for me for a minute?
B: No, of course not.

For more information on making offers, see G31.
For more information on making requests, see G16.

G35 | Questions with *how long* (page 138)

Look at these questions using *How long* and the ways of answering them:

Present perfect

A: How long have you been living here?
B: Since 1992 / For about fifteen years now.

A: How long have you worked there?
B: Since I left school / Since 1986 / For thirty years.

There is not much difference in meaning between *How long have you lived here?* and *How long have you been living here?* The second sentence suggests you think the person you're talking to might move soon. The first suggests you think they will probably stay where they are. Remember that we use *since* with a point in the past and *for* with a period of time.

***Going to* + verb**

A: How long are you going to stay here?
B: Till next September / Until next year / For six more weeks.

We use *until* / *till* with a point in the future.

G36 | Describing changes (page 139)

We use the present continuous to talk about changes that have already started and that haven't finished yet. We often also use the time expression *at the moment*:

The weather's getting colder, isn't it?
My wife's working too much at the moment. She's going crazy!

We use the present perfect simple to describe a change from the past to now. Notice the time expressions we use to show when this change happened:

The situation has got worse since the end of the war.
Unemployment has risen a lot over the last few months.

Over the last few months / years is exactly the same as *Over the past few months / years*.

G37 | Used to (page 143)

Look at these examples of *used to* / *didn't use to* and notice the language that goes with them:

When I was a kid, I used to love table tennis.
I didn't use to like sushi, but I've grown to like it.

Expression organiser

This section helps you to record and translate some of the most important expressions from each unit. It is always best to record words in phrases, rather than individual words. Sometimes you can translate very easily. Sometimes you will need to think of an equivalent expression in your own language. In each section, there is space for you to add any connected expressions or collocations you want to remember.

Unit 1

Where are you from? ....

Whereabouts exactly? ....

Is anyone sitting here? ....

What's it like? ....

It's in the west of the country. ....

It's about 60 miles from Madrid. ....

Are you from London originally? ....

I've no idea where it is. ....

I've been there. ....

I moved when I got married. ....

There's a lot of unemployment. ....

We moved because my dad got a
  new job. ....

There are lots of places to visit. ....

Sorry I'm late. I missed my bus. ....

....

....

....

....

Unit 2

What kind of music do you like? ....

Lots of things, really, but mainly classical. ....

I can't stand game shows! ....

I've never heard of her! ....

I find it a bit boring. ....

I'm thinking of going to the cinema later. ....

I'm thinking of going to their concert
  next week. ....

I cook dinner for my dad every Sunday. ....

I ring my mother every week. ....

He sounds really nice. ....

How long have you known each other? ....

How did the exam go? ....

I'm going swimming later. ....

I'm too busy to do it now. ....

It's too late to call him now. ....

....

....

....

....

Unit 3

Have you got a rubber? ....

Have you got any scissors? ....

There's some in my bag somewhere. ....

Have you got time for a coffee? ....

Have you got the time on you? ....

What's their place like? ....

It's really nice. It's got six bedrooms. ....

It's OK, but it's a bit cramped. ....

I'm thinking of getting a new computer. ....

My old one is a bit out of date. ....

I haven't got a TV. ....

It's a good film, but the first one was
  better. ....

This one's too bright. Have you got a
  cheaper one? ....

....

....

....

....

Unit 4

It's just gone three. ....

It's almost a quarter to six. ....

It's half past nine. ....

I'm going to a party later. Do you
  want to come? ....

How about half past seven? ....

Shall we say in front of the station? ....

I'm having my hair cut this afternoon. ....

I'm meeting my brother later. ....

I'm going out tonight. ....

in a few weeks' time ....

a few weeks ago ....

the day before yesterday ....

I hope it doesn't rain. ....

I hope your exam goes OK. ....

I've got a doctor's appointment at five. ....

....

....

....

....

Unit 5

Who's the guy with the baseball cap? ....

Who's the woman with the red top? ....

I like those shoes. Where did you get them? ....

I like that top. Where did you get it? ....

It's just round the corner from here. ....

It's right next door to the bank. ....

He does all the cooking. ....

I hate doing the hoovering! ....

Can I do anything to help? ....

Could you lay the table, please? ....

Could you help me tidy up this mess? ....

Don't you think it's a bit too tight? ....

No, not at all. I think it looks OK. ....

It doesn't fit me. It's too small. ....

It really suits you. ....

....

....

....

....

Unit 6

I'm just phoning to see how you are. ....

I've got a really bad cough. ....

I've got a bit of a cold. ....

Have you taken anything for it? ....

Have you been to see anyone about it? ....

I was up till two last night, studying. ....

I couldn't get to sleep last night. ....

I couldn't understand what he was talking about. ....

I can't eat this. It's horrible! ....

I can't drive. ....

What about you? ....

I'm really excited about it. ....

Hey, guess what? I'm getting married next month! ....

Hey, guess what? It's my birthday today. ....

Oh really? Congratulations! ....

....

....

....

....

Unit 7

Could you play the tape again, please? ....

Could you turn your mobile off, please? ....

What do you need to get into that university? ....

What year are you in? ....

I'm going to do a Master's next year. ....

I graduated from London University. ....

I graduated in law. ....

She dropped out of the course. ....

I've got to hand my essay in today. ....

I get a grant from the government. ....

I've got to pay back my loan. ....

She's doing computing and IT. ....

I'm not sure about that. It depends. ....

Is it OK if I open the window? ....

Well, actually, I'd rather you didn't. ....

....

....

....

....

Unit 8

So what do you do? ....

I'm an estate agent. ....

I do temping work. ....

Do you enjoy it? ....

I get a bit bored with it sometimes. ....

I get three weeks' holiday a year. ....

He got sacked. ....

How long does it take you to get there? ....

I have to start work at seven in the morning. ....

It's great. I don't have to start until ten. ....

Do you have to work weekends? ....

He got promoted last year. ....

Have you done this kind of work before? ....

Yes. I worked in a bank last year. ....

She's very good with people. ....

....

....

....

....

Unit 9

It's too sweet. ....

The service was very slow. ....

Do you want to go and get something to eat? ....

Have you got anywhere in mind? ....

Would you like something to eat? ....

I don't really like anything spicy. ....

I couldn't eat another thing! ....

sometime next week ....

I spilled coffee all over my desk. ....

It was a disaster! ....

The waiter mixed up our order. ....

There was a really long queue. ....

Are you ready to order? ....

I'm afraid we don't have any left. ....

Well, in that case, I'll have the fish. ....

....

....

....

....

Unit 10

Have you got any kids? ....

Are your grandparents still alive? ....

She died of a heart attack. ....

He died in his sleep. ....

What's he like? Do you get on? ....

They're identical twins. ....

My mother's more relaxed than my father. ....

My brother's a lot older than I am. ....

We've got a lot in common. ....

I grew up by the sea. ....

They got divorced when I was a kid. ....

I left home when I was 21. ....

I live on my own. ....

He's a friend from school. ....

I booked the tickets on-line. ....

....

....

....

....

Unit 11

Do you know if this is the way to the station? ....

Do you know where she lives? ....

It's miles away from here. ....

It's just past the bridge on the right. ....

Keep going straight on down this road. ....

You can't miss it. ....

It usually takes me about 20 minutes. ....

I usually cycle to school. ....

Let's get a taxi. It'll be quicker. ....

Let's get the bus. It'll be cheaper. ....

Is this the right platform for Leeds? ....

I got off at the wrong stop. ....

Can you tell me which stop to get off at? ....

Single or return? ....

....

....

....

....

Unit 12

So what did you do last night? ....

I went to see this new play at the theatre. ....

Oh right. Was it any good? ....

Do you go to the cinema a lot? ....

Yes, quite a lot. ....

Maybe three or four times a month. ....

No, hardly ever. ....

Maybe once or twice a year. ....

Who do you support? ....

Who's your favourite player? ....

He's the laziest person I've ever met! ....

She's one of the nicest people I know. ....

I'd like to learn how to play the guitar. ....

When does the course end? ....

The film starts at half eight. ....

....

....

....

....

Unit 13

We travelled round the country a lot. ....

We stayed with some friends. ....

Our room looked out over the beach. ....

What's the expiry date? ....

If you wait, I'll go and get you one. ....

I'll help you if you want. ....

I'll do it later if I have time. ....

The hotel had internet access. ....

I've got satellite TV at home. ....

There's hardly any crime there. ....

It cost us hardly anything! ....

I'm almost ready. I just need to comb
my hair. ....

I need to have a shower and get
changed. ....

Do you mind if I use your phone? ....

Of course not – as long as you're
quick! ....

....

....

....

....

Unit 14

What was your holiday like? ....

It was brilliant. We had a great time. ....

Finland was amazing! ....

Have you ever been to Norway? ....

Yes, quite a few times. ....

No, never, but I'd like to. ....

Yes, I went there on business last year. ....

I'd like to go to Italy. ....

The food there is supposed to be
delicious. ....

The bus drivers are on strike. ....

I had a big argument with someone
I work with. ....

I had the day off yesterday. ....

What's the area you live in like? ....

What're the people you live with like? ....

They're great. We get on really well. ....

....

....

....

....

Unit 15

I don't really like horror films. ....

I love action movies. ....

What's it about? ....

Where's it on? ....

Who's in it? ....

That sounds very serious. What else
is on? ....

She's a famous TV personality. ....

There's a good documentary on later. ....

My favourite soap opera's on later. ....

There's a new sitcom on tonight. ....

I don't like him. I think he's very
over-rated. ....

I'm afraid we don't accept that kind of
credit card. ....

I'm afraid your card has been rejected. ....

My car was stolen last night. ....

....

....

....

....

Unit 16

I just need to make a quick phone call. ....

I might give you a ring tonight. ....

I was so angry I put the phone down
on him! ....

Can I leave a message? ....

Do you know when he'll be back? ....

You could try again this afternoon. ....

It was really embarrassing! ....

It was really horrible! ....

I'll text you later. ....

I'm really excited about it. ....

It was a really shocking programme. ....

John told me to say hello. ....

John told me to ask you if you could
call him. ....

I need to recharge the battery. ....

Are you insured? ....

....

....

....

....

Unit 17

You should have it X-rayed. ....

I had to have two fillings. ....

I had to have five stitches. ....

It was horrible. There was blood
everywhere! ....

I've still got the scar today. ....

I need to put some cream on it. ....

The floor was wet and I slipped. ....

I tripped and fell over. ....

I hit my head. ....

I broke my arm in two places. ....

I was cooking and I cut my finger. ....

I was cycling and I fell off my bike. ....

I'm really sorry. I'll pay for it. ....

Don't worry about it. It was an
accident. ....

Let me take your coat. ....

....

....

....

....

....

Unit 18

I've got a problem with my landlord. ....

I've got a problem with my flatmate. ....

It's such a pain! ....

Have you tried changing the batteries? ....

Yes, but it didn't make any difference. ....

That's a good idea. I'll try that later. ....

Not yet, but I'm going to later. ....

Have you sorted out that problem yet? ....

It'll sort itself out. ....

I need to sort out what I'm going
to take. ....

We had to queue for hours! ....

Can you save my place? ....

Listen. I must go or I'll be late. ....

It's not working properly. ....

I need to get it fixed. ....

....

....

....

....

....

Unit 19

Can you lend me £10 until Monday? ....

Do you want to borrow some money? ....

I'll pay you back tomorrow. ....

He owes me £40. ....

It's a waste of time! ....

Do you want me to drive you there? ....

Would you mind? ....

That'd be great. Thanks. ....

I'd like to pay this into my account,
please. ....

They charge three per cent
commission. ....

Can you just sign here, please? ....

I can't afford to. ....

It's cheaper here than it is there. ....

How are you paying? ....

I need to pay my phone bill this week. ....

....

....

....

....

....

Unit 20

The economy is in a mess. ....

The cost of living is really high. ....

Inflation is going up at the moment. ....

The quality of living is great. ....

Tax is very high. ....

The situation has improved a lot. ....

over the last few months ....

since the last election ....

He retired a few years ago. ....

They're destroying the environment. ....

She's going a bit deaf. ....

He's losing his memory. ....

She's doing very well at school. ....

I used to love going out, but I don't
any more. ....

I never used to like it, but now I do. ....

....

....

....

....

....

Student A: Unit 12, page 87, activity 8

St. Peter's College offers two cookery courses

The first is Chinese Cookery. This is an Intermediate–Advanced course for people who have some previous experience of cooking, but want to learn more about Chinese food. It runs every Tuesday from 7–9pm and the course lasts for ten weeks. Start dates: January 5th, April 6th, June 29th and September 7th. It costs £200. You will have to bring your own food as well. There are seven places left.

The second course is called Elementary Cooking and is for people who have never really cooked before. It runs twice a week – on Tuesdays and Thursdays, from 6.30–8pm and the course lasts for six weeks. Start dates: January 5th, March 2nd, May 4th, July 13th, September 7th and November 2nd. The course costs £120, which includes everything you will need. There are still eleven places left on the next course. A deposit of £50 is needed.

Student B: Unit 13, page 93, activity 3

You work in the Metropole Hotel.
Single rooms are £80.
Twin rooms are £110.
Double rooms are £135.

Twin and double rooms have en-suite bathrooms.
Single rooms have shared use of the bathrooms on each floor.

Student B: Unit 14, page 100, activity 3

Text B:
Patrick's from Guinea Bissau, a small country in West Africa.

WHAT'S my life like? Well, Guinea Bissau is one of the poorest countries in the world, so, of course, life is quite hard. I live in a small metal house which is about 20 square metres. I can get some electricity, but there are often power cuts. As I live in the capital, Bissau, I also have running water for part of the day, which lots of people don't have, so that's quite good. I don't actually spend that much time at home – it's just so horrible and hot inside the house – it's often over 35 degrees. When I'm not teaching, I just sit around outside, chatting in the shade. But I don't have lots of free time. I work about ten hours a day, five or six days a week. I teach English in a small school in a poor suburb. The school where I work has only one big room, which we divide into four classes with curtains, so the younger students come in the morning and the older children come in the afternoons. I also have to work on a farm sometimes to earn enough money to live. I only get around £20 a month, but I really like my job. People know me and respect me as a teacher. It can be frustrating, because we don't have many books and I don't even have a blackboard, but the children are good and want to learn. I don't know whether I'll stay here, though, or even if I'll continue teaching. The money's just not good enough and I'd like more from my life.

Student C: Unit 14, page 100, activity 3

Text C:
Olga's from Latvia, one of the Baltic States in northern Europe.

IN LOTS of ways, I love my life here. My family are here; I have lots of friends here; it's my home. The big problem is money and work. I've been teaching for 15 years now and I only earn $125 a month. We still live with my parents because we can't afford to buy a place of our own. Rents in Riga, the capital city, are around $200 a month, so it's really difficult to live on my salary, especially as we have two young children. The school day lasts from eight till three, but most teachers here have got second jobs, or have to find other ways of earning extra money. I work as a barmaid some evenings and I also give private classes sometimes in English, which I speak a bit of. I'd like to go to the UK one day, and work there and improve my English. I could earn more money in England and I think in the future being an English teacher would be better for me. I teach history most of the time now, but nobody is really interested in history these days. My students just want to know about business and money. Some of them learn it because they have to pass the exam, but most of them just don't care. They either don't come to class, or when they do, they just come to meet their friends and they talk all through the class. Then, at the end of the year, they find ways to get through the exam.